Pornography

Pornography

THE PRODUCTION
and CONSUMPTION
of INEQUALITY

Gail Dines

Robert Jensen

Ann Russo

ROUTLEDGE
New York and London

Published in 1998 by
Routledge
29 West 35th Street
New York, NY 10001

Published in Great Britain in 1998 by
Routledge
11 New Fetter Lane
London EC4P 4EE

Printed in the United States of America on acid-free paper
Design: Jack Donner

Library of Congress Cataloging-in-Publication Data

Dines, Gail.
  Pornography: the production and consumption of inequality / by Gail Dines, Robert
Jensen, and Ann Russo.
       p.   cm.
  Includes bibliographical references and index.
  ISBN 0−415−91812−X. — ISBN 0−415−91813−8 (pbk.)
   1. Pornography—Moral and ethical aspects. 2. Pornography—Social aspects.
3. Women—Crimes against. 4. Oppression (Psychology). 5. Feminist theory.
I. Jensen, Robert, 1958− . II. Russo, Ann, 1957 . III. Title.
HQ471.D55   1997
363.4'7—DC21   97−18263
                                                   CIP

For Andrea Dworkin,

whose writing and commitment to fighting the
pornography industry have made this work possible;
and for all the women who have struggled against
pornography, survived to tell their stories,
and flourished in the face of oppression.

Contents

Acknowledgments

Although the chapters (with the exception of Chapter 4) were written individually, this book is a collaborative effort, the product of conversations that have been going on among us for several years. We work from similar, though by no means identical, theoretical and political bases; we endorse each others' work while reserving the right to take issue with each other on the finer points. In the three concluding chapters, we reflected separately on our experiences in the anti-pornography movement and in the academy and wrote more personal accounts. While we are responsible individually for claims made in our separate writings, we accept collective accountability for the evidence and analysis presented in this book.

Gail Dines: Reading, writing and speaking about pornography over the past ten years or so has been emotionally draining. I have been fortunate enough to have around me friends who share my beliefs and are as outraged as I am about pornography and violence against women. Rhea Becker, no matter what the time of day, is always there to listen, protest, organize, and be angry at the violence, degradation, and pain that pornography produces in the world. Jackson Katz, Lesley Lebowitz, David Lisak, Lundy Bancroft, and Sandy Goodman continue to be generous with friendship, conversation, and insights. Sophie Goodenough was a truly remarkable research assistant, and Sue Kaler's patience as I ordered yet another book on interlibrary loan was greatly appreciated. Above all, I would like to thank David Levy, who always offers unending support and love, from reading the manuscript to cooking dinner, yet again.

Robert Jensen: I would like to thank Donna McNamara, Jeanne Barkey, Sally Koplin, and all the women from (the late) Organizing Against Pornography in Minneapolis for their role in educating me as they worked for a better world. Thanks also to Nancy Potter, Elvia Arriola, and Naomi Scheman for their contributions to my understanding of gender, sexuality, philosophy, and law. And special thanks to Jim Koplin, also of OAP, whose intelligence, humor, compassion, and friendship have enriched my life and work in ways that are beyond words.

Ann Russo: My continuing process of change and transformation over the years with regard to the issues of pornography, violence, and sexuality has not been an individual one. While I take full responsibility for the ideas herein, I would like to specifically acknowledge the inspiration, challenges, and support of Lourdes Torres, Barbara Schulman, Cindy Jenefsky, Suzi Hart, Barry Shuchter, Rhea Becker, Pam Loprest, and Cheris Kramarae. Through many conversations and sometimes heated arguments, they each helped shape my perspective on these issues. I would like to thank all the women who I have met through my activism, teaching, educational slide shows, and writing who have shared their stories of violence and resistance, grief and anger, despair as well as hope.

Parts of Chapter 4 were originally published as Jensen, 1994a. Chapter 5 is based in part on Jensen, 1996, 1995b, 1994b.

ONE

Introduction

Pornographic Dodges and Distortions

ROBERT JENSEN

For all the talk about pornography that has gone on in the past two decades in society and the academy, the silences still can tell us much. An example:

For several years I helped lead presentations of an anti-pornography slide show to school and community groups. After one of those discussions, a woman came up to me and said that the analysis in the slide show had reaffirmed her gut feelings about pornography and its message about women and sexuality, but she had not found a way to talk to others about those views. She said her boyfriend wanted her to watch pornographic videos with her, which she reluctantly did a few times. When she tried to explain to him why she didn't like to watch, the boyfriend countered with arguments about how liberating pornography was and told her she had a problem. She found ways to avoid having to watch the videos, but her boyfriend continued to watch and she eventually stopped arguing with him. She was confused by his claim that something that felt so degrading to her was supposed to be liberating, worn down by his insistence that she was the one with a problem, and troubled by nagging questions about how he saw her after he had watched one of the videos. Feeling overwhelmed by it all, she fell silent. Silence was, at least in the short term, easier than the struggle to find a way to communicate with him.

I don't know how the woman resolved her conflict with her boyfriend. But the writing of this book has been motivated by the desire to continue the work of finding ways to fill those kinds of silences. Building on the work of radical feminists and the anti-pornography movement, this book takes a systematic look at the production, content, and use of pornography and provides further evidence and analysis of pornography's role in the sexual and social subordination of women. However, filling those silences can be difficult. The debate over pornography, both within feminism and in the culture more broadly, has become so heated that honest and open discussion of such evidence and analysis is often derailed. Over several years of work on this issue, both in public and in the academy, I have seen productive discussions about pornography undermined by various diversions. In this introduction I want to identify some of those traps and suggest ways they can be avoided before we move on, in subsequent chapters, to an analysis of contemporary mass-marketed heterosexual pornography.

THE DODGES AND DISTORTIONS

Part of any political debate is a struggle for control of how the issue is framed and how terms are defined, and the pornography debate is no different. A radical feminist anti-pornography critique, which will be described in more detail in Chapter 2 and throughout the book, argues that the sexual ideology of patriarchy eroticizes domination and submission and that pornography is one of the key sites in which these values are mediated and normalized in contemporary culture. Domination and submission are made sexual, sometimes in explicit representations of rape and violence against women, but always in the objectification and commodification of women and their sexuality.

But that critique often is misunderstood, unintentionally or deliberately, and as a result key evidence and analysis gets lost in the shuffle. This is the result of what I have come to call the pornographic dodges and distortions, which I saw emerge consistently in discussions after the anti-pornography slide show. [This slide show, one of several presented across the country beginning in the late 1970s, was produced by Organizing Against Pornography (originally called the Pornography Resource Center), a Minneapolis group that existed from 1984 to 1990.] The three common dodges—definitional, constitutional, and causal—often derail conversations and crowd out analysis of the production, content, and use of pornography with diversionary arguments. The two common distortions—mislabeling the critique as being about offensiveness and suggesting that anti-pornography feminists are anti-sex prudes—serve to trivialize the feminist critique and warn people away from it.

Before examining these issues in more detail, it is important to step back and deal with a crucial term: feminism. It has become common to talk not of feminism but of feminisms, of multiple ways of approaching questions about sex, gender, and power. Amid the diversity of approaches—which has generally been a healthy catalyst for increasingly more nuanced and useful theory, research, and politics—we suggest there can be common ground for a project that can speak to feminists of many stripes. Put succinctly, the core understanding of feminism that informs this book is that women in the contemporary United States (as well as other places and in other historical moments) are oppressed in a patriarchal system and that one of the key sites of oppression is sexuality. Gender oppression plays out in different ways depending on one's social location, which makes it crucial to understand men's oppression of women in connection with other systems of oppression. The feminist struggle, then, must be linked to struggles against heterosexism, racism, class privilege, and histories of colonial domination. The goal of feminism is to understand men's oppression of women in order to change it and move toward a more just and compassionate world. Such change requires not only individual action, but also collective social and political action aimed at challenging institutionalized misogyny and systematic abuse and discrimination.

That may seem like a simple or self-evident description, but it is important to be clear about the basic assumptions in which we are grounded. With that framework in mind, the remainder of this chapter looks at ways the pornography debate often has been derailed.

THE DODGES

Definitional Dodge

If we can't define the term with precision, some argue, then we can't, or shouldn't try to, say much of anything about pornography. As D.H. Lawrence (1955, p. 195) put it, "What is pornography to one man is the laughter of genius to another"—in other words, it is subjective, all a matter of taste. Attempts to discuss pornography and its role in the world repeatedly are torpedoed by definitional debates. What is pornography? How is it different from erotica? Who decides which is which? All of these are relevant questions, but they become diversionary when they keep us from engaging other issues. Such diversions are easily avoided if we can make some basic distinctions in the way we use the term.

In this book, we will talk about pornography in two basic senses. First, there is a widely understood definition of pornography in the culture: Pornography is the material sold in pornography shops for the purpose of producing sexual arousal for mostly male consumers. While this does not define the term with absolute precision, it is sufficiently clear to make conversation possible. Second, from a critical feminist analysis, pornography is a specific kind of sexual material that mediates and helps maintain the sexual subordination of women. In Chapter 4, we analyze pornography (in the first sense, as a description of a type of material from which we draw a sample) to determine if it is pornographic (in the second sense, as an expression of male-supremacist sexual ideology).

For our purposes, this definition is adequate. In legal settings, something more exacting may be necessary (Dworkin and MacKinnon, 1988, pp. 36–41), but concerns about legal definitions need not derail a wider conversation in the culture. And, it is important to remember that pornography is not necessarily more difficult to define legally than any other term. One of the jobs of the law is to define words; legal terms do not simply drop from the sky with clear meaning but are instead defined through application and use. The struggle over definitions is a political, as well as a legal, battle, one that takes place both inside and outside the legal arena.

Constitutional Dodge

Much of the debate around pornography in the feminist community has centered on the civil rights anti-pornography ordinance authored by Andrea Dworkin and Catharine MacKinnon (1988, pp. 99–142). That ordinance was rejected by the federal courts on First Amendment grounds in *American Booksellers Association v. Hudnut* [771 F.2d 323 (7th Cir. 1985)], and any future attempts to implement the ordinance will have to answer the constitutional concerns raised in that case. We support the ordinance and believe such arguments can be made. Our purpose in this book, however, is not to argue the law but to expand our understanding of pornography.

In public discussions, the First Amendment is often invoked as a talisman to shut down critiques of pornography itself. Because the Constitution obviously prohibits legislation, some argue, there is little need for extensive analysis of how pornography works because collective action has been ruled out. But two points are important. First, that interpretation of the constitutional guarantees of freedom of speech and press is but one interpretation, and interpretations change over time (Jensen, 1995c). Second, even if the First Amendment, for the foreseeable future, blocks the implementation of the ordinance, society still faces the same social questions about pornography and its effects in the world. The rejection of a legislative strategy by the courts does not erase the important questions about how we, as individuals and as a society, deal with pornography outside the legal arena. Again, a narrow focus on the legal and constitutional questions can derail important discussions.

Causal Dodge

Because "science" has not yet conclusively shown a causal link between the use of pornography and sexual violence, some pornography supporters argue, no collective action is possible. Chapter 5 addresses the issue of causation in more detail, but here I will simply assert that such a link is beyond the capacity of science to determine. Holding out such proof as a requirement before we act is the equivalent of saying we can never act. Instead of being paralyzed by the limitations of social science, we can pay attention to testimony about the ways in which people act out pornographic sexual scenarios, which gives us some understanding of how pornography works in the world. And, rather than constraining the discussion with simplistic notions about how mass communication causes specific behavior, we can think about how pornography cultivates certain views about sexuality.

Borrowing from Gerbner's model of the influence of television, pornography's most important effects can be thought of as "the specific independent (though not isolated) contribution that a particularly consistent and compelling symbolic stream makes to the complex process of socialization and enculturation" (Gerbner, 1990, p. 249). Such a model can help us past the obsession with causation and point us toward questions about how the pornographic symbolic stream is produced, what it says about culture, and how it shapes people's worldviews. So, even if definitive judgments about causation are difficult to make, there is much to be said about the role of pornography in our culture. Discussions need not be derailed.

THE DISTORTIONS

Offensiveness and Oppression

Opponents of the feminist critique of pornography often frame the issue as a question of offensiveness, suggesting that the critique is based on the subjective experience of feeling repulsed by pornography. This is either a fundamental misunderstanding of the critique or a deliberate attempt to distort it. The feminist critique is an analysis of power and harm that focuses on oppression, not offensiveness. As MacKinnon (1984) put it in the title of one of her essays, it's not a moral issue, meaning that the critique of pornography is not based on a judgment that depictions of sex are dirty or blasphemous. The feminist critique focuses on the role of pornography in a system of sexual subordination and oppression of women.

A definition of oppression is useful in making this distinction clear. Marilyn Frye (1983, p. 33) defines oppression as "a system of interrelated barriers and forces which reduce, immobilize and mold people who belong to a certain group, and effect their subordination to another group (individually to individuals of the other group, and as a group, to that group)." This concept is crucial to understanding the critique of pornography instead of simply caricaturing it as the result of some people being offended. The feminist analysis of pornography is a political critique, which, of course, has a connection to morality, but it is not about offenses to conventional sexual mores.

In a pluralistic society, I expect to be offended on a daily basis. I do not expect all people to adhere to my sense of what is beautiful, appropriate, or pleasing. However, practices that are connected to systems of oppression are the proper topic for discussion, collective judgment, and political action.

Against Sex?

Anti-pornography feminists are often labeled anti-sex or prudish; critique of a sexual system of eroticized domination and submission is equated with a fear of sex. I have yet to meet anyone in the anti-pornography movement who fits this caricature, though I have met many people in that movement who are, as Susan Cole (1989, p. 107) puts it, "against sexual pleasure as pornography and mass culture construct it." To work for change in an oppressive sexual system is to work not against sex, but for justice.

So, in one sense, the charge that anti-pornography feminists fear sex is simply false. But in another sense, perhaps we all should fear the way in which a patriarchal culture defines and practices sex (Jensen, 1997a). We live in a culture in which sexualized violence—primarily perpetrated by men against women and children—is so routine that it has to be considered "normal," that is, following the norms of patriarchy. If sex in contemporary culture is fused with domination, cruelty, and violence, isn't fear of that kind of sex reasonable?

There is another level of fear at work in the pornography debate. It is not a fear of sexuality, but rather a more pervasive fear within the culture that if we tell the truth about just how deeply many of us have been affected by a pervasive patriarchal sexual system, we may be left for the moment with nothing to take its place. If patriarchal sex—the kind of sex that pimps and pornographers have had so much success marketing—is the sex many of us have learned, we face the challenge of reconstructing sexuality, which implies that for some time we might have to face great uncertainty about who we are as sexual beings and what kind of sex we want to have. In a hypersexualized, pornographic culture—a world in which to not have sex is a sign of deviancy—such a process can seem frightening. But we could also see it as an opportunity for invention. The project of unweaving "the pattern of dominance and submission which has been incarnated as sexuality in each of us" (A Southern Women's Writing Collective, 1990, p. 145) is formidable, but the rewards are likely far greater than we can know at this moment. The work of creating a world in which sex and justice are not in conflict can be a source of much passion, excitement, and hope as we move forward.

OUR TASK AND GOAL

There is work to be done on many fronts if we are to live in a world in which sex and justice are not at odds. Our task here is the analysis of one type of mass communication that tells stories about what sex is, can, and should be. Our approach is simple: To fully understand a media artifact, three elements are key—production, text, and consumption—all examined in a social, economic, and political context. Like Douglas Kellner (1995, p. 37), we believe the task of what he calls "media cultural studies" is "analyzing the complex relations between texts, audiences, media industries, politics, and the socio-historical context in specific conjunctures." Beginning in Chapter 2 with an overview of the social and political history of the anti-pornography movement, this book looks at just those relations. Chapter 3 examines one element of the pornography industry and its marketing strategies. Chapter 4 offers an interpretive analysis of contemporary pornography. In Chapter 5, the effects of the use of pornography are explored through narratives. Finally, in the concluding chapters we offer more personal thoughts on how to make sense of some of the difficult issues that pornography raises.

An important caveat: In this book we take a systematic look at pornography, but the project is limited. This is a study of contemporary mass-marketed heterosexual pornography—we do not address issues around gay male or lesbian pornography. The anti-pornography critique is valuable in analyzing gay and lesbian material, as some writers have demonstrated (e.g., Stoltenberg, 1989; Reti, 1993). But an analysis of gay and lesbian material is not our task here.

We hope this book contributes to the project of creating a more humane and just sexual system, a world in which sex is a site not of oppression but of liberation. Even though some of the debates we address may remain unresolved indefinitely, the analysis of pornography can go forward, and political and moral judgments can be made. For as much as some of us might at times wish we did not need to make judgments on this subject, there is no neutral ground on which to stand. In a culture saturated with pornography, we all have a political and moral obligation to seek to understand, to judge, and to act on that judgment.

TWO

Feminists Confront Pornography's Subordinating Practices

Politics and Strategies for Change

ANN RUSSO

For anti-pornography feminist activists, writers, and scholars, pornography has never been simply an intellectual, academic debate over the interpretation of images; rather, the struggle has been against a multibillion-dollar industry that contributes to pervasive social inequalities and endemic sexual violence. It has never been a campaign to ban sexually explicit material; its object has been to challenge and to eliminate the pornography industry's participation in discrimination, bigotry, and violence. The salient issue in the feminist fight against pornography has not been an objection to sexual activity or representations but, rather, to the sexism and racism of pornography, the structure and dynamics of eroticized inequality, and the sexual mistreatment, abuse, and violence that occur in connection with its production, distribution, and consumption. The belief in the possibilities for resistance and change compels feminists to target the pornography industry and its ties to other cultural, economic, social, and legal institutions that reproduce social inequalities. The purpose of this chapter is to challenge the many misconceptions and distortions of feminist political analyses and strategies against the pornography industry. I seek to place the feminist anti-pornography movement into historical, intellectual, and political perspective.

VIOLENCE IN WOMEN'S LIVES IS THE ISSUE

Social inequality is created in many different ways. In my view, the radical responsibility is to isolate the material means of creating the inequality so that material remedies can be found for it (Dworkin, 1988, p. 265).

The feminist analysis of the pornography industry grew out of the U.S. grassroots anti-violence movement of the 1970s, when U.S. feminists met in small and large groups across the nation and began to speak out about the seemingly individual, private, isolated experiences of sexualized violence. Prior to this breakthrough in public consciousness, rape and wife-battery were constructed as individual women's problems to be borne in silence and shame. Through consciousness-raising and feminist politicization of women's "private lives" came the knowledge that pervasive violence exists in women's lives. Thousands of women and increasing numbers of men have come forward with testimony to the many forms of violence in their lives (e.g., Kelly, 1988; Russell, 1984; Stanko, 1985), including intrafamilial and interpersonal battery and rape (Dworkin, 1988; Herman, 1981, 1992; Martin, 1976; Richie, 1996; Schechter, 1982; White, 1985, 1990); sexual harassment and assault on the street, in the workplace, and in educational, medical, and prison institutions (New York Radical Feminists, 1974; Griffin, 1986; Herek and Berrill, 1991; MacKinnon, 1979, 1987; Sumrall and Taylor, 1992); sexual assault, battery, and torture in wars and in the service of colonial domination (Anzaldúa, 1990; Castañeda, 1993); incestuous assault and child rape in and outside of families (Armstrong, 1978; McNaron and Morgan, 1982; Queer Press Collective, 1991; Russell, 1986); prostitution, female sexual slavery, and pornography (Barry, 1979, 1995; Barry, Bunch, and Castley, 1984; Dworkin, 1989; Lederer, 1980; Russell, 1993a). One out of three women report that they have experienced some form of sexual abuse; up to 70 percent of rape cases are perpetrated by acquaintances, dates, coworkers, friends, lovers, husbands, employers, doctors, therapists, and/or fathers of women (Sanday, 1990; Warshaw, 1988; Buchwald et al., 1993). Women of color are more vulnerable to rape than white women (hooks, 1981). Women are battered by men in approximately one-half of all heterosexual marriages and partnerships (Jones, 1994), and recent studies show a similar level of violence in same-sex relationships (Lobel, 1986; Renzetti, 1992; Renzetti and Miley, 1996). Most women experience sexual harassment, many times in combination with racial and homophobic harassment, in work and educational environments, on the streets, and in their neighborhoods (Sumrall and Taylor, 1992; Herek and Berrill, 1992; Matsuda, Lawrence, Delgado, and Crenshaw, 1992; Morrison, 1992; Lederer and Delgado, 1995). Harassment, abuse, rape, and sexual torture contribute to the realities of poverty, homelessness, women's job instability, poor health and lack of access to health care, sex and race segregation in the workforce, and lack of educational opportunity, as well as to women's involvement in pornography and prostitution (Kelly, 1988; Richie, 1996; Silbert and Pines, 1984; White, 1990).

Feminists have sought to theorize this violence. Violence in women's lives is not simply linked to male domination, but is intricately connected with racial, colonial, postcolonial, heterosexual, and class domination (Castañeda, 1993; Davis, 1981; Crenshaw, 1994; Hernandez-Avila, 1993; hooks, 1981, 1984). Structural inequalities of gender, race, class, and nation and their attending ideological justifications shape the incidence of violence, its personal and social effects, and the ways in which social, medical, cultural, and legal systems and institutions respond to violence. Dominant sociocultural stories, mythologies, and ideological constructions continue to reproduce the structural inequalities in these practices, responses, and institutions.

Feminists involved in recognizing, challenging, and trying to stop violence are concerned with what creates a social context of pervasive violence that is denied, minimized, and trivialized, and simultaneously is legitimated and defined as normative, consensual sexual relations. Feminists working against violence ask: Why is men's privatized violence against women considered "just life"? Why are women often blamed for men's behavior? Why is there such shame, stigma, and secrecy attached to women who've been sexually assaulted? Why is there so little empathy and concern for victims of sexual violence, except in circumstances of interracial or interclass violence? Why is there such apathy or hostility in response to claims of sexualized mistreatment and violence, particularly that which occurs within groups? Why is so much of the violence sexual? Why are sexual desire and aggression so linked in the culture? How does violence against women get legitimated and made to seem natural and inevitable? When is sexualized violence not legitimated in the dominant culture? How are the constructions of legitimate and illegitimate violence connected with structural inequalities existing in the society?

Feminists have looked to pornography along with mass media culture, fairy tales, music, literature, and other cultural forms for help with the answers to these and other questions (Betterton, 1987; Cole, 1989; Dines and Humez, 1995; Dworkin, 1974, 1989; Faludi, 1991; hooks, 1990, 1992; Millett, 1971). Feminists have been interested in how ideological constructions of gender, race, and sexuality, and their resulting practices, participate in naturalizing, legitimating, and perpetuating sexualized and racialized violence. For instance, the pervasiveness of violence in women's lives can be connected to the construction of a naturalized (hetero)sexuality of dominance and submission in many forms of mass media and culture, which is also connected to the resulting victim-blaming and apathy in response to the pervasive violence.

The feminist analysis of the pornography industry begins with the problem of pervasive violence against women, not with the pornographic images themselves. The compelling issues and questions have to do with mistreatment, harassment, rape, battery, and murder, not sex per se. The imaginative feminist vision is a society free of inequality and violence, not a society free of sexual desire and expression.

PUBLICIZING THE HARM AND ISSUES OF ACCOUNTABILITY

In the mid- to late 1970s, anti-pornography and anti-rape groups took on the title of Robin Morgan's essay "Theory and Practice: Pornography and Rape," as a leading slogan. Morgan argued that rape was "merely the expression of the standard, 'healthy' even encouraged male fantasy in patriarchal culture—that of aggressive sex. And the articulation of that fantasy into a billion-dollar industry is pornography" (Morgan, 1980, p. 137). Across the country, feminists formed groups such as Women Against Violence Against Women (WAVAW) and Women Against Violence in Pornography and Media (WAVPM) to educate people about sexist and violent images in media and to demand social responsibility from media institutions. Feminists organized protests, marches, and group tours of pornography districts; picketed and boycotted films that made sexual abuse and violence into entertainment; and presented slide shows on the pornography industry's participation in the perpetuation of misogyny and violence (Lederer, 1980; Russell, 1993a). For instance, throughout 1979 the New York Women Against Pornography led biweekly tours of the New York pornography district in an effort "to expose women to the thriving pornography industry." They believed that "when women see for themselves the brutality of the industry they will be better equipped to fight it" (Lederer, 1980, p. 15). Some groups engaged in direct-action politics and civil disobedience against the industry to dramatically draw attention to its activities and harms to women (Delacoste and Newman, 1981; Russell, 1993a).

The slide shows documented how pornography constructs and perpetuates sexualized and racialized bigotry, exploitation, harassment, and violence against women. By deconstructing the ideology of white, male, heterosexualized domination, the shows illustrated how pornography presents sexual force and coercion as what women want and desire, and how it legitimates discrimination, mistreatment, and abuse by making it arousing and entertaining (Dworkin, 1989; Russell, 1993b). The slide shows demystified the secrecy and the taboo aspect of the pornography industry. This has been important, particularly for many women who have not been directly involved in the industry, since pornography has historically been produced for the privatized sexual entertainment of men and because the women involved in pornography have often been stigmatized, criminalized, and, at the very least, excluded from mainstream recognition and respect. This critical public viewing of pornography encouraged women and men to recognize that the industry does not simply traffic in "sexual expression" but rather in misogynist and racist discourse and practices. The feminist protests, marches, educational campaigns, and boycotts created an unprecedented public discussion of pornography's sexism, racism, and connections to violence against women.

As the movement developed, so did knowledge of and perspective on the impact of the pornography industry on women's lives. More and more women began to speak out about their own direct experiences with the production and use of pornography: women who had been coerced into the industry as adults and/or as children; women who were in relationships with men who used pornography as a method of sexual coercion and abuse; and women who had had pornography forced on them in their workplaces, neighborhoods, and/or social groups as methods of intimidation and exclusion (see Chapter 5). Through the stories that women and men tell about how pornography functions in their lives, the relationships between pornography, its social constructions of sexual identities and desires, inequality, discrimination, abuse, and violence are made manifest. These stories shift the discussion of pornography from one about the conflicting interpretations of abstract images to one focused on practices of discrimination and harm impacting the lives of women and men.

Contrary to most critiques of the feminist anti-pornography movement, the strategies have not been directed toward criminal laws to ban pornography or sexually explicit material in general. The goals have been critical analysis and discussion, as well as accountability by the industry for the harms created through pornography. In 1983, grounded in the accumulated knowledge of pornography's direct involvement in the subordination of women, feminists Catharine MacKinnon and Andrea Dworkin proposed a novel feminist legal perspective that conceptualized pornography as active practices of gender subordination. Rather than focusing on pornography as offensive images or speech, the ordinance targeted the harmful practices involved in pornography's production, consumption, and distribution and defined these as forms of sex discrimination. Individuals could seek legal redress for the harms of coercion, force, assault, defamation, and generalized subordination of women (Dworkin and MacKinnon, 1988; Baldwin, 1984; Itzin, 1992). Like sexual harassment law, the ordinance would offer women the chance to stop the specific discrimination and seek compensation for the harm caused.

The anti-discrimination ordinance conceptualizes pornography as:

> the graphic sexually explicit subordination of women through pictures and/or words that also includes one or more of the following: (a) women are presented dehumanized as sexual objects, things or commodities; or (b) women are presented as sexual objects who enjoy humiliation or pain; or (c) women are presented as sexual objects experiencing sexual pleasure in rape, incest, or other sexual assault; or (d) women are presented as sexual objects tied up or cut up or mutilated or bruised or physically hurt; or (e) women are presented in postures or positions of sexual submission, servility, or display; or (f) women's body parts—including but not limited to vaginas, breasts, or buttocks—are exhibited such that women are reduced to those parts; or (g) women are presented being penetrated by objects or animals; or (h) women are presented in scenarios of degradation, humiliation, injury, torture, shown as filthy or inferior, bleeding, bruised or hurt in a context that makes these conditions sexual (Dworkin and MacKinnon, 1988, p. 138–139).

This description and set of characteristics related to content, however, would not on its own determine whether the material in question would be considered a form of sex discrimination; the complainant would have to prove that the pornography not only fits into the above definition, but also is connected to the harms of coercion, force, assault, defamation, or trafficking (Dworkin and MacKinnon, 1988, pp. 41–52). Dworkin explains:

> There is nothing actionable about something meeting the definition. It has to be trafficked in, somebody has to be forced into it, it has to be forced on somebody or it has to be used in a specific kind of assault; so that the hypothetical question about whether I think that is subordination or not depends a great deal—has the woman been forced into it? I want to know. What is the sociology around it, is it being used on people, are women being forced to watch it and then do it; and those are the kind of issues, that is what is required to trigger this law (Dworkin, 1988, pp. 298–299).

Women[1] who have been coerced, intimidated, or fraudulently induced into performing in the production of pornography would have the opportunity to prove the coercion and, if proved, to seek monetary damages from the pornographers and to obtain an injunction to stop the further marketing and distribution of the specific pornographic materials. Women who have had pornography, as defined in the ordinance, forced on them in their jobs, education, homes, or public places as a form of harassment and intimidation could bring action against the person doing the forcing. Women who have experienced violence and can prove that specific pornography is directly implicated would have the opportunity to sue the perpetrator as well as the maker, distributor, and/or exhibitor of the pornography for damages. The trafficking provision would allow a woman to bring a complaint against specific pornographers for subordinating women as a class. While in this case, unlike the others, it would not be necessary for a woman to show direct harm to her as an individual, she would have to prove that the pornography harmed women as a class, including being targeted for rape, sexual harassment, and battery. The cause of action, in this case, would be directed toward producers and/or distributors of pornography. Finally, the ordinance would make it possible for a woman to sue pornographers who defamed her name, image, or recognizable personal likeness in a way that caused harm.

The ordinance's conception of pornography is completely different from obscenity law. Obscenity laws do not address gender discrimination, sexual subordination, or violence and are concerned with sexual morality and the incitement of "prurient interests." The ordinance is a civil law, not a criminal law. An individual woman, not the state or the vice squad, would file a civil complaint for compensatory damages with a Human Rights Commission or court. The material or actions would be deemed pornography, and therefore sex discrimination, only if they were proven to be involved in a practice of subordination as outlined.

Despite the defeat of the ordinance in the courts so far, feminists against pornography continue to organize support for the ordinance and to politicize pornography and the inequality and violence involved in its production, consumption, and distribution (Torrey, 1992, 1993). The work on the ordinance firmly shifted the feminist analysis of pornography from an analysis of abstract, decontextualized images to a focus on how the pornography industry is involved in coercion, force, assault, trafficking, and defamation that reproduce and perpetuate social relations of inequality, discrimination, and abuse.

PORNOGRAPHY AS INDUSTRY

The breadth of the pornography industry is comparable to mainstream corporate institutions, although it is difficult to find reliable and accurate figures. The authors of one book on the pornography business cite estimates from $4 billion to $7 billion a year in U.S. sales (Hebditch and Anning, 1988, p. 71). In 1985, the industrial profits from pornography were estimated to exceed the $6.2 billion combined gross of ABC, CBS, and NBC (Charles, 1985, p. 104). And it was estimated that Reuben Sturman, the head of only one of the major pornography empires, "rang up about $4 billion in sales last year [1986]." (Williams, 1987, p. 22). As noted in I Spy Productions:

> Pornography gains maximum distribution because it is accepted by the business world. It is recognized as an important and profitable section of the publishing industry. Pornography is bread and butter to the commercial printers, the magazine distributors and wholesalers. It has acquired a strategic significance for tabloid newspaper barons and go-getting magazine companies (I Spy Productions, 1992, p. 76).

The pornography industry has grown at an incredible rate since the 1950s and continues to make enormous profits selling to a huge, and growing, market. When *Playboy* began in the 1950s it was the only one of its kind, but by 1978 it had close to 100 competitors (see Chapter 3). Advances in communication technology in the past two decades have resulted in significant changes in the pornography market, with videocassettes replacing the once-dominant magazines as the center of the industry. Computers and the Internet also have become vehicles for disseminating pornography; interactive CD-ROMs and Web sites are still in their infancy, but are growing in popularity. In short: Pornography is not a fringe business in the U.S. economy.

While feminists critical of the pornography industry focus on the products and practices of an industry, sexual liberals[2] who have been involved in attacking the feminist anti-pornography movement define pornography as any sexually explicit expression. They include, for example, a wide range of materials, including greeting cards, "great" literature, feminist materials on sexuality, birth control, and reproduction, as well as lesbian and gay artistic expression (Strossen, 1995; Kipnis, 1996). Drawing upon such a broad definition serves to obscure the target of the feminist anti-pornography critique and makes it seem as if feminists against pornography are against all forms of sexual expression.

Sexual liberals tend to focus on issues of sexual restriction and repression, rather than oppression, and thus rarely define (heterosexual) pornography, which is the target of the feminist anti-pornography movement, as a mass-market industry. When speaking about pornography they tend to talk about its "deviance" and its rebellion against sexual repression and mainstream values (Strossen, 1995; Kipnis, 1996). They minimize its social power by describing it in terms of small, struggling businesses in run-down areas of town, whose owners, managers, distributors as well as consumers are powerless, if not pathetic, because of the stigma associated with sexually explicit materials (Duggan, 1984; Benn, 1987). Given the breadth of the pornography industry, however, it cannot realistically be considered a deviant and taboo enterprise.

In their defense of pornography, feminist sexual liberals tend to focus their analysis on pornographic publications that cater to "sexual minority" communities (Williams, 1993a, 1993b). They focus on the bigotry that individual members of sexual minorities face from the larger society for their presumed choice of sexual fantasies. Sexually explicit material produced for, and by, sexual minorities is seen as vital because it is one of the only arenas available for sexual expression (Bronski, 1984; Rubin, 1984; Califia, 1986; Kipnis, 1996). The term "sexual minorities" refers to a wide variety of groups, including lesbians, gay men, bisexuals, transvestites and transsexuals, and individuals and groups involved in "intergenerational sex," voyeurism, fetishism, sadomasochism, and bondage, as well as prostitution (e.g., Rubin, 1984).

The unqualified defense of the pornography industry on the grounds of a concern for the rights of sexual minorities has been effective in many progressive communities concerned with individual rights and privacy, and protection from governmental interference. The defense resonates among some feminists, particularly in lesbian and gay communities, because of the rampant homophobia and heterosexism being spread by right-wing forces in the country. Many of the materials and groups targeted for state-orchestrated stigmatization, suppression, and criminalization, defined by the hegemonic society as "deviant," are often gay, lesbian, and transgender sexual identities, practices, and publications (Rubin, 1984).

These are real issues of concern. However, the uncritical acceptance of the defense of pornography needs more discussion. Use of such an overarching term as "sexual minorities" deflects attention away from the substantial social differences between the groups and decontextualizes their various relationships to the mass market and international industry of pornography. For instance, by referring to adult/child sexual relations as "intergenerational sex," sexual liberals neutralize the power dynamics involved between adults and children, ignore sexual abuse, and minimize the illegal trafficking of children by labeling all those who raise questions "moralists." By classifying women who work in the sex industry as members of a "sexual minority," sexual liberals imply that the work is a voluntary activity, representative of the woman's (or man's) own freely chosen sexual identity and desire; they ignore the economic conditions of the sexual exchange, the social and economic power of the producers and consumers, and the poverty, economic exploitation, and sexual abuse that may underlie the lives of those involved in the sex industry (Jeffreys, 1990; Summer, 1987). This is not to deny the possibility that some women's work and their sexual identities and desires are overlapping, but only to acknowledge that this automatic assumption evades the social and economic contexts of women's work in the industry.

Using the identity label of "sexual minorities" to refer, without distinction, to private consensual relationships, to public contractual relationships, as well as to mass-market capitalist enterprises is evasive and misleading; it makes the critical and social analysis of the pornography industry, a major capitalist enterprise, into an attack on the personal choices of individual members of sexual minority communities. By classifying pornography as expressive of sexual minority identities, sexual liberals ward off criticism of the social inequalities, coercion, and/or violence connected to the structure and practices of the multibillion-dollar, heterosexual white male-dominant pornography industry. This perspective reduces the social critique of a profitable capitalist mass-market industry into a personal attack, which they claim is targeted against the expression of personally chosen, though socially stigmatized, identities (Jeffreys, 1990).

The feminist critical analysis of pornography, however, is not about pornography as a deviant form of sexual expression, but rather about a powerful mass-market industry that normalizes, sanctions, and participates in sexist, racist, anti-Semitic, and other forms of discrimination that are made into sexualized entertainment. The analysis challenges normative and institutionalized sexual relations connected to structural inequalities, not sexual deviance per se. This does not mean that the reproduction of inequalities in gay, lesbian, bisexual, feminist, or other truly marginal groups' sexually explicit media is not problematic, only that the feminist analysis is about social inequalities, not sexual expression. It has been a feminist tradition to critically analyze and protest inequalities perpetuated within the movement's organizations, movements, and media. It is important to recognize that the focus is not sexual expression or sexually explicit materials, but sexualized exploitation, discrimination, abuse, and violence as they manifest themselves in pornography's production, consumption, and/or distribution. The homophobia, heterosexism, and other forms of bigotry that underlie right-wing and state-orchestrated campaigns against "sexual deviance" are not connected to the feminist struggle to challenge violence and social inequalities.

SEXUALIZATION OF INEQUALITIES

Feminists who initially targeted the pornography industry did so because its mass-distributed products so clearly illustrated the ideological justification of men's mistreatment of women. From even a cursory review of pornography's structure and content, the mainstream pornography industry, directed toward white heterosexual men, constructs women as sexualized objects of discrimination, harassment, and abuse for the purposes of sexual arousal and entertainment (Dworkin, 1989; Kappeler, 1986). The ways in which pornography sexualizes gender and racial inequalities are connected to the ways in which men, and often women, tend to deny, minimize, trivialize, and defend themselves against women's public criticism of sexual harassment, abuse, and violence. Through the consumption of products that produce sexual pleasure and entertainment, men learn to sexualize inequality and objectify women's bodies such that the mistreatment and abuse that these products are predicated upon become invisible or socially insignificant (Dworkin, 1989; Gardner, 1980; Kappeler, 1986; Itzin, 1992). Ideological arguments that legitimate practices of gender and racial inequalities are woven into the stories, cartoons, and pictorials found in the pornography industry's cultural products. Pornography gives the message that women within and outside of the pornography industry are inferior and deserve sexual mistreatment (see Chapter 4).

The mass distribution of pornographic magazines, books, videos, and computer programs perpetuates sexual abuse and discrimination in the real world of social inequality because it legitimates sexual and racialized harassment and abuse as forms of sexual pleasure and entertainment. It creates an environment in which men (and women) have difficulty believing women who speak out about rape, battery, child sexual abuse, and sexual harassment. The messages in pornography about women's pleasure in submission and pain contribute to men's beliefs that sexual assault victims derive sexual pleasure from the experience (see Chapter 5). In response to women's claims of assault, men and women assume that the women consented to the sex (assault) or in some way were responsible for the sexual experience (assault), especially in the cases of women of color, poor women, and/or prostitutes (Itzin, 1992; Baldwin, 1984). By placing inequality and bigotry in a sexual and entertainment arena, pornography serves to protect its makers and consumers from sustained public scrutiny (relying on individual rights to speech and consumption to stave off criticism).

The pornography industry is not creative or original in its exploitation of historical and social power dynamics to create a profitable product. It takes existing inequalities and makes them sexy and entertaining. The discourses and images target specific groups of women depending on status and occupation, race, color, and ethnicity, and/or on size and shape, age, disability, for specific types of sexual violence and torture, which feed back into structural inequalities operating in the society (Gardner, 1980; Walker, 1980; Teish, 1980; Collins, 1990; Forna, 1992; Mayall and Russell, 1993). For example, pornography makes racism sexy, thereby legitimating, nourishing, and reinforcing racist stereotypes, bigotry, and mistreatment (Russell, 1993; Forna, 1992). The racist representations that permeate this society are integral to the lack of response on the part of social institutions to violence against women of color. The eroticization of black women's skin in pornography contributes to the racist history and stereotype that black women exist for the sexual use of men, especially white men, and the myth that they are always sexually available (Dworkin, 1989).

Products of the pornography industry, because so much of their sexual appeal relies on the dynamics of dominance and subordination, draw upon these historically constituted structures and institutionalized forms of inequality, discrimination, and violence (Gardner, 1980; Dworkin, 1989). Thus, (heterosexual) male pornography's profitability is dependent on gender, racial, economic, political, and social inequalities and bigotries at several levels: the structure of the industry's labor force; the constructed stories and images surrounding sexual identities and desires in the industry's products; and the mass-market appeal it has for male audiences who identify at some level with this hegemonically constructed, heterosexual white male, masculinity.

This analysis has been challenged by feminist sexual liberals in the debate over the pornography industry and its connection to inequality and violence. By defining pornography as sexual representations and images, separate from material realities and social structures, feminist sexual liberals foreground issues of individual interpretation. They evade discussions of the social inequalities upon which pornography relies, promotes, and legitimates (Burstyn, 1985). They distinguish pornographic speech from its making or use. As Deirdre English explains:

> The fact remains that no matter how disturbing violent fantasies are, as long as within the world of pornography, they are still only fantasies. The man masturbating in a theater showing a snuff film is still only watching a movie, not actually raping or murdering. . . . There is something wrong with attacking people, not because of their actions, but because of their fantasies—or their particular commercial style of having them (English, 1980, p. 48).

Pornography, according to feminist sexual liberals, is a "mere" representation belonging to the minds of the individual producer or consumer. They speak about pornography as if it does not have to be produced and as if its effects only exist by choice in the realm of individual privacy and sexual fantasy. From their perspective, conflict over pornography is one of individual interpretation, not social and institutionalized practices of discrimination.

By conceptually framing the issue as one of interpretation, they appeal to a liberal tolerance for personal tastes and pleasures. Paula Webster, for example, criticizes the links made between the cultural product and the reality of the women used in its production by a Women Against Pornography tour of 42nd street in New York. She criticizes the tour guide for describing the photo of a young adolescent girl who is portrayed as she is about to have anal intercourse with an adult male as rape. Webster challenges the equation of a "mere representation" with an "actual event recorded by some Candid Camera" (Webster, 1981, p. 48). She disagrees with the guide's interpretation because it "indicated certain biases about pain and pleasure and preferred positions." According to Webster, the guide claimed that anal intercourse would be quite painful for the young girl. In her discussion, she never acknowledges the social context of the photograph's production or consumption (e.g., child sexual abuse, power differences between adults and children), nor the exploitation of children in pornography and prostitution in the United States and around the world. Pornography becomes private sexual fantasies and choices that are a matter of individual tastes and preferences. Therefore, the feminist anti-pornography analysis is interpreted as a personal attack on an individual's personal choice of sexual practices and fantasies.

For feminists critical of the industry, it is the practice of inequality and subordination, not simply sexual images or abstract speech, that is of concern. Rhetorically this is important, as Dworkin and MacKinnon (1988, p. 24) recognize: "Once pornography is framed as concept rather than practice, more thought than act, more in the head than in the world, its effects also necessarily appear both insubstantial and unsubstantiated, more abstract than real."

Reconceptualizing pornography in terms of the practices involved in producing, consuming, and mass distributing the cultural products, rather than isolated images and speech, focuses feminist attention on the sociology of an industry. The analysis takes up the structures and practices involved in the production and consumption of pornography and their connection to and interaction with social inequalities in all other areas of life. Anti-pornography feminists are interested in such questions as: How are the images produced? Who is used in the production? What are the social conditions of the production? Who owns and controls the media? Who determines what is produced? Who controls the distribution? How do the women become involved in the production? How are women treated in the industry? Once images are made with human models, who controls what is done with these images? What are the effects on women and men used in the production? What is the relationship between the structural dynamics contained within the pornography industry and the social structures of gender, race, and class? How do the social constructions of gender, race, national, and class identities in pornography resonate with those in mainstream media, the criminal justice system, and other social institutions? Who has access to pornography? How much does it cost? Where is it consumed and how? How is it used? Anti-pornography feminists put these questions into the larger contexts of social relations and structures of inequality.

WOMEN IN PORNOGRAPHY'S PHOTOGRAPHIC REPRESENTATIONS

A major issue raised in the debates over pornography is whether or not the women who are photographically represented in pornography are there by choice or coercion. Feminists critical of the pornography industry analyze women's participation in the industry in terms of social and historical contexts, systems of economic exploitation, racism, and/or sexual coercion (Barry, 1995; Summer, 1987; Itzin, 1992), while sexual liberals view women's involvement in pornography in terms of individually chosen sexual identities and practices (Delacoste and Alexander, 1987; Strossen, 1995; Kipnis, 1996). Because sexual liberals define women's participation as a matter of individual choice, they interpret the feminist anti-pornography analysis to be one leveled at the individual women, rather than a social analysis of the mass industry of pornography.

Feminists who fight the pornography industry often find themselves addressing the role of women models who work in the industry and their level of responsibility for the industry's products. First, myths about "free choice" abound in mainstream media, in sexual liberal discourse, and in pornography. The assumption is that people have free choice over their employment and, in this case, over the nature of the products produced and marketed by their employers. These myths serve to erase the social conditions of women's lives—myths that say that all women freely choose to be in the pornography and that pornography accurately represents women's identities, sexualities, desires, hopes, and dreams. Pornographers and their defenders sometimes claim that pornography accurately represents the photographed woman's own sexual identity, "that the use of women in pornography is the sexual will of the woman, expresses her sexuality, her character, her nature, and appropriately demonstrates a legitimate sexual function of hers" (Dworkin, 1988, p. 232). What is left out of the discussion are the social conditions of pornography's production, the working conditions of women in the industry, and the levels of control and/or autonomy that workers have over the end products.

The assumptions of "free choice" and consent, in combination with the ideology of free market enterprise, make harm to women invisible. As Sarah Wynter points out about prostitution:

> Prostitutes are afforded neither the status of victim nor survivor, but are defined as fully consenting participants that in an industry if viewed objectively would be understood to be the commerce of sexual abuse and inequality. . . . [but] because an exchange of money occurs, irrespective of whether the woman herself maintains control of, or benefits from this exchange, the client is given permission to use the woman in a manner that would not be tolerated in any other business or social arrangement (including marriage); and the woman's acceptance of the money is construed as her willingness to engage in such commerce (Wynter, 1989, p. 7).

Defenders of pornography sometimes assume that women eagerly choose to participate in the industry out of a vast range of opportunities; they minimize the importance of unemployment, low and unequal pay based on sexism and racism, educational and employment opportunities; and they too often ignore the constraints of a capitalist industry that is owned and controlled by men (who are the vast majority of producers and directors), whose targeted audience is predominantly male. Young girls and women make decisions to work in the pornography industry, but the contexts of their decisions are not ones of economic opportunity and social freedom; their decisions are not socially neutral. Economic necessity, limited economic and educational opportunities, and sexual abuse, among other social factors, often compel women, who may not be able to secure a living wage and or have young children to support into sex work, in contrast to other jobs, because on the surface it seems very lucrative (Nelson, 1992). Some young women enter the industry in response to false advertising and promises of future wealth. As Evelina Giobbe (1993, p. 3) points out, "In the same way naive young women are lured into prostitution through ads for 'Escort Services' which omit mentioning the sexual component of the 'job,' others are lured into pornography by misleading advertisements for 'models' or 'actresses.'" They may be told that such modeling will be a stepping stone to a better acting career. Once in the industry, however, women are socially stigmatized and isolated, which reduces the span of opportunities available to them.

Some women get work in the pornography industry because they are attracted to the promises of glamour, adventure, and excitement that the media portrays about the sex industry. Sex work is made to seem like a way out of current social and/or economic circumstances. One woman describes:

> I hated the way I was treated, but the job seemed glamorous, sophisticated; it was a far cry from the drudgery of minimum-wage office work. I was fascinated by the glimpses of corporate and male wealth, the call girls, the whole atmosphere of "adult" sexuality.... In a culture where female self-esteem still depends on sexual attractiveness, on male "appreciation" of our looks, this job felt like the big time.... To be *paid* for being beautiful and sexy was the ultimate reassurance.... In the end of course, economic power usually controls. They [the businessmen] could buy whatever they chose; we were interchangeable purchases ("Working in the Body Trade," 1981, pp. 19–20).

As she says of the power disparity, "No amount of wealth or power gives men the right to buy us, but the lack of our own wealth or power means that we can be bought."

Some women work in the pornography industry because they are running away from sexually and physically violent homes, and pornographers offer them food, shelter, money, promises of love, and a home. Some may get into it because their fathers, uncles, husbands, brothers, or boyfriends prostitute them or make pornography of them, and then act as their "agents"; sometimes the pornography is used to blackmail young girls into continuing their life in the sex industry (Giobbe, 1993; Barry, 1979). In a study by Mimi Silbert and Ayala Pines of 200 street prostitutes in San Francisco, 10 percent of the women stated that they had been used in pornographic films and magazines as children [under age 13], and 38 percent reported that explicit photographs had been taken of them when they were children for commercial reasons or the personal gratification of the photographer (Silbert and Pines, 1984).

A growing number of women and children are photographed and videotaped by their husbands, boyfriends, and/or relatives without their consent, and sometimes without their knowledge. As Judith Gaines (1992, p. 26) points out, "What separates this new genre from standard pornographic fare is that these films are made by novices, usually without scripts, in their own homes. After the raw footage has been shot, it typically is sold for prices ranging from $250 to $2,000 to any of about 100 U.S. companies that provide minor editing and packaging and distribution services." While marketers claim that these are harmless fantasies, women survivors speak about the coercion, abuse, rape, and battering involved in video production, and about their fear and humiliation in knowing that people are buying videos of their abuse for plea-sure and entertainment. According to proprietors who sell adult videos, these home-made videos account for approximately 20 to 60 percent of video sales in New England. The women have no legal redress; as Gaines (1992, p. 26) writes, "women abused in this way are often too ashamed to seek public redress, consent can be obtained under duress and, in any case, no state or federal law prohibits marketing pornographic films of adults, even films showing the commission of crimes." As in other parts of the industry, the pornography may be a documentation of the harassment, abuse, rape, and torture the women are experiencing (Lovelace, 1980; Bogdanovich, 1984).

Defenders of pornography argue that the feminist anti-pornography analysis feeds into society's restrictive and repressive approach to women's sexual practices. Women in pornography should be seen as women choosing to make a living through performing sexual acts. As Anne McClintock (1993, p. 2) writes, "Far from 'selling their bodies' to men, sex workers—of whom very large numbers are men themselves—exchange specific services, often for very good money, carefully negotiating the time, the terms, the amount, and the exact service, demanding, though too seldom receiving, the respect that other workers in the social service sector can receive." Performing sex is a skill, like any other one, sexual liberals argue, and can be indicative of a woman's power and creativity. Thus, feminists should recognize women's performance in pornography as individual sexual choices, rather than a result of economics and/or gender and racial inequalities. This view fails to address the reality that the producers and directors have economic and social control and power, sometimes enforced through violence or the threat of violence, to determine the conditions and substance of pornogra-phy's production.

When confronted with evidence that many women in prostitution and pornography have histories of sexual abuse and economic exploitation, sex-ual liberals say that feminists who fight the industry are making the women into victims (Strossen, 1995). Some suggest that work in pornography may provide sexually abused women with opportunities to take back power in sex. Priscilla Alexander writes:

The connection many prostitutes report ... is that the involvement in prostitution is a way of taking back control of a situation in which, as children, they had none. Specifically, many have reported that the first time they ever felt powerful was the first time they "turned a trick" (Alexander, 1987, p. 188).

In these arguments, sexual liberals fail to address the difference between "feeling powerful" and material social and economic power, especially in terms of the structure of the industry, where the women often have little real power. A sex industry primarily defined through the economic interests and social power of capitalists, who are mostly white and male, does not offer women control over their bodies, souls, and lives.

The stories of women who have left the industry are evidence of the mistreatment, coercion, and violence that many experience (*Pornography and Sexual Violence*, 1988; Radinson, 1986; Bogdanovich, 1984). No doubt, there are also stories of women who do sex work and feel it offers them an arena in which to express their power. However, these are in sharp contrast to stories of others who report that the sex often is experienced as "abusive" and "like rape," others who learn to cope with it by disassociating themselves from their bodies by using drugs and alcohol to numb physical and emotional pain. Many women do not make substantial sums of money, and they are often abused by those who profit from their work ("Statement of WHISPER Action Group Members," 1992, p. 3). Micki Garcia, former director of Playmate Promotions, was for six years a supervisor, friend, and confidante to the "Playmates." She "saw and felt the grim realities of the Playboy lifestyle: alienation from family and friends, drug abuse, attempted suicide, prostitution, unnecessary cosmetic surgery, mental and physical abuse, rape, attempted murder and murder." Peter Bogdanovich's biography, *The Killing of the Unicorn* (1984) also documents *Playboy*'s exploitation of women.

While Kipnis (1996) portrays Althea Flynt as someone who took control of *Hustler* publisher Larry Flynt's empire after he was shot in 1978 and who compared herself to a "rogue version of *Washington Post* publisher Katharine Graham," Dorchen Leidholdt (1987) provides a very different perspective. Leidholdt contrasts Althea Flynt's public defense of pornography as women's "free choice" with the facts of her life: When she was 8 years old, her father murdered her mother and two others, and then killed himself; she was shuttled between relatives who didn't really want her until she was 17 years old; she began shooting heroin as a teenager and got a job at $90 a week as a dancer in one of Flynt's Ohio clubs to support her habit. This story suggests that Althea Flynt's own entry into prostitution and pornography cannot, with any honesty, be characterized as "free choice."

Feminist sexual liberals seem also to suggest that it is sexist to use economic inequality, poverty, or sexual violence as explanatory frameworks for understanding women's participation and experiences in the industry. According to their logic, the claim that women do not always freely choose to be involved in pornography disempowers all women because it implies that we are always victims (i.e., different, inferior to men) when it comes to sex. They say claims of coercion assume that women would never willingly choose sexual activity as a profession. These claims, they say, increase the stigma of women in the industry as "bad girls," and this stigma is the "real" source of women's oppression in and out of the industry (Bell, 1987; also see Strossen, 1995). As McClintock (1993, p. 7) writes, "The social depiction of all prostitutes as victims and sex slaves not only obscures the myriad contexts and experiences of sex work, but, more hazardously, exacerbates the dangers of assault." However, the dismissal of women's claims to coercion makes the lives of the many women who *are* coerced invisible and politically insignificant.

I am not suggesting that stories of coercion automatically cancel out the stories of empowerment and choice. But to simply accept the argument of "free choice," when there are competing and conflicting narratives of economic exploitation, abuse, and violence, serves only to shield the industry from public scrutiny, and thus accountability for those women who are being harmed. To ignore, evade, and deny the attendant issues of discrimination, abuse, and violence does not help to validate women who work in the industry. The struggle against pornography must not, in any case, be directed toward the women themselves, but rather focused on the industry and its participation in the production and reproduction of inequalities. The feminist critical analysis of pornography is a socio-structural critique, not an individual one.

The feminist sexual liberal analysis, however, does raise the important issue of the sexual stigmatization and criminalization of women in the industry. They argue that sexual injustice stems from the societal intolerance that labels, stigmatizes, and/or criminalizes individual sexual practices like prostitution as deviant (McClintock, 1993; Pheterson, 1993). Feminist sexual liberals suggest that the exploitation of women in the sex industry arises from the social stigma associated with "sex work," not the material conditions of poverty, coercion or abuse, nor the economic and social structure integral to the work (Pheterson, 1993). Mary Johnson, a woman who has worked in prostitution, explains:

If in fact we are those "poor, downtrodden women," it is because a prostitute can be evicted from her home for being a prostitute, because a dancer is arrested for doing her job, because our rights as human beings in this society are being taken away from us because of our chosen employment. It's not so much that we're being exploited by our trades or by the individuals that are in our trades, namely, the agents in the dancing industry or even the pimps in prostitution. We are free individuals that do have a choice. It is society that stops us at every turn (in Bell, 1987, p. 118).

There is no doubt that the stigma attached to women in the sex industry increases the intensity of discriminatory and inhumane treatment by the social system. The stigmatization, however, cannot be separated from the material conditions of economic exploitation and physical and sexual violence. Women who are connected, or alleged to be connected, with the sex industry in the United States are not granted credibility when they report and seek redress for sexual coercion, abuse, or rape. According to the sexist, racist, and classist socio-cultural system operating in the United States, women's participation in prostitution or pornography lessens their value as human beings. In most cases of serial murders of women, the media and the police express little outrage when the victims are identified as prostitutes (Scholder, 1993; Russo, in press). They focus on the women's identities as prostitutes to diffuse the public's concern and rarely discuss the women as full human beings (Kornack, 1989).

The question is whether the stigma can be challenged without simultaneously addressing the gender and racial inequalities and bigotry, sexual coercion, and violence that are integral to the industry and to its function and meaning in the society. To me, the stigma is intricately connected with sexualized mistreatment and abuse, misogyny and racism, social and economic inequalities, and criminal injustices. The individual women involved in the pornography industry are not the source of the problem; rather, it is the mass industry of pornography, which is built upon and perpetuates the conditions of mistreatment, economic exploitation, sexual abuse, and violence that underlie many women's lives. The abuses against women in the industry, which emanate both from within the industry and from outside (e.g., criminal justice system), are significant and should be addressed, rather than denied or minimized. The goal is not to deny an individual woman's right to choose to participate in the industry, but to target the structural inequalities both within the industry and in the social relations, structures, and institutions that shape the industry. This would include the problems of poor working conditions, coercion, and harassment, as well as criminalization and stigmatization of women by social institutions outside of the pornography industry.

CONSUMPTION OF PORNOGRAPHY AND HARM

Pornography as a product cannot be separated from its use and function in people's lives. The feminist analysis of pornography grounds its analysis on the recognition that the consumers of pornography are affected by their consumption. Feminist sexual liberals minimize the impact, saying that the pornography must be distinguished from the behavior and attitudes of those who consume it—that the discourses and images have no influence on the consumers' social relations and that the realities in pornography are separate from the realities in women's lives. And yet concrete evidence shows that pornography is created and used in ways that contribute to women's inequality and subordination and violence.

Some consumers of pornography use it to harass, intimidate, humiliate, and silence women (MacKinnon, 1987; *Public Hearings,* 1983; Russell, 1993). Some men have used pornography as a method of sexual intimidation and abuse in their heterosexual relationships; women have also reported having had pornography forced on them in their workplaces, neighborhoods, and/or social groups as methods of intimidation and exclusion (Lederer, 1980; Lederer and Delgado, 1995; Russell, 1993a; *Public Hearings,* 1983; Torrey, 1992). In education and in the workplace, the public presence of pornography may significantly undermine women's efforts toward gender equality and mutual respect.

Pornography has functioned as a method to motivate, orchestrate, justify, and guide sexual abuse and violence against women. While there are important questions to be asked about how this happens, there can be no doubt that pornography has effects in the world (for a detailed discussion of these issues, see Chapter 5).

PORNOGRAPHY, SEXUAL REPRESSION, AND THE RIGHT-WING

Sexual liberals often treat feminist anti-pornography analysis as if it was indistinguishable from right-wing perspectives and campaigns against pornography. For instance, Duggan, Hunter, and Vance (1985) link right-wing efforts to ban literature and pass anti-gay legislation with the feminist anti-pornography ordinance, suggesting that the right-wing attacks on gay and lesbian communities, abortion rights, and sex education programs are fueled by feminist criticism of sexual practices, including pornography and prostitution. However, feminists against pornography do not accept, agree, or support the right-wing's analysis. In fact, some feminists against pornography link the tremendous growth of the pornography industry with the anti-feminist backlash of the right-wing. MacKinnon argues:

> Might not the growth and viciousness of the pornography industry be an example of that repressiveness, directed specifically against women? The internal values of pornography are fascistic on every level. It has grown astronomically parallel to the rise of the Right, which deplores it openly but gets off on it covertly, even as the Left defends it openly while deploring it covertly. Maybe it's time we stopped buying the institutional Right's public rap about itself and listened to what their wives and children and the prostitutes who service them say: they love it, they use it (MacKinnon, 1985, p. 18).

Feminists against pornography recognize that the sexual repression and oppression of women are interconnected. Rather than accept the right's public anti-sexual agenda as indicative of its actual behavior, it must be deconstructed. I would suggest that the right's public agenda of anti-sexual morality does not inhibit their private sexual abuse and violence against the women and children to whom they have access. Their anti-sexual morality is particularly destructive to women because it targets women as sexually suspect and responsible for sexual activity, whether coerced or consensual. In their public rhetoric, they reinforce the strict virgin/whore dichotomy to blame, stigmatize, and segregate the class of women they associate with prostitution and pornography. This morality specifically functions to silence the women and children who have been sexually abused by infusing them with guilt and shame. The right's agenda focuses on fears of intergroup sex with and violence against "their women," especially that which crosses racial (e.g., men of color against white women) or sexual (e.g., gay/lesbian against heterosexual) lines. Their discourse deflects attention from the intimate sexual violence that occurs both in the privacy of their homes and families and in public contexts like prostitution that are made private because of access to power and money. Research indicates, for instance, that fathers who sexually assault their daughters often adhere to strict sex roles and gender power (Herman, 1981). And recent cases within the Catholic Church show that child sexual abuse and violence are not necessarily inhibited by anti-sexual ideology.

Sexual repression and right-wing moralism are dangerous, but must be analyzed in the contexts of inequality and violence. For example, sexual repression contributes to the privatization of sexual violence and abuse. The sexual liberals' tendency to focus exclusively on the social and moral restrictions on women's sexuality enables them to ignore the many women who are actively engaged in sexual relations despite public rhetoric to the contrary. Restrictions on autonomous sexual activity do not inhibit sexual abuse, but do serve to blame and punish women for both consensual and nonconsensual sexual activity. As documented in the anti-violence movement, many women (and men) are forced into sexual relations by men (and women), often as children, yet because these experiences occur in the context of silence and stigmatization, they are not discussed as public social issues. Women do not speak out because of victim-blaming no matter what the degree of force, in conjunction with the stigma and double standard attached to women's sexual activity.

Feminist sexual liberals do not address these complexities. They target public institutions and ideologies that restrict women's autonomous sexual desire and expression, while ignoring the sexualized oppression and exploitation of women. By defining the source of women's oppression solely in terms of the state and religious dogma, and the method of oppression as the public repression of women's sexual expression, their politics are limited to advocating women's individual rights to sexual desire and pleasure. This alone, however, is not enough given the prevalence of sexual violence in women's lives, particularly in intimate relationships, and given the current lack of legal redress against harassment and rape, especially for sexually active women who are further punished through the sexual double standard.

When feminist sexual liberals consistently link the feminist anti-pornography movement with the right-wing, a discussion of the sexism, misogyny, racism, and violence of the pornography industry remains unaddressed. The feminist anti-pornography movement does not have a right-wing agenda. The analysis and politics are directed against the (heterosexual) pornography industry and its connection to the endemic discrimination, harassment, and abuse in this society.

While feminist sexual liberals condemn feminists against pornography for supposedly colluding with the right, it is also important to recognize that some of them are not neutral with regard to the mainstream white heterosexual male dominant pornography industry; in some cases, they actively legitimize this part of the industry in their writings and work. Some have colluded with the pornography industry to undermine and destroy the feminist critical analysis and struggle against the industry's perpetuation of inequality and violence. Karen DeCrow, former president of the National Organization for Women and a member of Feminists for Free Expression, wrote an article for *Penthouse* condemning the feminist anti-pornography movement. This article was made into a flier and used by the Feminist Anti-

Censorship Taskforce (FACT) in their organizing efforts against the civil-rights ordinance. At the "Sex, Power and Desire" conference at Mount Holyoke, Carole Vance recalled her commiseration with representatives from *Penthouse* during the Attorney General's Commission on Pornography hearings and their shared disdain for the testimony of "self-proclaimed victims of pornography." Dworkin (1988) recalls being heckled by this group when she testified before the commission. Varda Burstyn was interviewed in *Penthouse Forum* about her book *Women Against Censorship* (1985).

The theoretical alliance with the hegemonic pornography industry is evident in FACT's publication of *Caught Looking,* which compiles photographs from "the last 100 years of pornography" with no analytic discussion of the images. The collage of images represent, for them, a "celebration of sexuality." There is no reference to the social, economic, or political conditions of their production, consumption, or distribution over the past 100 years. Nadine Strossen's *Defending Pornography* (1995) and Laura Kipnis' *Bound and Gagged* (1996) are not only explicit defenses of the industry, but also glorifications of the industry's contributions to women's sexual freedom and to the struggle against inequalities. Kipnis (1996) presents Larry Flynt as a pro-feminist, anti-classist, sexual liberator. In a very strange twist of logic, *Hustler's* racism, sexism, and classism are redefined as revolutionary and even feminist.

VICTIMIZATION AND EMPOWERMENT

Feminist sexual liberals argue that the feminist focus on sexual violence and pornography encourages women's fear and ignorance about sexuality and enhances the conservative right's anti-sexual rhetoric. They accuse feminists who focus on sexual violence of promoting ideas such as:

> Sex is degrading to women, but not to men; that men are raving beasts; that sex is dangerous for women; that sexuality is male, not female; that women are victims, not sexual actors; that men inflict "it" on women; that penetration is submission; that heterosexual sexuality, rather than the institution of heterosexuality, is sexist (Duggan, Hunter, and Vance, 1985, pp. 142–143).

Instead of trying to understand the levels of sexual violence in this society, sexual liberals claim that feminists disempower women by focusing on sexual violence. For them, documenting the realities of sexual violence minimizes women's sexual desire, autonomy, and subjectivity, magnifies male domination and misogyny, and denies women their own individual sexual choices, power, and pleasures. Ann Snitow suggests, "To bring sex and violence together is to deny that heterosexual women have a sexual interest in men. It denies women any place in the long history of heterosexuality" ("Porn: Liberation or Oppression?" 1983, p. 14). But speaking out, publicizing and protesting sexual violence, empowers women—it makes those harmed feel less alone and isolated, and it makes perpetrators more publicly accountable. Speaking out makes change possible because sexual abuse becomes a social and community issue, rather than an individual private tragedy. As Wendy Stock (1990, p. 152) writes, "Demanding change within institutions and within relationships is a crucial and effective way to push back the boundaries of patriarchy."

Feminist sexual liberals attribute the focus on sexual violence to socialized femininity and anti-sexual puritanism, not life experience; in so doing, they deny the realities of sexual violence. In fact, some argue that it is the feminist movement against violence, rather than the pervasive sexual violence that has been uncovered, that is responsible for women's fear and anger at men. They blame feminists for contributing to women's feelings of powerlessness and vulnerability. Snitow writes:

> Visibility created new consciousness, but also new fear—and new forms of old sexual terrors: sexual harassment was suddenly *everywhere*; rape was an *epidemic*; pornography was a violent polemic against women. It was almost as if, by naming the sexual crimes, by ending female denial, we frightened ourselves more than anyone else (Snitow, 1985, p. 112).

Instead of further exploring and protesting sexual violence, she argues, feminists should celebrate the development of rape hotlines and battered women's shelters as illustrative of women's power to change their social conditions. She fails to see the connection between women's, and increasingly men's, collective acknowledgment of a social problem and the development of these hotlines and shelters. Jean Bethke Elshtain challenges the claims that sexual violence is pervasive and on the increase. She argues that the literature of the feminist anti-pornography movement is characterized by "consistent overstatement of the problem and underplaying of the repressive potential in suggested solutions" (Elshtain, 1982, p. 43). In an incredible distortion of the realities of gender inequality, feminist sexual liberals blame feminists for women's fears of violence (as if the fears were not based on reality), rather than criticize the men (and women) who are perpetrating the violence and the public's social denial and lack of accountability. Their analysis misses the incredible power of women's individual and collective challenge and resistance to the sexual abuse and violence in intimate relationships. Women are empowered, not disempow-ered, when they demand the right to be treated as human beings. Hope for a better life is made possible when women struggle to change relationships, make decisions to leave relationships when equality and mutual respect are not forthcoming, and challenge and fight mistreatment and abuse in the workplace, in social institutions, and in capitalist enterprises whether or not they are connected with sexuality.

CONCLUSION

The feminist anti-pornography movement has been under attack since its inception. The debates over pornography among feminists, which some label the "sex wars," have had an incredible impact on feminist politics, especially around sexualized violence. What seems most evident in many of these fem-inist defenses of pornography is a movement away from a concern for pervasive violence against women. The arguments—as evidenced in Burstyn's *Women Against Censorship* (1985), FACT Committee's *Caught Looking* (1986), Gibson and Gibson, *Dirty Looks* (1993), Strossen's *Defending Pornography* (1995), and Kipnis' *Bound and Gagged* (1996)—emanate primarily from a frame-work of individual preferences and rights in relation to sexual exploration and expression. In brief, the arguments include: that pornography is made up of mere images and fantasies of sexuality that are created and interpreted differently by different individuals; that sexuality is separate from social inequality and violence; and that critical analyses of pornography are a form of censorship of individual ideas, creativity, and sexual identities and prac-tices and will inevitably lead to state censorship. Thus, the grounds of the defense are along the lines of individual choice and privacy in the realm of sexual identities and practices, completely separate from inequalities and social institutions.

Feminist critical analyses of the pornography industry are decidedly social, rather than individual; they locate the industry of pornography in social, economic, political structures and relations, rather than individual, interpersonal ones. The focus is on social structures and practices and the interlocking nature of social relations and institutions that perpetuate inequalities and violence in women's lives. The issue for feminists against pornography is violence, including mistreatment, harassment, rape, battery, and murder of women, and the ideological discourses and constructions that legitimate and rationalize such violence. The purpose of the grassroots feminist anti-pornography movement is to fight the pornography industry as part of a strategy to create broad-based social change, not simply individ-ual self-fulfillment. The hope is that by making public and visible the harms to women and to men in the production and mass consumption of pornography, it will help to bring the society one step closer to ending the inequalities. Through these efforts, feminists seek not only to challenge the social inequalities that pervade this society, but to create the conditions under which personal and sexual freedom will have real substance and meaning.

Unfortunately, the polarized debates have made the struggle against violence and toward sexual freedom opposing goals, rather than interdependent and mutually reinforcing movements. Feminist sexual liberals do not seem to recognize the power of resistance against social inequalities, discrimination, and violence when they are connected to sexuality. But it is also true that feminists against pornography sometimes seem to minimize the need for individual women to discuss and explore the complexities of women's relationships with sexualized power dynamics inevitable in such a social and historical context, as well as sexual desires and pleasures (see Chapter 6). Both are essential to any forward movement in this discussion and debate and are fundamental to social transformation. The sexual restrictions and punishments placed on women that often operate simultaneously with the coercion and violence must be equally addressed and challenged in order to create the conditions for social justice and freedom.

NOTES

1.　For the purposes of the ordinance, women are the generic; however, men, children, and transsexuals may utilize the ordinance if they can connect the harm they experienced to sex discrimination.

2.　For the purposes of this essay, I use the term "sexual liberals" to refer to feminist and progressive writers, scholars, and activists who criticize the feminist anti-pornography movement on the grounds of potential infringement on individual rights to sexual identity, sexual expression, individual interpretation, freedom of speech, and privacy. What makes their analysis "liberal" is their focus on issues of restriction or limitation, real or perceived, in relation to an individual's choices, which emanate, from a liberal rights tradition in U.S. social theory and politics.

THREE

Dirty Business

Playboy Magazine and the Mainstreaming of Pornography

GAIL DINES

The major trade publication of the pornography video industry, *Adult Video News*, stated in its 1996 *Adult Entertainment Video Guide*, "economically ... adult video sales are doing better than ever—and adult manufacturers have been working overtime to supply the demand for XXX product" (p. 8). Indeed, both production and sales are at an all-time high (rental and sales of videos reached the $3 billion mark in 1995), and the industry is moving into newer technologies such as CD-ROM and the Internet. The pornography industry[1] was not always a multibillion-dollar-a-year business with sales across the globe. Mass-produced, mass-distributed pornography is a relatively new phenomenon, growing out of the under-the-counter, poor quality pin-ups and stag movies that had previously dominated the market.

Charting the evolution of this industry has not been given priority in much of the work on pornography that grew out of the "porn wars," with scholars focusing instead on "the text," often decontextualized from its cultural and economic conditions of production (see especially Kaite, 1995; Kaplan, 1987; Rubin, 1993). One outcome of this type of work is a construction of pornography as free-floating sexual fantasy that belongs in the realm of the private, rather than as an industry that is historically located within a specific matrix of economic and cultural conditions. To examine the text outside of its politics of production is to miss how the pornographic text is itself shaped by the different ways production is financed and organized.

Given the staggering profits enjoyed by this industry, the time is ripe for an exploration into how it developed from its somewhat humble beginnings to its present-day global level. This is no easy task, since there are many factors that influenced the evolution of the pornography industry, ranging from technological advances in communications to changes in obscenity law fought by pornographers and mainstream media producers.

While there are many different paths that can be taken to explore the growth and development of the industry, many would lead to late 1953, when *Playboy* magazine first appeared on newsstands. The phenomenal success of the magazine played a major part in transforming the industry from an under-the-counter "sleazy" endeavor to a multibillion-dollar-a-year industry. Hugh Hefner's brilliant marketing strategy, together with his willingness to fight the legal battles to gain access to mainstream distributors and outlets, paved the way for *Penthouse* and *Hustler*, the most successful "hard-core"[2] pornographic magazine in the world. These three top-selling pornography magazines (together with their imitators), in turn, helped to lay the economic, legal, and cultural foundations for the development and growth of the video pornography market, a market that threatens to swallow up the shrinking print pornography industry.

By any standards, *Playboy* was an overnight success, increasing its sales from 53,991 copies in its first month to 175,000 by its first anniversary issue, and by 1959 to a circulation of 1 million a month. At its peak in the late 1960s and early 1970s, the Playboy company was an enormous business concern with sales of over $200 million and more than 5,000 employees. Clearly, as Michael Kimmel argues, "*Playboy* struck a nerve with American men" (Kimmel, 1996, p. 255), and many books have attempted to describe exactly what that nerve was (see for example, Brady, 1974; Miller, 1984; Weyr, 1978). To explore the *Playboy* phenomena, and the magazine's role in laying the groundwork for the contemporary pornography industry, the magazine has to be historically located in the economic and cultural trends at work during the 1950s, which at different times and to varying degrees contributed to *Playboy* becoming the lifestyle magazine of choice for the upwardly mobile, white American male in the post-war years.

PLAYBOY MAGAZINE AND THE "PRO-FAMILY," ANTI-FEMALE 1950s

The 1950s was a time of enormous change in the United States, both economically and culturally. Historians of the 1950s point to the economic boom, the baby boom, women working outside the home, the growth of suburbia, the pressure to marry at an early age, and the push toward consumption as a way of life as trends that if not wholly specific to the 1950s, were magnified and legitimized to an unprecedented degree (Coontz, 1992; May, 1988; Miller and Nowak, 1977). *Playboy* magazine occupies an ambivalent place in relation to these trends—some it celebrated as the best things to happen to America, while others it condemned as the living embodiment of hell. It was its uncanny ability to pick and choose among these trends that made *Playboy* a success not only with readers, but also eventually with advertisers. But long before the advertisers realized that *Playboy* was reaching the very men that corporations sought (young, white, college-educated, upwardly mobile), the readers themselves made *Playboy* the lifestyle magazine of the 1950s.

From the start Hefner was clear about his targeted audience. He wrote in the first issue of *Playboy* published in late 1953:

> If you are a man between 18 and 80, Playboy is meant for you.... We want to make it clear from the start, we aren't a "family" magazine. If you are somebody's sister, wife or mother-in-law and picked us up by mistake, please pass us along to the man in your life and get back to the *Ladies' Home Companion.*

For a magazine to clearly state that it was not "a family magazine" in the 1950s was close to heresy. According to social historian Stephanie Coontz (1992), during this period there was an unprecedented rise in the marriage rate, the age for marriage and motherhood fell, fertility increased, and divorce rates declined. From family restaurants to the family car, "the family was everywhere hailed as the most basic institution in society" (Coontz, 1992, p. 24). Indeed, getting married and having children became a patriotic duty since America needed strong families to fight the Russian menace; in some cases, it was suggested that in the event of a nuclear war with Russia, the nation with the strongest family would be the victor (May, 1988, p. 154).

The mass media played a major role in legitimizing and celebrating this pro-family ideology by selling idealized images of family life in the sitcoms and women's magazines while demonizing those who chose to stay single as either homosexual or pathological. The most celebrated sitcoms of the period were "Leave it to Beaver," "Father Knows Best," and "The Adventures of Ozzie and Harriet." The ideal family was white, upper-middle-class, with a male breadwinner whose salary supported a stay-at-home-wife and a large well-appointed home in the suburbs. Both husband and wife were depicted as rooting their primary identity in the family, and the result was a well-run household populated with smart, well-adjusted kids.

While the broadcast media sold the happy-family image, the print media provided tales of woe for those who had the misfortune to remain single. *Reader's Digest* ran a story entitled "You Don't Know How Lucky You Are to Be Married," which focused on the "harrowing situation of single life" (quoted in Miller and Nowak, 1977, p. 154). Similarly, *The Woman's Guide to Better Living* told its readers that "the family is the unit to which you most genuinely belong. . . . The family is the center of your living. If it isn't, you've gone far astray" (quoted in Miller and Nowak, 1977, p. 147). One writer went so far as to suggest that "except for the sick, the badly crippled, the deformed, the emotionally warped and the mentally defective, almost everyone has an opportunity to marry" (quoted in in Miller and Nowak, 1977, p. 154). In the 1950s, "emotionally warped" was a coded way of saying homosexual, and indeed many single people were investigated as potential homosexuals and by extension communists, since the two were often linked during the McCarthy years (Coontz, 1992, p. 33).

The effects of this massive pro-family trend in the 1950s has been the focus of much feminist analysis, for as Douglas Miller and Marion Nowak argue, "Woman's role was the base of the domestic and sexual pyramid. If she refused . . . the whole structure collapsed. She was compelled to submit" (Miller and Nowak, 1977, p. 157). The women's magazines, the sitcoms, and the growing field of child development all collaborated to prove to the 1950s suburban housewife that women were most fulfilled when they were wives and mothers, and to feel otherwise was unnatural, sick, and a threat to the very security of the nation.

In 1963, Betty Friedan's *The Feminine Mystique* (1974/1963) provided one of the first major insights into what life was really like for the young, white, middle-class wives who found themselves in the suburbs, alone for most of the day with young children and limited transportation. The depression and despair that Friedan documented was profound, and, indeed, helped to form the liberal feminist movement of the second half of the twentieth century.

What seems to be less well researched by historians and sociologists are the effects of this suffocating domesticity on men. Just as women were being told to root their identity in the roles of wife and mother, so too were men being instructed to see themselves as primarily husbands and fathers. To be a real man meant being the breadwinner, a nurturing but disciplining father who spent his spare time tinkering in the garage or in the yard rather than out with the guys.

Magazines ran stories on how to be a good dad, and the sitcoms were no less a socializing agent for men than they were for women. Just as Harriet enjoyed being house-bound, so too did Ozzie look forward to spending the evening in his comfortable living room surrounded by his adoring family. One episode of "Ozzie and Harriet," aptly titled "Ozzie's Night Out," shows Ozzie being cajoled into a night out by his next-door neighbor, a man who clearly does not take his fathering role as seriously as Ozzie. Ozzie at first declines because he has to help the boys with their homework and Harriet with balancing her checkbook. However, after much reassurance from his family, Ozzie goes bowling. The result in the home is chaos—the boys can't do their homework and Harriet ends up $50 overdrawn. When Ozzie returns home we find that the evening was equally disastrous for him. The bowling alley was closed, and he spent the evening wandering the streets alone until he plucked up the courage to come home and admit what an awful evening he had without Harriet and the boys. It is no surprise that after the media bombardment, *Life* magazine declared 1954 as the "year of the domestication of the American Man."

This ideology of domestication was given further legitimation by social scientific theories. The 1950s was the heyday of the "scientific" study of juvenile delinquency, especially in sociology. One of the main causes of delinquency in boys was said to be the lack of a father figure, and, according to Talcott Parsons (1963), one of the most influential post-war sociologists, delinquency could be avoided by a strong nuclear family with a father at the head. Men who did not take up their proper role as head of the family were suspect. One of the best-selling books of the 1950s argued that "bachelors of more than thirty, unless deficient, should be encouraged to undergo psychotherapy" (Farnham and Lundberg, 1947, p. 370–371). This policing of men's behavior was carried over into the corporate world, where lack of a wife could mean loss of a job or a promotion (Coontz, 1992, p. 33). Corporate America also required its own type of homogeneity on the job: loyalty to the company, group conformity, and willingness to take orders from bosses.

The pressure on men to conform to both domestic life and corporate life was not without its critics. Existing side by side with the pro-conformity ideology of the mass media was a growing body of literature, academic and popular, that began to voice concerns about what effect domestic and corporate conformity might have on the American male. In the academic discourse, C. Wright Mills (1953) and David Reisman (1950) talked about how the American male was made to feel "dwarfed and helpless" by corporate America (Mills, 1953, p. 47) and was forced to be a cog in a wheel, stripped of his identity and agency. The mainstream media echoed some of these fears, talking about the conformist male as "a psychopath, a mechanized, robotized caricature of humanity," "a slave in mind and body" (Ehrenreich, 1983, p. 30). According to Ehrenreich, *Life, Look,* and *Reader's Digest* all carried stories suggesting that "Gary Gray" (the conformist in the gray flannel suit) was robbing men of their masculinity, freedom, and sense of individuality.

While the social scientists and pop psychologists criticized the corporate world for reducing American men to "little men" (Kimmel, 1996, p. 240), it was women in the form of wives and mothers who were really singled out as the true destroyers of American manhood. As Barbara Ehrenreich has argued, because "the corporate captains were out of the bounds of legitimate criticism in Cold War America" (Ehrenreich, 1983, p. 36), women were the more acceptable and accessible villain. Described as "dumb," "greedy," "rapacious," and as "an idle class, a spending class, a candy craving class" (Wylie, 1942, p. 48), American women were accused by best-selling authors, magazine writers, and social scientists of turning American men and boys into cross-dressing, sexually frustrated wimps who left all the manly decisions to their overbearing wives (Miller and Nowak, 1977, pp. 164–167).

The most vicious, and indeed popular, of woman-hating books was Philip Wylie's *Generation of Vipers*, first published in 1942 but frequently reprinted after World War II. The source of modern ills, according to Wylie, was "mom" who "is everywhere and everything and damned near everybody.... Disguised as good old mom, dear old mom, sweet old mom ... she is the bride at every funeral and corpse at every wedding" (Wylie, 1942, pp. 187–188). As a wife, "mom" was no better—she worked her husband into an early grave so she could have increased leisure time and the trappings of middle-class life. As Wylie so eloquently put it, "It is her man who worries about where to acquire the money while she worries about how to spend it, so he has the ulcers and she has the guts of a bear" (Wylie, 1942, p. 99, quoted in Kimmel, 1996, p. 254).

This anti-woman ideology was being picked up in public discourse. For example, *Industrial Design*, when tackling the perplexing question of what women do all day, echoed Wylie's rantings:

> Automatic ranges and one-step washer dryers leave the housewife with a precious ingredient: time. This has come to be regarded as both her bonus and her right, but not everyone regards it with unqualified enthusiasm. Critics belonging to the woman's-place-is-in-the-home school ask cynically what is she free for? The bridge table? Afternoon TV? The lonely togetherness of telephone gossip? The analyst's couch? Maybe (*Industrial Design*, 4(12), pp. 33–34, quoted in Haralovich, 1989, p. 68).

Typical of woman-hating ideology, women couldn't win no matter what their choice. Should women choose to go out to work rather than play bridge, watch TV, or gossip on the phone, they were destroying the American family. Another best-selling book of the period, *The Modern Woman: The Lost Sex* (1947) by Marynia Farnham and Ferdinand Lundberg, called feminism a "deep illness" (p. 24) that caused women to deny their true femininity by seeking paid employment. According to these two writers, women's paid employment resulted in confused children, unfulfilled husbands, and sexual frustration on the part of women. A few years later, Merle Miller defined working women as "that increasing and strident minority of women who are doing their damndest to wreck marriage and home life in America, those who insist on having both a husband and career. They are a menace and they have to be stopped" (*Esquire*, July 1973, p. 126, quoted in Miller and Nowak, 1977, p. 164). According to Coontz (1992), corporate America did as much as it could to stop this menace. However, women were not so quick to give up on their independence, and, by 1952, there were 2 million more wives in the labor force than there had been at the peak of war-time production.

It was during these woman-hating, pro-family years that *Playboy* hit the newsstands. Picking up on the growing anti-woman, anti-domesticity ideology of the 1950s, *Playboy* editors, from the first issue, defined women—married and single—as a menace to the *Playboy* reader because they were out to get him financially. The first major article in the first issue of *Playboy* was called "Miss Gold-Digger of 1953." Bemoaning the good-old days when alimony was reserved for "little floosies," the *Playboy* editors wrote, "When a modern day marriage ends, it doesn't matter who's to blame—its always the guy who pays and pays and pays and pays" (p. 16). Echoing Wylie, that women had taken over America, the article continues, "A couple of generations ago, this was a man's world, [now] nothing could be further from the truth in 1953" (p. 16).

This was a theme that was to be expressed again and again in the early years of *Playboy*. Burt Zollo, writing in the June 1954 issue, told *Playboy* readers to "take a good look at the sorry, regimented husbands trudging down every woman-dominated street in this woman-dominated land" (p. 38). For those men who had been lucky enough to escape marriage, Zollo warned them to beware of June, the marriage month, since "woman becomes more heated, more desperate, more dangerous" (p. 38). Dangerous women were the focus of Wylie's article, "The Womanization of America," published in *Playboy* in September 1958. Starting from the now familiar themes developed in his book, Wylie accused American women of taking over the business world, the arts, and, of course, the home. It is the home, according to Wylie, where men especially cease to be men since the "American home, in short, is becoming a boudoir-kitchen-nursery, dreamed up for women by women, and as if males did not exist as males" (*Playboy*, September 1958, p. 78). It appears that the position of American men continued to deteriorate; by 1963, according to an article in *Playboy*, the American man was being worked so hard by his wife that he was "day after day, week after week . . . invited to attend his own funeral." This state of affairs could not continue, according to writer William Iversen, because "neither double eyelashes nor the blindness of night or day can obscure the glaring fact that American marriage can no longer be accepted as an estate in which the sexes shall live half-slave and half-free" (*Playboy*, September 1963, p. 92).

While the anti-woman ideology of *Playboy* was not new, what was new was the way it was tied in to an anti-marriage position. Rather than suggesting new and more sophisticated ways of controlling the time and labor of the lazy, greedy, overbearing housewife, *Playboy* was throwing the baby out with the bath water. American wives were beyond salvation; they had been given too much power, and the only solution was to refuse to conform to the ideal of domesticity. However, telling men simply not to conform by staying single would not have been enough in the 1950s, since nonconformity was taken as a sign of either homosexuality or social pathology. What was needed was an alternative to "Gary Gray," an image of a man who refused to conform but was no less a man, a man who would work hard but not for his family, rather for his own needs and wants, a man who was actively heterosexual but not with a wife, rather, with lots of young, beautiful women. Such a man, Zollo informed readers in the June 1954 issue of *Playboy*, did indeed exist and he was the "true playboy," the well-dressed, sophisticated guy who could "enjoy the pleasures the female has to offer without becoming emotionally involved" (*Playboy*, June 1954, p. 38). *Playboy* magazine was to become the manual for men who aspired to be a playboy, and these men, born and/or raised in a time of material deprivation (the Depression and World War II) and sexual conservatism, needed all the help they could get on how to become a big-spending, up-market consumer of goods and women.

Part of *Playboy*'s overnight success can be explained in terms of lack of competition, since the men's magazine industry was dominated by magazines that specialized in what was referred to as "blood, guts and fighting" (Weyr, 1978, p. 2). After the war, this industry enjoyed record-breaking profits with sales increasing 62 percent from 1945 to 1952 (Barko, 1953, p. 29). At the time there was some concern over the increasingly violent content of these magazines. Naomi Barko, for example, writing in 1953 complained that men's magazines were dominated by "war, big-game hunting, women, speed sports and crime," a world where "jobs, families, careers, education and civic problems are never mentioned"(Barko, 1953, p. 30). While these magazines were offering escape from the suburban world of the 1950s, it was an escapism founded on danger and adventure rather than sex. Even *Esquire* conformed to the sexually conservative 1950s by reducing its sexual content in an attempt to redefine itself as a more upscale literary magazine.

Hefner understood that the magazine market was enjoying a boom (he worked as an entry-level clerk at a number of magazines, including *Esquire*), and that *Esquire*'s move away from sex had opened up a niche in the market. While there was a print pornography market, it was dominated by the poorly produced, under-the-counter pin-up magazines, the type that men would hide in a brown-paper bag rather than display on a coffee table. Hefner was well aware that the financial potential of these magazines was limited in the 1950s, and, moreover, he did not want to create just a pornography magazine; rather, he wanted to develop an up-market lifestyle magazine that would have the pornographic pin-up as its centerpiece. This was the core of the magazine, but unlike the other pornography magazines of the time, this pin-up would be delivered to the readers in a package that celebrated upper-middle-class bachelor life, the type of life that the 1950s male dreamed of having, be he a college student, a married man living in the suburbs, or an upwardly mobile corporate male.

SELLING *PLAYBOY* TO THE PLAYBOY

Hefner's desire to create a pornographic lifestyle magazine with mainstream distribution, readership, and status meant he had to carefully construct the public image of *Playboy* as a "quality life-style magazine" (Miller, 1984, p. 23) that had "tasteful" pictures of women, rather than as a pornographic magazine that carried articles on consumer items and current events. The fact that *Playboy* was in the business of constructing and reconstructing its image is apparent in the way it marketed itself to different target groups. It appears that Hefner's initial marketing strategy was to sell *Playboy* as a soft-core pornography magazine to the potential distributors and as a lifestyle "men's" magazine to the targeted audience. In April 1953, six months before the first copy of *Playboy* hit the stands, Hefner sent a letter to 25 of the largest newsstand wholesalers throughout the United States inquiring about potential interest in the magazine, which was originally to be called *Stag Party*.[3] The letter read:

> *Dear Friend,*
> STAG PARTY—a brand new magazine for men—will be out this fall—and it will be one of the best sellers you have ever handled. . . . It will include male pleasing figure studies, making it a sure hit from the very start. But here's the really BIG news! The first issue of STAG PARTY will

include the famous calendar picture of Marilyn Monroe—in full color! In fact every issue of STAG PARTY will have a beautiful full page, male pleasing nude study—in full natural color. Now you know what I mean when I say that this is going to be one of the best sellers you have ever handled ... fill out the postage paid Air Mail reply card enclosed and get it back to me as quickly as possible (Miller, 1984, p. 39).

While the pictorials were emphasized in the letter to wholesalers, it was the lifestyle section of the magazine that was promoted to readers. In the first edition of *Playboy*, Hefner told his readers that:

Within the pages of Playboy you will find articles, fiction, pictures, stories, cartoons, humor and special features ... to form a pleasure-primer styled to the masculine taste. ... we plan [on] spending most of our time inside.

We like our apartment. We enjoy mixing up cocktails and an hors d'oeuvre or two, putting a little mood music on the phonograph and inviting in a female acquaintance for a quiet discussion on Picasso, Nietzsche, Jazz, Sex.

Notice that when addressing the reader, the pictures are just one of many attractions, rather than the attraction. The reader is invited, not to masturbate to the centerfold, but rather to enter the world of the cultural elite, who discuss philosophy and consume food associated with the upper-middle class. To sell the magazine primarily in terms of its pictorials, as was done to distributors, would have constructed a very different image for the reader to identify with. The markers of upper-class life, which appear causally thrown in as afterthoughts (cocktails, hors d'oeuvres and Picasso), were more likely deliberately placed to cloak the magazine in an aura of upper-middle-class respectability.

The centerfolds would barely raise an eyebrow today, with their carefully concealed pubic hair and coy gazes at the camera. However, in the 1950s, they were considered daring, and many in publishing felt that Hefner was heading for jail (Weyr, 1978, p. 8). That these were the selling point of the magazine, however, was never doubted by Hefner and the early editors of *Playboy*. One such editor, Ray Russell, commenting on the importance of the pictures, stated in an interview that:

we could have all the Nabokovs in the world and the best articles on correct attire without attracting readers. They bought the magazine for the girls. We couldn't take the sex out. The magazine would die like a dog (Weyr, 1978, 35).

However, given the time period, Russell would have been equally correct if he had reversed the order and said that the magazine will die like a dog if we take the articles out. These were crucial in providing a cover for the reader and allowed the self-defined middle-class American male to indulge in an activity that had been defined as "low-class."

One effective technique that Hefner employed to give *Playboy* an up-market image was to develop the literary side of the magazine. For the first few years of *Playboy*, Hefner or one of his editors would select the literary content, often choosing materials that were in the public domain, for economic reasons. However, as sales increased toward the end of 1956, Hefner started looking around for a managing editor to help run the magazine. His eventual choice was Auguste Comte Spectorsky, who had been an editor for *The New Yorker* and was an aspiring author. On taking the job, Spectorsky claimed that he would devote his efforts to the literary side of the magazine, and within a few years *Playboy* became a magazine that attracted the most respected American writers. The problem for Hefner was that Spectorsky became increasingly uncomfortable with the sexual content of the magazine and wanted Hefner to put more money and effort into developing the literary and service features. It seems that Spectorsky was not aware of the role that the literary side was to play in legitimizing *Playboy* and mistakenly assumed that Hefner was interested in *Playboy* becoming more of a literary magazine than a pornographic one. According to Miller (1984) and Weyr (1978), the relationship between Hefner and Spectorsky became very conflicted, with editors splitting up into Hefner's "pro-sex" camp and Spectorsky's "pro-literature" camp.

While the two factions fought over the content of the magazine, they were careful to construct in the magazine an ideal reader who bought *Playboy* for the articles, interviews, humor, and advice columns. If Spectorsky can be faulted, it is for believing in the image of the ideal reader that *Playboy* constructed, the playboy. Although articles and editorials often made reference to the playboy who reads *Playboy*, it was in the April 1956 issue where Hefner most clearly laid out his image of the ideal *Playboy* reader. He wrote:

> What is a playboy? Is he simply a wastrel, a ne'er-do-well, a fashionable bum? Far from it. He can be a sharp minded young business executive, a worker in the arts, a university professor, an architect or an engineer. He can be many things, provided he possesses a certain kind of view. He must

see life not as a vale of tears, but as a happy time, he must take joy in his work, without regarding it as the end of all living; he must be an alert man, a man of taste, a man sensitive to pleasure, a man who—without acquiring the stigma of voluptuary or dilettante—can live life to the hilt. This is the sort of man we mean when we use the word playboy.

The actual *Playboy* reader of the 1950s looked nothing like the playboy described above. More than half the readers were married (54 percent) and more than one quarter were undergraduate college students. As for being a man of taste, most of the readers had, as discussed earlier, grown up during a time of material deprivation and were not used to high-level consumption. Thus, these men needed to be schooled in the ways of living "life to the hilt" and especially in how to spend money. Clearly, given the experiences of the older generation, these young men could not turn to their parents for guidance on how to spend their discretionary income. A new, modern teacher was needed and Hefner was only too willing to became a major player in this campaign, providing to men an image of what constitutes a *Playboy* lifestyle. Toward this end, all the products offered by the magazine were to be of the highest quality: the short stories, the interviews with famous people, the cars, the alcohol, the clothes, the food, the advice about consumer items to buy, and, of course, the women.

From the very first issue of *Playboy*, pages and pages of editorial comment instruct readers as to what products to buy to become a playboy. In the early years, mainstream advertisers avoided *Playboy* because of its "raunchy" image, thus the products were discussed in articles rather than advertisements. In the first *Playboy*, for example, a special feature on desk designs informs the reader which desks make the best impressions. Arguing that big desks and heavy cabinets are depressing and old-fashioned, the editors suggest that the new, more sleek-looking desk tells clients that "this executive and his firm are as up-to-date as tomorrow, know where they are going and will use the most modern methods to get there" (*Playboy*, 1953, p. 41). The comparison of the old with the "modern" is a standard theme in the early years of *Playboy*, with the reader being told again and again that a real playboy buys only modern lampshades, ties, clothes, and ice buckets [the Fiberg ice bucket being the one to "please any playboy" (*Playboy*, January 1954, p. 4)].

Playboy was not the only media product to sell the 1950s young adult an ideology of consumption. According to George Lipsitz, the main function of television in the 1950s was to provide "legitimation for transformations in values initiated by the new economic imperatives of postwar America"

(Lipsitz, 1990, p. 44). One way to do this, according to Ernest Dichter, the marketing guru of the 1950s, was to demonstrate "that the hedonistic approach to life is a moral one, not an immoral one" (Dichter, quoted in Lipsitz, 1990, p. 47).

While *Playboy* was one of many media corporations to employ Dichter, it was the only one whose clear aim was to turn the male into a consumer. In the *Playboys* of the 1950s, every area of the reader's life was discussed, dissected, and marketed. Elaine May (1988) has argued that the 1950s was in general the period of the "expert," when increasing numbers of people turned to professionals for advice on what to buy, how to bring up children, even on how to prepare for a nuclear war. *Playboy* editors certainly played the role of the expert with gushing enthusiasm, telling readers "what to wear, eat, drink, read and drive, how to furnish their homes and listen to music, which nightclubs, restaurants, plays and films to attend, what equipment to own" (Weyr, 1978, p. 55).

However, as with all advertising, the actual product on offer was not the commodity being advertised but rather the fantasy of transformation that this product promised to bring to the consumer's life. Within *Playboy*, the high-quality products would transform the reader into a "playboy" who could then have the real prize: all the high-quality women he wanted—just like the ones who populated the magazine. The women in the *Playboy* pictorials were designed to be "teasers," demonstrating to the reader what he could have if he adopted the *Playboy* lifestyle of high-level consumption. In an interview, Hefner revealed this strategy of sexualizing consumption when he explained: "*Playboy* is a combination of sex . . . and status . . . the sex actually includes not only the Playmate and the cartoons and the jokes which describe boy-girl situations, but goes right down in all the service features" (Brady, 1974, p. 95).

Hefner, by sexualizing consumption, provided an extremely hospitable environment for advertisers looking to expand markets in the post-war boom. By the end of 1955, advertisers had overcome their initial fear of advertising in a "men's entertainment" magazine and were "clamoring to buy" (Weyr, 1978, p. 32). During the 1950s and 1960s, *Playboy* continued to increase its readership and its advertising revenue, and by the late 1960s the circulation figures reached an all-time high of 4.5 million. An article in *Business Week* in 1969 titled "Playboy Puts a Glint in the Admen's Eyes," discussed the enormous popularity of *Playboy* magazine with the advertisers and quotes a media man at J. Walter Thompson Co., the world's largest advertising agency at the time, as saying that years ago none of their clients would have touched *Playboy* but "today, it's a routine buy" (*Business Week*, June 28, 1969, p. 36). The magazine then informs its readers that "last year JWT expenditure in the magazine increased 70 percent."

Despite the increased advertising revenue that *Playboy* enjoyed well into the 1960s, its relationship with advertisers was stormy. The main reason for this was *Playboy's* somewhat split personality as a lifestyle magazine and a pornography magazine. The advertisers loved *Playboy's* readership (mostly white, college-educated, upwardly mobile men) yet disliked its sexual content for fear of being associated with a sleazy pornography magazine. In the early years, Hefner and his major associates regularly flew to New York for emergency meetings with advertisers whose clients felt that the pictorials or stories had gone too far (Brady, 1974; Weyr, 1978). Many of these meetings ended in a promise from the *Playboy* staff to limit the overt sexual content, and no revenue was lost. One such battle occurred over a story by Calder Willingham which appeared in the July 1962 issue. Called "Bus Story," it focuses on the rape of a 17-year-old girl by an older man. However, as in much of pornography, the story is written in a way that sexualizes the brutality:

> There are times to be tender and times to be just a little rough. This was a time to be just a little rough. Left forearm heavily across her breasts and left hand gripping her shoulder so hard she winced, Harry used his knees like a wedge, grey eyes hypnotic above her. "Open your legs," he said in a cold, hard and vicious tone. Lips apart and eyes empty with shock, the girl did as she was told. A moment later, hands limp on his shoulders, a gasp came from here. Then another gasp (Quoted in Weyr, 1978, p. 128).

A number of companies, including Ford Motor and Hart, Schaffner, and Marx, threatened to cancel contracts with *Playboy,* and a number of newsstand wholesalers refused to carry the July issue. Fear of losing the advertisers prompted Hefner to write a letter of apology to all the major corporations that advertised in the July issue, and he offered to meet personally with their representatives (Brady, 1974, p. 129). This kind of economic power has meant that advertisers have policed (and continue to police) the sexual content of *Playboy*. Thus, built into the magazine is a conflict between the need to attract advertising revenue and the need to keep the readers interested in the sexual content. When there was no competition, keeping the readers was relatively easy since the readers' only other option was the poorly produced, down-market variety of pornography, which certainly did not offer the reader a "playboy" image of himself. However, as the pornography market began to develop, other magazines adopted the *Playboy* formula, while pushing for more explicit imagery in the pictorials. Chief among these competitors was *Penthouse*, a magazine that specifically aimed to replace *Playboy* as the best-selling pornography magazine in the country. The competition between *Playboy* and *Penthouse* in the early 1970s not only hurt *Playboy* financially, it also changed the mainstream print pornography industry by pushing the limits of what was deemed as acceptable, both legally and culturally.

THE COMPETITIVE DYNAMICS OF THE MASS-DISTRIBUTED PORNOGRAPHY MAGAZINE INDUSTRY

In the summer of 1969, the *New York Times*, *Chicago Tribune*, and *Los Angeles Times* all carried full-page advertisements showing the *Playboy* bunny caught in the cross hairs of a rifle. The caption of the advertisement for *Penthouse* magazine, which would be on the newsstands later that year, read, "We're going rabbit hunting." According to Miller (1984), the news, at first, was greeted with some amusement on the part of the *Playboy* staff. *Playboy*, in 1969, had a monthly circulation of 4.5 million, a figure unmatched by competitors. Robert Guccione, the editor-publisher of *Penthouse* magazine, aimed to topple *Playboy* from the number-one slot by following its literary and service format while making the pictorials more sexually explicit. By foregoing advertising revenue in the short term, he planned to draw in the advertisers after he had put *Playboy* out of business. In a *Newsweek* article on *Penthouse*, Guccione is quoted as saying, "I'm not coming to America to be number No. 2 . . . in five years, *Playboy* and *Penthouse* will be locked in a toe-to-toe competition" (*Newsweek*, March 2, 1970, p. 71).

Penthouse started with a circulation of 350,000. By February 1970, the figure had grown to 500,000. Miller argues that one major reason for the increase was that *Penthouse* photos were more explicit, especially in their willingness to reveal pubic hair. *Playboy* meanwhile continued to resist showing pubic hair and instead focused on what they called the "girl next door look," which largely consisted of a photographic convention Kuhn (1985) calls "caught unawares."[4] The more explicit imagery in *Penthouse* was the focus of a number of articles in mainstream magazines, with *Forbes* (March 1, 1971, p. 19), *Business Week* (August, 9, 1969, p. 98), and *Time* (Nov. 7, 1969, p. 88) commenting on the willingness of *Penthouse* to go beyond *Playboy*'s levels of explicitness. *Forbes*, for example, describes *Penthouse* as being "much bolder. Whereas *Playboy* bared breasts in the mid-fifties, now *Penthouse* has introduced pubic hair . . . and kinky letters to the editor on subjects like caning and slave parties" (*Forbes*, March 1, 1971, p. 19). These articles could be seen as free advertising for *Penthouse* since they often discussed the competition in a tongue-in-cheek manner, with no analysis of how this publishing war, with its battleground being the female body, could have consequences for the way women's bodies are represented in pornography and mainstream media. Rather, the articles gave titillating accounts of Guccione's *Penthouse* ["his girls (sic) look less airbrushed—and hence sexier—than *Playboy*'s and the copy in *Penthouse* is more bluntly erotic" (*Newsweek*, March 2, 1970, p. 71)], and gave quotes as teasers from *Penthouse* magazine stories: "Her eyes sparkled 'We are in a birchwood. Perhaps you want to birch me. Yes?'" (*Time*, November, 7, 1969, p. 88). The only topic that is treated with any seriousness in these articles is the impact that this war is having on the financial health of the magazines.

By the end of 1970, *Penthouse*'s circulation had reached 1.5 million. Hefner decided that he could no longer ignore Guccione, and there "began a contest between Hefner and Guccione to see who could produce the raunchier magazine" (Miller, 1984, p. 194). When *Penthouse* came out with the first full frontal centerfold in August 1971, *Playboy* followed suit in January 1972. This change in policy must be seen as having some success for, by September 1972, *Playboy* broke all previous circulation records by selling 7,012,000 copies. By 1973, however, *Playboy*'s circulation began to decline while *Penthouse*'s was increasing past the 4 million mark. Miller (1984) argues that what followed could only be defined as an all-out circulation war fought over who could produce the most "daring" pictures.

To make matters worse for *Playboy*, the magazine's advertisers were beginning to complain again about the explicit nature of the pictorials. A number of high-level *Playboy* executives flew to New York to meet with advertising agents who were concerned about what they saw as the increasingly pornographic content of the magazine. Hefner had been one of the original proponents of keeping up with *Penthouse*, but because of the pressure from advertisers, internal battles with editors, and the appearance of other competitors such as *Gallery* and *Hustler*, which captured the more hard-core market, Hefner capitulated, sending a memo to all the department editors informing them that *Playboy* would cease to cater to those readers interested in looking at "gynaecologically detailed pictures of girls" (Miller, 1984, p. 204) and would instead return to its previous standards.

Current circulation figures suggest that Hefner made the right decision. In 1995, *Playboy* had a monthly circulation of nearly 3.5 million and an advertising rate of $61,680 for one page while *Penthouse* reported just over a million circulation with an advertising rate of $39,510. One possible explanation for this is that *Playboy*, by staking out its terrain as the "respectable soft-core" magazine, still has no real competitor. With its airbrushed shots of women's bodies sandwiched in between the interviews, political articles, and service features that presume a privileged male reader, *Playboy* continues to sell itself as a lifestyle magazine. Indeed, in their promotional material aimed at potential advertisers, *Playboy* compares itself to *Sports Illustrated*, *Rolling Stone*, *Esquire*, *GQ,* and *Details,* and describes its magazine as being about "the way men live in the nineties . . . . Entertainment, fashion, cars, sports, the issues, the scene, the people who make waves, the women men idealize" (*Playboy* Advertising Rate Card # 44). What is clearly absent from *Playboy*'s list of competitors is its real major competitor, *Penthouse,* and what is thus rendered invisible in its promotional description is the pornographic content that sells the magazine.

Penthouse, on the other hand, because it tends to be more explicit in its focus on women's genitals, simulated sexual intercourse, sexual violence, and group sex, has only one foot in the acceptable "soft-core" market, and the other in the more hard-core market. This is probably the worst situation to be in since the magazine can compete with neither; it cannot attract the writers or interview subjects that provide *Playboy* with its markers of respectability and thus its advertising revenue, nor can it attract the readers away from the hard-core magazines by being even more explicit, for fear of offending the advertisers it already has.

The magazine that was largely responsible for drawing readers away from both *Playboy* and *Penthouse* with the promise of delivering the real pornography was the more hard-core *Hustler*. Within three and a half years of publishing, *Hustler* reached a circulation of more than 3 million, and after four years was showing a profit of more than $13 million. It is no coincidence that Flynt published the first issue of *Hustler* in 1974, five years into the *Playboy-Penthouse* circulation war. One of the results of the war was a growing acceptance in the mainstream soft-core market of more explicit imagery, thus opening the way for mass distribution of more hard-core materials. Without a doubt, Flynt has had to fight many legal battles (he wrote the editorial for the 10-year anniversary issue from his prison cell), but the groundwork laid by *Playboy* and *Penthouse* facilitated Flynt's aim of being the "first nationally distributed magazine to show pink" (Flynt, 1984, p. 7).

Understanding the pivotal role that product differentiation plays in capitalism, Flynt wrote in the first issue of *Hustler*, "Anyone can be a playboy and have a penthouse, but it takes a man to be a Hustler" (*Hustler*, July 1974, p. 4). Flynt repeatedly writes in *Hustler* that his target audience is "the average American" (Flynt, 1984, p. 7) whose income makes it impossible to identify with the high-level consumption and life-style associated with *Playboy* and

Penthouse. Taking shots at *Playboy* and *Penthouse* for being too up-market, for taking themselves too seriously, and for masquerading the "pornography as art by wrapping it in articles purporting to have socially redeeming values" (Flynt, 1983, p. 5), *Hustler* has carved out a role for itself in a now-glutted market as a no-holds-barred magazine that tells it how it is, "unaffected by the sacred cows of advertising" (*Hustler*, July 1988, p. 5). From the very first issue, Flynt has limited advertising in his magazine mainly to those companies involved in the sex industry (phone sex, vibrators, and penis enlargers being the main wares advertised).

The decision to sacrifice advertising revenue and instead rely on subscription-financed revenue appears to have paid off, since *Hustler* is the most successful hard-core magazine in the history of the pornography industry and Flynt is a multi-millionaire today. Moreover, given the type of magazine Flynt wanted to produce, he had no choice; it seems unlikely that even the most daring of advertisers would select *Hustler* as the place to market its products. Flynt has created a magazine that looks different from *Playboy* and *Penthouse* in parts of its print and image content. The first few pages of the magazine are often given over to advertisements from the phone sex industry with very explicit pictures of women's genitals and men's ejaculating penises. While *Penthouse* may publish shots of women's internal genitalia, leaking or ejaculating penises are strictly taboo in any section of *Playboy* and *Penthouse*. Within the first 10 pages of *Hustler* is a regular feature called "Asshole of the Month," whose centerpiece is a photograph of a male bending over, testicles in full view and the picture of a politician or celebrity superimposed onto the anal opening.

Although *Hustler*'s key marketing strategy has been its claim to be the most "outrageous and provocative" (*Hustler*, July, 1984, p. 9) sex magazine on the shelves, its centerfolds and pictorials tend to adopt the more soft-core codes and conventions (young, big-breasted women bending over to give the presumed male spectator a clear view of her genitals and breasts), than the hard-core ones which specialize in rape, torture, bondage, bestiality, defecation, and incest. One of the main reasons for this is that *Hustler* has to be careful not to alienate its mainstream distributors with pictorials that might be considered too hard-core and thus relegated to the pornography shops, a move that would severely limit its sales (*Hustler*'s success is mainly due to its ability to gain access to mass-distribution outlets in the United States and Europe).

However, *Hustler* also has to keep its promise to its readers to be more hard-core or else it would lose its readership to the more glossy, expensively produced soft-core *Playboy* and *Penthouse* or to the more hard-core pornography sold in adult bookstores. One way that *Hustler* has negotiated this built in conflict is to use the cartoons as the place to make good on its promise to its readers to be "bolder in every direction than other publications" (*Hustler*, July 1988, p. 7). Cartoons, because of their claim to humor, allow *Hustler* to depict "outrageous and provocative" scenarios such as torture, murder, and child molestation, which may, in a less humorous form such as pictorials, deny the magazine access to the mass-distribution channels.

Given the pivotal role that the cartoons play in promoting the image of *Hustler*, it is no surprise that there are frequent articles in the magazine on the cartoonists and especially the long-standing cartoon editor of *Hustler*, Dwaine Tinsley. The creator of the "Chester the Molester" cartoon (a white, middle-aged pedophile who appeared monthly until Tinsley was arrested on child sexual abuse charges in 1989) and some of the most racist cartoons, Tinsley is described by *Hustler* editors as producing "some of the most controversial and thought-provoking humor to appear in any magazine" (*Hustler*, November 1983, p. 7) and in some cases cartoons that are "so tasteless that even Larry Flynt has had to think twice before running them" (*Hustler*, November 1987, p. 7). We are, however, reassured by *Hustler* that the "tastelessness" will continue since "Larry is determined not to sell out and censor his creative artists" (*Hustler*, November 1983, p. 65). Indeed, in an editorial responding to critics of *Hustler* cartoons—titled "Fuck You if You Can't Take a Joke"—Flynt tells his readers that "more often than pussy . . . [*Hustler's*] cartoons have got us into controversy and court" (*Hustler*, July 1988, p. 7), and that *Hustler's* unwavering commitment to its cartoonists is its way of upholding the Constitution of the United States of America.

One recurring element of *Hustler's* articles about its own humor is the construction of the reader as a man who likes "tasteless" humor and no-frills pornography, and lacks the financial ability to live like a playboy and own a penthouse. Encoded in this image of the "ideal reader" is a clear class location, one that trades on the most classist of stereotypes and one that *Hustler* has worked hard to promote, both in and out of the magazine. In the 1970s, *Hustler* regularly ran a full-page picture of an overweight middle-aged white male leaning on a bar, with shabby looking clothes, a beer gut that spilled over his worn jeans and a glass of beer in his hand. The caption read "What Sort of Man Reads Hustler." The answer, of course, is a fat, unkempt working-class male who drinks beer all day. Adding further weight to this image of the "ideal" reader, Flynt told *Newsweek* in 1976 that *Hustler* is more interested in getting to truck drivers than professors and that "we sell to the Archie Bunkers of America" (*Newsweek*, February 16, 1976, p. 69).

This ideal reader of *Hustler* is as accurate a description of *Hustler's* readers as the playboy is of *Playboy* readers. Both constructions are marketing ploys, though they work in very different ways. *Playboy* is an advertising-driven magazine, and like all such magazines, has to present an "idealized image . . . for potential readers to desire, identify with, and expect to attain through consuming the magazine" (McCracken, 1993, p. 15). Thus while *Playboy* continues to sell an image of the reader as an upper-middle-class executive, the median income for *Playboy* readers (less than 50 percent of whom have been to college) is $26,000 a year for single men and $41,000 for married men (*Playboy* Demographic Profile, Fall 1995). This is hardly a salary that allows a playboy to play at the level depicted in *Playboy*.

The *Hustler* reader is also unlike the classist working-class image of the hustler. The *Hustler* reader's median income is $38,500 (*Hustler* Reader Profile, Fall 1995), which puts him in the middle-income bracket of the *Playboy* reader rather than the lower-income levels associated with "Archie Bunker." Moreover, given *Hustler*'s caricatured image of working-class men, few, if any, would see themselves as belonging to the same class as the beer-swigging hustler inscribed in the text. One possible reason for *Hustler*'s unusual marketing strategy of presenting the "ideal reader" in anything but ideal terms is to allow the real reader to *not* see himself as the intended reader. This allows the reader to buy *Hustler* while at the same time distancing himself from this "outrageous" magazine, filled with cartoon images of semen, feces, child molesters, and women with leaking vaginas. For the duration of the reading and masturbation, the reader is slumming in the world of the "white trash," an observer to the workings of a social class that is not his.

Hustler seems to have been successful in its marketing ploy because mainstream publications and academics have bought into the image of the *Hustler* reader. *Newsweek* referred to *Hustler* as appealing to "beer-belly macho" (*Newsweek*, March 20, 1978, p. 36), while *Time* defined it as being the most "vulgar" of sex magazines (*Time*, March 20, 1978, p. 20). In a recent article on *Hustler*, Laura Kipnis suggests that neither she nor the reader of her article (printed in a collection on cultural studies that targets an academic audience) are *Hustler*'s "implied reader" (Kipnis, 1992, p. 378). Rather than shedding light on who actually buys the magazine, Kipnis is actually reinforcing the marketing strategy of *Hustler*, since no one is meant to see themselves as the "implied reader."

The "implied reader" constructed in *Hustler* is someone to be either avoided or ridiculed, certainly not someone with whom to identify. However, in *Hustler*'s advertising promotional material, the reader is defined as the "hard-working middle-class American Male" who "makes substantial purchases through mail-order services." It would seem that while *Hustler* publicly calls its readers "Archie Bunkers," they want to make sure that their advertisers understand that he is in fact middle class by writing "middle-class" on the first line of the promotional material as well as prominently displaying the median income ($38,500) in the reader profile box situated in the center of the sheet.

THE PLAYBOY AND THE HUSTLER:
MARKETING HEFNER AND FLYNT

Each publisher is represented as the ideal reader inscribed in their text. Hefner is marketed by his magazine and the press as a smooth playboy, jet-setting across the world with a young attractive female on his arm. Flynt on the other hand is portrayed as a sexually perverted, low-class hustler whose failure to get a real woman leads him to desperately seek out harder and harder pornography. Again, the way these images are constructed is one more (successful) marketing technique.

Hugh Hefner is probably the only pornographer in America who has achieved mainstream celebrity status. Like the magazine itself, Hugh Hefner was marketed as an up-scale, high-quality commodity in order to reduce the sleaze factor normally associated with pornographers. Articles on Hefner rarely picture him outside of his opulent surroundings and are nearly always accompanied by photographs of him lounging on his famous round bed surrounded by the "bunnies," flying in his customized plane, or dancing the night away in the fully staffed Playboy mansion. Writers have gone into great detail about Hefner's daily life, praising the gourmet food and excellent service at the mansion that "has a staff of twelve which functions around the clock" (*Newsweek*, January 6, 1964, p. 48), the kidney shaped pool "with inviting nook called Woo Grotto" (*Saturday Evening Post*, April 28, 1962, p. 28), and his "rotating round bed" (*Forbes*, March 3, 1971, p. 18). Hefner's life is cast as the playboy American dream come true, a man who works hard, plays hard, and has achieved the ultimate goals in life. A *Forbes* article on the success of Hefner actually ran under the headline, "Hugh Hefner Found Complete Happiness Living the Playboy Life" (*Forbes*, March 1, 1971, p. 17).

Hefner is presented as the all-American businessman who is "modern, trustworthy, clean, respectable" (*Time*, March 3, 1967, p. 76), and is not afraid of hard work, since, according to *Newsweek*, "he works as much as 72 hours at a stretch" (*Newsweek*, January 6, 1964, p. 48). In the late 1950s and early 1960s, most of the major newspapers and news magazines carried articles on Hefner the businessman, rather than Hefner the pornographer. In these articles the centerfolds are backgrounded and the business success of *Playboy* and Hefner is foregrounded. Part of this playboy image also involved his support for liberal organizations such as the ACLU (American Civil Liberties Union) and NORML (National Organization for the Reform of Marijuana Laws). *Playboy* magazine has often run stories on Hefner's attendance at parties held in honor of his financial contributions to various causes.

Flynt, on the other hand, is presented as a working-class ex-con who carries his poor Kentucky background with him wherever he goes. He is portrayed as low-class, uneducated, and sexually peverted, and, unlike Hefner, Flynt has been demonized by the press as a sleazy pornographer. Many of the articles on Flynt highlight his poor beginnings as a way to link his class background with his sexual tastes. *Time,* for example, in an article on the 1978 shooting of Flynt, tells their readers that:

> ever since Flynt came out of the Kentucky mountains to escape the poverty of his sharecropper family, he has led an aggressive life. He quit school in the eighth grade, entered the army at 14, worked nights at a General Motors assembly plant, whizzed through two marriages, two divorces and a bankruptcy by age 21 and finally opened eight "Hustler" go-go bars around Ohio (*Time*, March 20, 1978, p. 20).

In a similar vein, *People* magazine refers to Flynt as "a nightmare version of the American dream come true. Born into an impoverished Kentucky family, he never completed high school" (*People*, August 2, 1993, p. 92). Whereas Hefner is represented as a man who has a playboy sex life (good, clean heterosexual sex with young attractive females), Flynt is cast as a pervert who at the age of eight "lost his virginity to a chicken on his grandmother's farm" (*Newsweek*, January 14, 1983, p. 16) and now runs the "most vulgar of the leading sex magazines" (*Time*, March 20, 1978, p. 20). Flynt's late wife Althea is described as an ex-go-go dancer who was "brazenly debauched" (*People*, July 20, 1987, p. 32), drug addicted, and destroyed by AIDS. While Hefner has been linked to women who were either murdered (Dorothy Stratten) or committed suicide (Bobbie Arnstein), he is the "Teflon pornographer" in that his reputation as a fine upstanding American citizen remains intact.

Some of the more recent articles on Flynt and Hefner suggest that these two men are heroes of an era gone by, a time when showing pictures of naked women was still considered risky business. While reference is made to the fact that both men are now no longer the young trend-setters of the pornography industry, Flynt is portrayed as a pathetic wheelchair-bound ex-junkie, while Hefner is talked about as a doting father to his daughter and loving husband to his young wife (see, for example, *Spy*, March/April 1996;

People, August 2, 1993). This celebration of Hefner and demonization of Flynt help to obfuscate the connections between *Playboy* and *Hustler* as the two magazines that staked out the parameters of the once hugely successful mass-distributed pornography magazine industry. The success of this industry is measurable not only in terms of its past sales and advertising revenue, but also as an industry that helped pave the way for the contemporary multibillion-dollar-a-year market. Because the pornography industry, like other industries under capitalism, evolves dynamically in response to external and internal forces, the magazine section of the industry is fast becoming obsolete and in its place is an exploding video market (and a growing CD-ROM market), which appears to be following a somewhat similar path to the one blazed by Hugh Hefner's *Playboy* magazine.

MICHAEL NINN AND THE VIDEO PORNOGRAPHY INDUSTRY: THE HEFNER OF THE 90s?

The video pornography industry generated $3.1 billion in rental and sales in 1995, up from $2.5 billion in 1994 and $1.2 billion in 1991. There has also been a major increase in the number of hard-core titles released to the market, going from 1,275 in 1990 to 2,475 in 1993 to 5,575 in 1995 (*Adult Video News Adult Entertainment Video Guide*, 1996, pp. 67–70). The majority of these videotapes are cheaply made and poorly produced with minimal conversation, plot, or camera work. As discussed in the following chapter, the purpose of these videos is to show sex.

Until 1994, the top-selling and renting videos of the pornography industry have tended to be of low production quality, which helped cast an aura of nonrespectability over the video pornography industry. The last two years, however, have seen a major change, brought about by Michael Ninn, the producer of two of the best-selling and renting videos of 1994 and 1995, *Sex* and *Latex*. The use of computer graphics, high-tech images, and fast-paced editing gives both *Sex* and *Latex* the feel of standard mainstream fare. Indeed, there are parts in *Latex* that resemble MTV videos, complete with clothed dancers in the background. The women in these videos (especially the star of both, Sunset Thomas) conform to the mainstream standard of beauty with a sleek body, fashionable hairstyles, and professional as opposed to exaggerated make-up. Also the men tend to have muscular, tanned bodies and sleek hair-cuts, in place of the often flabby men who are standard fare in the more cheaply produced videos.

The marked differences between Ninn's videos and the rest of the industry have been discussed a number of times in *Adult Video News*. Writing about the success of *Sex*, *Adult Video News* described the video as "relentlessly close to the technically flawless pinnacle of eclectic, sexual, cinematic expression as one would hope to imagine ... much more than just an excellent film" (*Adult Video News Adult Entertainment Video Guide*, 1995, p. 177). On the box of *Sex, Adam Video Guide* (a lesser known trade publication), calls it "The best erotic film of all time." The reputation that *Sex* earned Ninn helped to make *Latex* a major success, winning 11 Adult Video News awards (the industry's version of the Academy Awards) including Best Picture. Discussing the awards ceremony, *Adult Video News* wrote, "[D]irector Michael Ninn, who has given birth to a renaissance in rubber dressers, morphing, gregorian chants and revolutionary post-production technology, swept all contenders with *Latex* for VCA Platinum" (*Adult Video News Entertainment Monthly*, March 1996, p. 27). Michael Ninn's next video, *Shock*, was released in June 1996 and was heavily advertised in *Adult Video News* in the months leading up to the release. Along with the advertisement (full-color inside page costing approximately $3,000) for the video, Ninn was advertising his site on the World Wide Web for those interested viewers who wanted a sneak preview of future offerings.

The fact that Ninn's videos were best-sellers and award-winners clearly demonstrates to the industry that there is a huge market for high-quality pornography videos. His success in the '90s can be compared to Hefner's success in the '50s; both men have been trend-setters in the pornography industry by opening up the market for more upscale and technically superior products. Moreover, Ninn's videos, similar to *Playboy*, push the boundaries of acceptable content since *Latex*, while placed in the "features" section of pornography stores—a section that traditionally contains "non-violent" material—actually borrows liberally from the bondage subgenre, both in its focus on the fetishized latex clothing and in scenes that depict sadomasochistic sex. While in the 1950s, the thinking behind *Playboy* was that "quality takes some of the shock off nudity" (John Mastro, product manager of *Playboy*, quoted in Weyr, 1978, p. 33), it appears that for Ninn in the 1990s, quality takes some of the shock off bondage.

Ninn does indeed see himself as a trend-setter. The promotional material on the box of *Latex* describes Ninn's videos as having "redefined cinematic eroticism and raised the stakes for future filmmakers." Unlike other promotional material on pornography video boxes, the word pornography is missing and in its place we have eroticism, a class-coded way of saying pornography for the middle-class consumer. This marketing technique has not been lost on *Hustler,* which criticized *Latex* for using "longhair fancy boys with English accents, Fashion-shoot photography of preening, posing, primped-up women" which could only appeal to "faggots and 14-year-old girls" (*Hustler*, June 1995, p. 22). The suggestion here is that *Hustler* readers, with their "Archie Bunker" tastes, will not be interested in a more arty, high-tech porn videos that, like *Playboy*, masquerades the "pornography as art" (Flynt, 1983, p. 5).

At this point, one can only speculate on the impact Ninn's videos will have on the industry. However, given the growth in video sales and rentals, the movement of pornography shops to the suburbs, and the increasing ownership of VCRs, there is a push to make the industry more home-centered. Rather than traveling to urban centers to see pornographic movies, men can now go to their local pornography shop or mainstream video stores to rent pornography and bring it home to watch on video. For this reason, the industry has been pushing videos for heterosexual couples, and Ninn could be seen as helping to shift the industry in that direction. *Latex*, with its attempt at a more coherent narrative, drawing on a New-Age style discourse on sexual shame and guilt, and slick production techniques, has the potential to be passed off to girlfriends and wives as a chic movie with sex, as opposed to a porn flick. This image may, however, be difficult to sustain as the video progresses to bondage, and woman after woman is penetrated anally, vaginally, and orally (often at the same time) with penises and objects, and ejaculated on by numerous men to the point that semen is dripping from her face.

Given the way that product differentiation works in the pornography industry, it appears that even if Ninn-type videos become more commonplace, there will still always be a market for the lower-budget videos that dispense with any technological "foreplay." Just as *Playboy* magazine did not replace the more low-budget magazines but rather opened up the market to a range of magazines, so it seems that Ninn's videos will help to expand the video pornography market for all types of videos. Men may take *Sex* and *Latex* home for their female partners or to show in couples settings, but will continue to use *Anal Maniacs* or *Dirty Debutantes* in private or with other males. Given the continuing increase in sales and rentals of the videos, all segments of the industry appear to have the potential to make enormous amounts of money, and it remains to be seen whether Ninn will do for the video pornography market what Hefner did for print pornography in the 1950s.

THE MISSING LINKS:
PUTTING THE WOMEN BACK IN PORNOGRAPHY

In the wake of the "porn wars" that raged through the feminist movement, many books and articles were written that explored the ways in which pornography, as a regime of representation, constructs meaning. Scholars have analyzed mainstream pornography magazines, stag movies, gay and lesbian pornography, and child pornography, paying close attention to the ways in which the text is not simply a vehicle for the dissemination of ideology but is itself a complex, cultural product. But, as argued in this chapter, any serious attempt to understand pornography must go beyond a text-based analysis to include research on the socio-economic conditions of pornography production. The earlier discussion suggests just one way of looking at the dynamics and processes involved in pornography production. Indeed, there are many different paths that could be taken, each of which will add to our understanding of the industry and the text.

Pornography is often mistakenly referred to as "fantasy," as if the images just appeared from nowhere and are produced in the private head of a consumer. Missing from this position is an analysis of the actual workings of the industry, located in the concrete world of capitalism. Because methods of financing will ultimately affect the nature of the content of pornography, it is a mistake to assume that analysis of the text can take place divorced from analysis of the economic realities of pornography production. *Playboy*, because of its dependence on advertising revenue, has had to limit the explicitness of its pictorials, articles, and cartoons. *Hustler*, however, because of its market niche as mass-distributed hard-core pornography, had to forego mainstream corporate advertising and has had to keep up with the more hard-core market to keep sales steady.

By ignoring production, much of the scholarly work on pornography has failed to analyze the most important group in the production process, the women whose bodies are used as bait—the bodies that are penetrated by penises, bottles, rodents, bull whips, dogs, and hair dryers; that are ejaculated on, spit on, defecated on, urinated on; that are strung up, burnt with cigarettes and hot wax; women who are ultimately presented to the consumer as "Pet," "Playmate," or "Beaver" of the Month, or Debby, Suzi, Sunset, Annabel.

When women in "pro-sex" work are discussed, there is a tendency to limit the discussion to either a first-person account by a "sex-worker" (often Nina Hartley) or to focus on woman-owned/produced pornography (often Candida Royalle or Annie Sprinkle). While this type of research sheds light on the workings of the various sectors of the industry, it cannot stand in for a critical macro-level approach that explores how capitalism, patriarchy, racism, and first-world economic domination provide the economic and cultural space for international, mass-scale pornography production. To focus only on those women who have the resources to produce and distribute pornography is as limited as looking at worker-controlled cooperatives to explore how labor is organized under capitalism.

The aim in developing a political economy of pornography is to examine the complex ways in which the pornography industry is located within a society stratified by class, gender, and race. This foregrounds the structured inequalities that exist on the level of production, inequalities that cannot be rendered away by polysemous texts that allow for multiple readings. The slide toward celebration of the text in scholarly works on pornography posits pornography as a mode of representation rather than as a global capitalist industry that trades in female bodies. Failure to explore the dynamics and processes involved in the production of pornography will result in a superficial analysis that has little to say about how the industry functions in world where a few control the majority of resources and where women continue to be the most exploited, economically and sexually.

NOTES

1.   Pornography is defined here as any product that is produced for the primary purpose of facilitating arousal and masturbation. While there may be other uses for the product (for example, *Playboy* as a magazine to teach men how to live a playboy lifestyle), its main selling feature for the producer, distributor, and consumer (whether overtly or covertly) is sexual arousal. For more on the definitional issue, see Chapter 4.

2.   For the purpose of this discussion, hard-core pornography is any material that is made and distributed for the purpose of sexual arousal that depicts, in pictures or words, at least one of the following: internal female genitalia, the penis, ejaculate, S/M, or sexual activity between two or more people. The distinction is made because to include any one of the above elements would prevent access to mainstream distribution outlets. To be denied access to these channels means that the material will be relegated to the "adults-only" bookstores, which negatively affects sales. The only "hard-core" magazine to have mainstream distribution is *Hustler* magazine, and publisher Larry Flynt has had to fight many legal battles to hold onto his distribution network.

3.   Hefner intended to call his magazine *Stag Party*, but shortly before the publication date he received a letter from a lawyer representing a field-and-stream magazine called *Stag*, saying that there could be possible confusion between the two magazines. Hefner agreed to change the name, and *Playboy* was born (Miller, 1984, pp. 42–22).

4.   Here the woman appears not to know that she is being photographed since her head is turned away from the camera and she is lost in her own thoughts. Her partially naked body is positioned, however, to give maximum viewing ability to the spectator.

FOUR

The Content of
Mass-Marketed Pornography

ROBERT JENSEN AND GAIL DINES

What is pornography? In the first chapter, we argued that the definitional question often derails important conversations about pornography and its role in shaping sexuality. If we can't define the term with precision, some argue, then we can't, or shouldn't try to, say much of anything about pornography. In this chapter, we want to avoid such diversions. We will talk about pornography in two basic senses. First, there is a widely understood definition of pornography in the culture: Pornography is the material sold in pornography shops for the purposes of producing sexual arousal for mostly male consumers. While this does not define the term with absolute precision, it is sufficiently clear to make conversation possible. Second, from a critical feminist analysis, pornography is a specific kind of sexual material that reflects and helps maintain the sexual subordination of women. In this chapter, our task is to analyze pornography (in the first sense, as a description of a type of material from which we draw a sample) to determine if it is pornographic (in the second sense, as an expression of male-supremacist sexual ideology).

We began with trips to pornography shops, where we asked clerks and managers what was popular with consumers. Our sampling method was market-driven. That is not to say, of course, that things sold outside those stores are not pornography, only that the material in such shops is widely defined as pornography. In this study, we focus on those materials that depict sex between men and women and are marketed primarily to a heterosexual male audience (which is not to deny that women sometimes buy or rent the material as well, but only to acknowledge the primary market). We did not examine child pornography, which is illegal in the United States and generally available only through underground sources. Also, we did not look at sexually explicit material marketed to gay men or lesbians; analysis of that material is important, but outside the scope of this project.

Our primary goal was to identify the codes and conventions used in pornography. How is sex depicted? Are feminist critics correct in their analysis of what makes pornography pornographic? A number of feminists have identified such gendered codes as bodily fragmentation, sexual availability, and submission in mass-marketed pornography (e.g., Kuhn, 1985). Similarly, Andrea Dworkin (1988, pp. 266–267) has argued that the sexualization of subordination in pornography—which makes it an important site of the oppression of women—has four main parts. These can be thought of as the elements of the pornographic, and our research, building on the work of Dworkin and many others, suggests this is a compelling way in which to understand contemporary, mass-marketed pornography. These elements are:

1. Hierarchy: a question of power, with "a group on top (men) and a group on the bottom (women)."
2. Objectification: when "a human being, through social means, is made less than human, turned into a thing or commodity, bought and sold."
3. Submission: acts of obedience and compliance become necessary for survival. Members of oppressed groups learn to anticipate the orders and desires of those who have power over them, and their compliance is then used by the dominant group to justify its dominance.
4. Violence: when it becomes "systematic, endemic enough to be unremarkable and normative, usually taken as an implicit right of the one committing the violence." The first three conditions make violence possible.

Dworkin argues that subordination, made sexual in these four ways, is one central component of the oppression of women:

> In the subordination of women, inequality itself is sexualized: made into the experience of sexual pleasure, essential to sexual desire. Pornography is the material means of sexualizing inequality; and that is why pornography is a central practice in the subordination of women (Dworkin, 1988, pp. 264–265).

If this kind of feminist critique is accurate, it is important to discuss the ethical implications of describing or reproducing pornographic images, even in a critical framework and in a scholarly book. Are we not just adding to the amount of pornography in the world with this chapter? Can that be justified?

As we have taught and lectured about pornography over the past 10 years, it has become clear to us that some people—especially women, who typically have seen less pornography than men—have little understanding of contemporary pornography. Many seem to believe that the bulk of the market is *Playboy*-style pictures of naked women or videos that simply show "normal" sex between men and women. Many women, for example, are surprised to find out that in contemporary pornographic videos anal sex and multiple penetration are common and that virtually every sex scene ends with a man ejaculating onto a woman's body (see discussion below). Because there has been little systematic interpretive work on the content of pornography, and because the work that has been done is often marginalized, discussion of theoretical and policy issues often is disconnected from the reality of the material.

So, while such description is crucial, there are risks, even with the summaries and abbreviated excerpts presented here. First, once this book is published, we have no control over how the material is used. Put more bluntly: Some men who read this book may use the excerpts and descriptions to facilitate masturbation, just as consumers of pornography do. Second, women and men who are survivors of sexual abuse and intrusion may find that these descriptions trigger reactions of fear, sadness, or arousal—all of which can be difficult to negotiate psychologically. Obviously, our goal is not to unwittingly be pornographers nor to retraumatize survivors. Yet, we know of no way to engage in useful public discussion about pornography without grounding it in an understanding of the material that exists in the world. We realize that others may weigh the pros and cons differently, and we invite discussion of this issue as well as of our findings.

The chapter begins with a description of the material on sale in a typical U.S. pornography shop. From there, we explain our method and summarize existing literature on the content of pornography before moving on to an analysis of contemporary video pornography and pornographic novels.

A TOUR THROUGH A PORNOGRAPHY STORE

We visited pornography stores in 1995–96 in Boston's "combat zone" and suburbs, and the university area of Austin, Texas. There was little variation in inventory among these stores; this description is of one of the suburban stores.

Like most shops, the bulk of the inventory was video cassettes for sale for $20–$50. This shop did not rent tapes, although many do. About three-fourths of the floor space of this store was devoted to videos divided into the following categories, for which we have listed examples of the titles (in rough proportion to the titles available in each section):

1. True Classics and Best Sellers: *Deep Throat, Talk Dirty to Me, Anal Intruder.*
2. Features: *Tit's a Wonderful Life, Pussyman Auditions, Blackbroad Jungle, Ski Sluts, Back Door Brides, A Cum Sucking Whore Named Francesca.*
3. Anal: *Rectal Reamers, Love Hurts, Hotel Sodom.*
4. European: *Swimming Pool Orgy, Insatiable Lust.*
5. Fetish: *Orgy of Pain, Slave Sisters, Exchange of Blows, Real Breasts Real Torment.*
6. TVs, TSs (transvestites, transsexuals): *Las Vegas She Males, T.V. Dick Suckers.*
7. Bisexual: *Swinging Both Ways, Fucker Bi Bi.*
8. All Men: *Beach Bums, The Stalker, Stiff Latinos.*
9. Wall to Wall (multiple partners): *The World's Biggest Gangbang, House of Sex, Ultra Kinky.*
10. Girls Only: *Double D Dykes, First Time Ever.*
11. Interracial: *Dark Desires, Up the Ying Yang, Bad Ass Bangin'.*
12. Gonzo (unusual sex acts): *Shave Tails, Kink, Ready to Drop* (featuring pregnant women).
13. Oral/Cumshots: *Gang Bang Jizz Jammers, Let's Suck, Swallow.*
14. Amateurs: *Nasty Newcummers, Up and Cummers.*
15. Compilations: up to four-hour collections of the sex scenes from other movies.

In addition to the videos, the store had a small selection of computer CDs (*Wet Nurses, Vagablonde*), which allow the viewer to direct the action. Clerks said these were increasing in popularity but still a small percentage of business. CDs ranged in price from $20–$40. (The digitizing of images and rapid advances in computer technology are changing, and will continue to change, the way in which pornography is delivered. Pornography has colonized, and likely will continue to colonize, new communication technologies. Whether it will change the nature of pornography is another question.)

The store also carried a small selection of paperback sex novels, with both heterosexual and homosexual themes, for $2–$3 each. There were about a dozen sex-oriented newspapers, both regional and national, for sale.

The store's display of magazines included individual issues and discount packs of older issues. These were divided into categories similar to the videos, and included some mass-marketed magazines such as *Hustler*, as well as more specialized magazines published quarterly or irregularly that focused on, among other things, women presented as young girls (*Baby Dolls*) and large-breasted women (*Busty*).

Finally, a small selection of sex toys was available, including dildos, vibrators, nipple clamps, whips, and latex clothing.

LITERATURE REVIEW AND METHOD

A number of traditional content analyses of pornographic cartoons and pictorials in magazines and pornographic movies have been done (Bogaert, Turkovich, and Hafer, 1993; Brosius, Weaver, and Staab, 1993; Brown and Bryant, 1989; Cowan et al., 1988; Cowan and Campbell, 1994; Dietz and Sears, 1987–88; Malamuth and Spinner, 1980; Matacin and Burger, 1987; Palys, 1986; Prince, 1990; Scott and Cuvelier, 1987; Slade, 1984; Winick, 1985; Yang and Linz, 1990). Most of these studies focused on depictions of violence, and from them no consensus can be reached on trends in contemporary pornography. Some find increasing levels of violence from the 1970s into the 1980s, while others find the opposite.

Because different methodologies and different definitions are used in these studies, direct comparisons are difficult. However, Dan Brown and Jennings Bryant (1989, pp. 18–19) suggest that three general observations are supported by those studies: (1) pornography tends to be less violent than other entertainment genres, but the degree of violence in pornography is increasing; (2) when violence is featured, females are usually victimized by males; and (3) the negative consequences of that violence are rarely shown. And despite the disagreements about violence, it is relatively uncontroversial, as researchers who studied pornographic videotapes made from 1979 to 1988 suggest, that the genre "spotlights the sexual desires and prowess of men" and "consistently and persistently portrays women as sexually willing and available" (Brosius, Weaver, and Staab, 1993, p. 169).

While these types of studies occasionally offer some insight into the world of pornography, they do little to help us understand the meaning of pornography in contemporary society. One key problem is the violent/nonviolent framework of the research. This obsession with dividing up the pornographic world says much about the culture's need to believe that if we can identify the "bad" category (violent), then we can uncritically enjoy what is left over in the "good" category (nonviolent). But violence of various types is present in almost all pornography, from the violent manner in which women routinely are penetrated, to more overt forms that involve hitting or weapons (see discussion below). Perhaps most important, beyond squabbles over categorization, this violent/nonviolent framework obscures the routine sexualized violence that must exist in the world *for pornography to be able to be made* (Giobbe, 1991).

Beyond that specific concern, traditional quantitative content analysis in general obscures as much as it illuminates. Despite the attempts at precision, in the end this kind of research tells us little about what images and words mean. A text is a structured whole, and fragmenting it into quantifiable units leads us away from, not toward, understanding. The meaning of a text can't be determined by simply counting the elements in it. Meaning is messy, open to interpretation, slippery; it can't be counted. Content analysis' method of creating categories so that things can be counted ignores the fact that the creation of the categories itself is a linguistic act that is messy, open to interpretation, slippery. As Stuart Hall (1989, p. 47) puts it, "Meaning is polysemic in its intrinsic nature; it remains inextricably context bound." Yet traditional content analysis is an act of context stripping, of removing fragments of a text from their context and searching for understanding in the void that results.

This critique does not lead to hopelessness about the quest to understand a text and its intersection with a culture's ideology; it simply means that importing techniques from the natural sciences to try to understand language, mass media, and interpretation is a failed project. That failure does not mean we are doomed to "the bottomless bog of relativistic apolitical postmodernism" (Frye, 1992, p. 63), where nothing coherent can be said about meaning. Again, following Hall (1986, p. 49), "there is all the difference in the world between the assertion that there is no one, final, absolute meaning—no ultimate signified, only the endlessly sliding chain of signification, and, on the other hand, the assertion that meaning does not exist."

One of the ways we can work toward a collective understanding of the meaning of a text (always with the caveat that no final, definitive reading will emerge) is by paying attention to context, both in terms of the society in which the text is produced and circulated and the specific context of the genre. Pornography is produced and circulated in a male-dominant society in which sexualized violence against women and children is routine. Pornography is a genre produced primarily for men as a masturbation facilitator. Whatever interpretations of the pornographic text one makes, they must be made within that context: Pornography is a product made primarily by men, primarily for men, in a patriarchal society.

So, there is a creative space between social science's sterile quest for objectivity and a postmodern abandonment of any hope for collective agreement on meaning. The solution lies in thick description and the struggle for compelling interpretation. Progress made through this kind of interpretive study is, as Clifford Geertz writes, "marked less by a perfection of consensus than by a refinement of debate. What gets better is the precision with which we vex each other" (Geertz, 1973, p. 29). In the debate over pornography people too often have vexed each other without much precision. This chapter is a step toward greater precision, not through categories and quantification, but through engagement with the text.

The chapter is based on this type of interpretive analysis of 14 pornographic videos (conducted by Dines and Jensen) and 20 pornographic novels (conducted by Jensen alone). With such small samples, the intent obviously is not to make generalizations about all of pornography. But what is lost in generalizability by this approach is made up for in the depth of analysis made possible by a close reading of the texts. While these videos and novels cannot be said to be representative in terms of traditional sampling requirements, our research and experience suggests that they are typical of the genre of pornography being investigated. In short, the goal is not to claim that "all pornography looks like this," but to say, "when pornography looks like this (and lots of it does), this is what we think is going on."

We chose the videos (see Appendix) with the help of clerks at several pornography stores in 1995–96. We asked simply, "What is popular? What sells and rents most?" The answer at each store was, "Most everything." In the store where we rented videos, the clerks said that almost any tape that is put on the shelf will rent and that the store turns over tapes quickly. We walked through the store with a clerk, selecting tapes from most of the sections, aiming for what the clerk considered to be a typical selection of popular material.

The novels analyzed (see Appendix) were purchased in 1989–90 from a Minneapolis news store that carries a wide variety of publications, including sexually explicit books, magazines, and videotapes. The novels were selected at random from a large display rack of books aimed at a heterosexual market, noting titles only to avoid selecting too many books with similar plots (although titles of books of this kind may have nothing to do with story lines).

One of the common criticisms of the anti-pornography critique is that it focuses on a small segment of the market that is particularly violent and degrading to women. The tapes and novels chosen for this analysis were "mainstream" pornography, the standard fare that is legally rented and purchased all over the United States every day from stores that operate within the definitions of obscenity law. As our analysis will point out, there are varying forms of violence in most pornography, from the violent pounding of pornographic intercourse to more explicit violence, but overtly violent sex was not the advertised focus, nor the predominant theme, of this material. (We rented one bondage-and-domination tape for comparative purposes, but that tape is not part of the analysis that follows.)

The viewing and analysis of the videos was conducted jointly not only for the usual benefits of collaborative work, but specifically in this case to provide a reading of the movies from a male and female perspective. This does not mean we are offering ourselves as representatives of simplistic, essentialized categories of man and woman, but simply acknowledges that because men and women are socialized differently and occupy different social locations, our reactions to the material in the videos may be different, and an analysis that incorporates both locations is potentially richer.

The analysis of the videos integrates our separate observations and insights. In general, we found ourselves in agreement about how to make sense of what we were watching, which reflects a common commitment to a radical feminist approach to politics and sexuality. Where we did read things differently, we paused and discussed the issues immediately; hence it is impossible to separate our individual insights from the collective analysis. Our notes from the viewing sessions reflect the free flow of conversation between us as we watched the videos.

THE VIDEOS

There is a dulling sameness to pornographic videos, a predictability that one might expect would eventually resulted in bored consumers and a declining market. Yet the number of pornographic videos released each year continues to increase. We suggest that consumers likely accept the repetitiousness of the genre because the tapes provide them with a kind of sex that men in this culture are routinely trained to desire. (This does not ignore the fact that some women may also find this kind of pornography arousing; it simply acknowledges that men are the primary consumers.) In the pornographic world, sex is divorced from intimacy, loving affection, and human connection; all women are constantly available for sex and have insatiable sexual appetites; and all women are sexually satisfied by whatever the men in the film do.

The tapes had varying levels of sophistication in plot, dialogue, and character development, though in every case the story-telling devices exist to connect sex scenes. For example, *Taboo VIII* was organized around a relatively coherent story about the struggle between a ranch owner and a developer over valuable real estate. *Latex* spun a somewhat convoluted fantasy story about a psychotic man who could see people's sexual fantasies. *More Dirty Debutantes #37*, however, was simply the videotaping of a series of sexual encounters between the producer/director and women who were supposed to be having their first experience in pornography.

The standard sexual script in these videos, from which there were occasional minor variations, began with the presentation of the female body to the camera for viewing, with a focus on the conventionally sexualized parts of the female body: the breasts, vagina, and buttocks/anus. There was relatively little attention paid to women's breasts compared with the focus on breasts in magazines such as *Playboy*. Because the explicit videos have almost no limits on what they can show, we speculate that they focus on the parts of the woman's body that can be penetrated.

From the camera's scanning of the female body, the scenes usually move to a short period (often no more than several seconds) of kissing or fondling. In some scenes, this was eliminated altogether. There appeared to be no expectation that nonsexual romantic interaction or foreplay would take place. When it did happen, it was so brief that it clearly was not necessary to begin the sex.

While some pornographic videos portray women as reluctant or prudish, in need of being coaxed or coerced into having sex, the women in the videos in our sample never said no and were always immediately ready for sexual activity. The presence of a man and the possibility of sex was sufficient to arouse women in the videos and spark them to initiate sex or receive sexual advances. In short, virtually all women in the videos were portrayed as "nymphomaniacs." (We put the term in quotes because we consider it to be a male fantasy about women's sexuality. Subsequent uses of the term refer to the "nymphomaniacs" that exist in men's minds and in pornography.)

Next in the progression can be a short period of cunnilingus (though some videos forego this) before the rotation, in various positions, of fellatio, vaginal intercourse, and anal intercourse. All sex scenes ended with the man or men ejaculating onto the woman's or women's bodies, most often on the face or in the mouth but also on her breasts, vagina, stomach, buttocks, or back.

Sex in these videos was male-centered. Sex was marked by the rise and fall of the penis, beginning with the male need to fuck, evidenced by an erection, and ending with his orgasm. Sex never continued after a man's orgasm. Even the "lesbian" scenes in these videos, which more accurately should be called scenes of women performing for male viewing, followed this dictate. First, in many of these scenes the woman-woman sex was prelude to a man entering the scene and penetrating the women. And in scenes in which no man appeared, the women almost always finished the sexual activity with the insertion of a dildo or some other substitute phallus into one or both of the women.

The physical appearance of the men and women in the videos varied. Some fit the traditional beauty standards of the culture in terms of facial features and body size, but many did not. There were no obese men or women in the videos we analyzed, but there was a range from the current standard of fashion-model thinness for women to what might be called more "normal" shapes (something other than the big-breasts/thin-hips standard). Some of the men had pumped-up hard-bodies and others displayed middle-age paunches. Perhaps the only clear pattern was that there were very few women with small breasts (see the section on sexualizing age for the exception).

There was a clear pattern, however, in dress. Men appeared most often in clothing that is common in public, from casual shirts and jeans to suits. Women, however, were typically dressed in clothing that maximized the visibility of their bodies, such as low-cut blouses and short, tight skirts. Women also frequently appeared in fetishized clothing that is highly sexualized in the culture: latex skirts or suits, garters, push-up bras, lace panties. Spike heels or knee-high boots were standard.

In addition, women often kept one of those fetishized items on during sex; for example, a lace bra might be pulled down to expose her breasts but not taken off. There are several plausible explanations for this. Annette Kuhn (1985, p. 32) has suggested that in a genre that hinges on the production of sexual difference, such clothing "functions as a cultural marker of femininity-as-sexuality." Also, because these garments are coded as sexual, leaving them visible while sex happens could simply be an attempt to heighten the sexual charge of the scene. If an unadorned female breast is sexy, a breast with a lace bra is potentially more sexy.

A typical example of these basics can be seen in *The Nympho Files*, a series of vignettes about female nymphomaniacs (again, as defined by male fantasy) stitched together through a parody of a TV newsmagazine. One of the video's five scenes concerned Louise, a nymphomaniac unsuccessfully trying to reform. She calls two all-night repair services to have them each send a man to fix things in her house. When the men arrive at the same time, she begins groping them and takes out their penises to perform fellatio. All of Louise's clothes come off, with the exception of high heels and a push-up bra to accentuate her breasts, which stay on throughout the sexual activity. From there, they move through various combinations of oral and vaginal penetration, ending with the woman being penetrated vaginally and anally at the same time before the men ejaculate into her mouth, one at a time. This is the standard fare of video pornography.

Finally, as the radical feminist critique of pornography has always emphasized, it is important to remember that pornography is made with the bodies of real women (and the bodies of men as well, though the role and risks for men are considerably different). In analyses of most media texts, it is risky to try to read the politics of production from the text. The final media product (a television drama, for example) is carefully constructed and edited, so that the actual conditions of production are hidden. Mass-marketed pornography, however, is somewhat different. Some of the videos we watched were similar to mainstream media in the sophistication of production values, especially bigger-budget efforts such as *Latex*. But in others, especially the more homemade-style videos, less care was taken to edit out events that one can reasonably assume give hints about the conditions of production. For example, women in pornography are expected to express pleasure during sex through facial expression and moaning. As the women in these videos had to deal with the bodily reality of the sex acts—especially anal sex or having more than one penis in them at once—they often seem to forgo the orgasmic acting to concentrate on getting through the scene. Expressions of pain that did not appear to be scripted were common during anal intercourse.

One question about conditions of production that can be answered by viewing the videos concerns the use of condoms. While safe sex practices have been widely adopted by gay pornographers (Burger, 1995, pp. 28–29), condoms were used in only one of the 14 videos we analyzed. Unprotected vaginal and anal intercourse were the rule.

From this sketch of the genre, we move to more detailed analyses of specific elements of these videos, with an eye toward gendered differences in portrayals, including discussions of (1) the presentation of the body; (2) depictions of sexual response; the importance of two specific sexual acts, (3) the cum shot and (4) anal sex; the depiction of (5) control and (6) violence; and the sexualization of (7) race and (8) age.

SCRUTINIZING THE FEMALE BODY

Despite much talk about the "couples market" for heterosexual pornography, producers clearly assume that the typical viewer is a man. The representational conventions of pornography are geared toward the presentation and maximum visibility of the female body, particularly the vagina, compared with an almost complete lack of concern for the male body. This can be seen in choices about what the camera takes in both before and during sexual activity.

As we have already indicated, in these videos the female body was typically scanned by the camera before sex begins. Sometimes men in the scene directed a stripping off of her clothes, telling a woman to "show me your tits" or "show me your pussy." Sometimes women held open their vaginas for the camera. This practice was particularly evident in the more home-made style, in which there was little or no attempt to create a narrative. For example, as director Rick Savage panned a woman's body in *New York Video Magazine Vol. 5*, he said, "My camera tends to act like a guy," acknowledging not only his preferences but the gender of the presumed audience.

The sexual activity between men and women occurred in various positions, but almost all were arranged for maximum visibility of the female body. The camera was positioned to show us things we don't see while having sex. That these sexual positions may be uncomfortable and are not likely to be common outside of pornographic sex is irrelevant; the goal is maximum visibility of the female body and genitals. For example, in describing one of these positions (called the "cowgirl," in which the woman is facing the man and sitting up, or the "reverse cowgirl," in which she faces away from him) a pornographic video director has said: "Very unnatural position. The girls hate it. It kills their legs, you know. But it shoots beautifully, because everything's opened up to the camera. It's very convenient" (Stoller and Levine, 1993, p. 133).

The male body was not scrutinized in this way. The camera did not linger on the male body, nor did men present their bodies for the viewer. Men removed their clothes only when necessary for sex. In addition, the penis was not explored with the obsession that the camera investigated the vagina. The camera rarely focused on the penis exclusively, except at the point of ejaculation, when recording the evidence of the male's pleasure was crucial.

One possible explanation for this involves a key problem for heterosexual pornography in a homophobic culture: To show explicit sexual activity, pornographers must show the male body and the penis. How can that be accomplished without raising the homosexual anxiety level for the straight men who are the primary customers? The videos we saw dealt with the severe restrictions on the viewing of the penis in this culture, especially by men, by never objectifying the penis in the way that the female body and genitals were routinely objectified. The penis showed up for action, but it appeared only in relation to the woman, to be consumed by her orally or to be used by him to penetrate her vaginally or anally. When that business was over, the penis was put away until the next sex scene.

In a culture that so severely punishes expressions of homoeroticism and in which heterosexual men's sense of masculinity is routinely connected to not being homosexual in any way, it is easy to speculate that many straight men may watch pornography in part to be able to see penises and indulge unspeakable homosexual fantasies. If this is this case, pornographic videos must avoid any focus on the penis and present it only in a context in which a male viewer has a cover story for viewing it.

Another way in which this difference in the presentation of the male and female bodies was evident was in the way oral sex was performed on men and on women. First, the scenes of men performing cunnilingus, if they appeared at all, were shorter in duration than those of women performing fellatio, which is in keeping with the male-centered construction of sex in pornography. Likewise, men remained unemotional and unresponsive while performing cunnilingus, while women performing fellatio responded as if having a penis in their mouths brought them to orgasm as well as the man. Also, cunnilingus scenes almost always were set up in such a way as to maximize visibility of the woman's vagina; men usually position their heads off to the side, rather than directly over the vagina, to make it possible for the camera to see the vagina. Fellatio scenes, on the other hand, are constructed and photographed to center on the female's providing of pleasure for the man (more on this later).

A clear example of these conventions was in *Rick Savage's New York Video Magazine Vol. 5*. In one scene a woman who is alone in a room stripped for the camera, then reclined on a coach and began masturbating. A man entered the room and sat on the other end of the couch, with the camera positioned over his shoulder. The viewer does not see the man's face as he masturbated and ejaculated onto her. Throughout this, the woman continued to masturbate and expose herself to the camera. The camera placed the viewer with the disembodied man; the implicit invitation was to masturbate with the man while watching the woman.

SEXUAL RESPONSE

There was an intriguing difference between the sexual responses of women and men in the videos: Women were constantly orgasmic, while men typically showed little reaction to sex. This is especially ironic because the only person we could be sure was experiencing sexual pleasure was the man, as evidenced by his orgasm; whether or not women felt much pleasure was unclear.

A man who watched these pornographic videos to determine what women want sexually would have been disappointed—everything a man did in the videos sparked an orgasmic response in the always insatiable women. Anything the man did to the woman was depicted as producing intense pleasure in the woman, and everything the woman did to the man also made her orgasmic. This was most noticeable when women perform fellatio, which consistently produced an orgasmic response in women. At times, the facial expressions and sounds women used to convey their pleasure were so exaggerated that they played like a parody of pornographic conventions. So long as the woman expressed pleasure with everything she did and everything done to her, the scene was acceptable to producers. As one of the men having sex with a woman in *Afro Erotica #17* said, "I know she's got to be feeling good. Look at the smile on her face." These visible and audible signs of pleasure were central to the narrative of female nymphomania and male sexual prowess.

While this observation holds for most of the videos, as we pointed out earlier women did sometimes fail to produce the signs of this orgasmic state, especially in the more homemade-style videos. It was as if the women forgot to act out the pleasure they were supposed to be feeling. In some cases, this involved not only an absence of expressions of pleasure, but noticeable expressions of fear or pain. It seemed that producers were willing to ignore failures in acting so long as the sexual activity happened as scheduled; directors didn't seem concerned enough to reshoot or edit to deal with such questions.

While women were constantly orgasmic, men were most often stoic in these videos. Men occasionally offered some facial expressions and grunting to indicate pleasure, but it was not unusual for the men to be silent and unexpressive throughout an entire sex scene. In this sense, women were the bearers of emotion and pleasure in pornography that is constructed for and around male pleasure. That may be one reason the women were always orgasmic—they had to express the man's arousal through their expressions of pleasure. The woman didn't exist outside of the man's arousal; she was a mirror of his desire. One obvious explanation for this practice is the rather banal observation that women typically are assigned the emotional work in contemporary culture. To be normatively masculine is to remain cool and in control. Such a pattern in pornography is perhaps unremarkable.

THE CUM SHOT

The most predictable event in these videos was the cum shot, the ejaculation by the man onto a woman. The target of the ejaculation varied with the sexual position: on the buttocks, back, vagina, stomach, breasts, or face, or in the mouth. The man removed his penis from the woman's mouth, vagina, or anus shortly before orgasm, masturbated himself (sometimes with help from the woman), and ejaculated in full view of the camera. Sometimes after the ejaculation, the man would slap his penis, with varying levels of force, against the woman's mouth, vagina, or anus. Women often played with the ejaculate, either rubbing it into their bodies or licking it off their fingers.

The absolute need for a cum shot in each sex scene can be seen in the way in which bodies were repositioned quickly to make sure the event was captured by the camera. For example, in *Buttman's Big Butt Backdoor Babes,* during a sex scene on a desk, when the woman realized that the man was going to ejaculate she scrambled to get below him so that he could ejaculate on her face and breasts. Likewise, in *Rick Savage's New York Video Magazine Vol. 5*, a man was having sex in various positions with a woman on a doctor's examining table in a tattoo parlor. When he approached an orgasm, apparently before he expected it, he was standing and penetrating her vaginally. To ensure that he could ejaculate on the woman's face, he pulled out of her vagina quickly and roughly pulled her body down the table, positioning her just in time for her face to catch the ejaculate.

The importance of the cum shot was also seen in *More Dirty Debutantes #37*, in which the ejaculation was replayed from different angles. Also, in one scene the director/actor ejaculated into woman's mouth, told her to open her mouth and show it to the camera, and then ordered her to swallow. The evidence of the sex, the semen, was displayed, not just swallowed quickly or deposited in an orifice unseen.

All of these common practices were carried out with even more intensity in *Latex*, an "upscale" 1994 video. First, the video contained more cum shots than any other we analyzed. The opening montage was a collection of quick cuts featuring ejaculating penises. Throughout the video, men ejaculated onto women, usually on their faces or into their mouths, but sometimes into the women's hands. The women then licked the ejaculate or rubbed it onto their bodies, or, if there was more than one woman in the scene, shared it with each other. When there was more than one man in a scene, each man ejaculated onto the woman or women. In the video's final scene, a woman performed fellatio on a man who was wearing a full latex suit, with only his penis visible. Editing together several ejaculations, the scene ended with the woman's face covered with ejaculate.

What does the cum shot mean? One hint appeared in *Taboo VIII*, in which the hero of the video had sex with a woman who was in collusion with the video's villain. When she requested that he penetrate her, he replied, "I don't fuck sluts. I jerk off on them. Take it or leave it." He then ejaculated onto her breasts. If this was an accurate description of the meaning of the cum shot, we conclude that in pornography, ejaculating onto a woman is a method by which she is turned into a slut, something (not really someone) whose primary, if not only, purpose is to be sexual with men.

Obviously, having ejaculate on one's body is not inherently dangerous or dehumanizing. Our comments here are concerned with the symbolic meaning of the act in the culture at this historical moment. In watching one of these shots after another, we were struck by how degrading and violent the practice felt. That experience was echoed by veteran pornographic director and actor Bill Margold, who said in an interview:

> I'd like to really show what I believe the men want to see: violence against women. I firmly believe that we serve a purpose by showing that. The most violent we can get is the cum shot in the face. Men get off behind that, because they get even with the women they can't have. We try to inundate the world with orgasms in the face" (Stoller and Levine, 1993, p. 22).

ANAL SEX

Interviews with clerks and pornography users suggested that anal sex had become increasingly common in pornography in the late 1980s and early 1990s. The majority of sex scenes in all the videos we analyzed included anal penetration. One possible explanation for the increase of anal sex in pornography is that as pornography exhausts one convention after another, producers are always in search of a sexual practice that can stimulate viewers. Because anal sex is a taboo practice in some segments of the culture, it no doubt appeals to many viewers.

It is uncontroversial to assert that anal penetration can be painful. The human body can adjust to accept a penis in the anus, and anal sex can be pleasurable for the recipient; clearly the commonness of the practice in the gay community attests to that adaptability. The popularity of anal sex in pornographic videos is potentially connected both to a viewer's interest in a sexual practice that is not commonly engaged in and that can cause female pain (though this is not to suggest that vaginal penetration is never painful; more on that later). The same can be said for the pornographic practice of penetration of the anus and vagina at same time.

Pornographers themselves acknowledge that women are likely to fear anal penetration. In a "Kinks" column in *Hustler* (July 1994, p. 58), the writer acknowledged the "common misperception . . . that women hate taking dick up the ass. Consequently, the thrust of most HUSTLER literature dealing with sphincter-probing is how to overcome a lady's fear of accepting prong in pooper."

The videos not only showed anal sex, but constructed the act as something that women like. In one scene in *Buttman's Big Butt Backdoor Babes*, a man penetrated the woman anally while the producer/cameraman says, "She likes it." The woman remains silent in that segment. In *More Dirty Debutantes #37*, the women in one of the scenes repeated several times, "I like it in my ass," even though her facial expression suggested otherwise. And when women rejected anal sex, men corrected them. In *Rick Savage's New York Video Magazine Vol. 5*, the man having sex with an 18-year-old woman asked, "Want me to fuck your ass?" When she replied, "Not really," he told her, "Yes you do."

A *Hustler* magazine interview with Max Hardcore, a pornography director and actor known for anal sex scenes, offered some insight into the appeal of anal penetration. "There's nothing I love more than when a girl insists to me that she won't take a cock in her ass, because—oh yes she will!" Max said. He described his trademark as being able to "stretch a girl's asshole apart wide enough to stick a flashlight in it," and went on to say that he doesn't hate all women, just "stuck-up bitches" (*Hustler*, June 1995, p. 22). Hardcore attributed his success to being "an average joe, someone any regular guy can relate to."

CONTROL

In these videos, men sometimes took direct control of the sexual encounter, ordering the woman to do specific things or using physical control to force her. But more commonly, such overt control was not necessary because the women "naturally" wanted sexual activity that was primarily directed at heightening and satisfying his pleasure.

An example of the former: In *Afro Erotica #17*, three men took turns having sex with one woman, who had a chain around her neck that the men hold during intercourse. Although the woman showed no signs of resisting the sex, the men keep a tight hold on the chain. An example of the latter, from the same video: A woman in her home turned to find three men entering the room. One of the men told the woman that her husband had been sleeping with his sister, and that they were there to pay him back by fucking her. The woman's initial fear of the intruders evaporated immediately as they touched her, and she went into a sexual frenzy. The sexual activity took place on a dining room table, beginning with her performing fellatio on two of the men while the third man performed cunnilingus. Then one of the men penetrated her vaginally from behind while she performed fellatio the other two. Finally, still on the table, she was penetrated orally, vaginally, and anally at the same time, with the man having oral intercourse occasionally removing his penis to slap her with it. When the man having anal intercourse pulled out to ejaculate on her back, one of her hands immediately moved back to masturbate him. At this point, virtually every part of the woman's body was employed to produce male sexual pleasure. The scene ended with each of the men ejaculating onto her body or into her mouth. In a scene such as this, the hierarchy was established without a need for men to exercise overt control.

Even when women took control of sex, pornography constructed them as eventually wanting to submit to a man. For example, in *The Nympho Files*, two women who had escaped from a girls' school entered the man's bedroom. The dominant woman announced that she was in charge and that they were "gonna use this cock" of the man for their pleasure. After the two women engaged in sex with each other for a short time, the standard script began, with the focus on the man's pleasure and the women servicing him orally. The dominance of the woman gave way to her more predictable role as submisive, needing the man to satisfy her sexually.

VIOLENCE

The function of violence in these videos was not typically to subdue a woman or secure her participation in sex. Because the women in these videos were always eager to engage in sex, overt violence to coerce was rarely needed. Instead, violence was portrayed as heightening the erotic charge of the scene. The most common forms of this kind of violence included men slapping a woman's buttocks during intercourse; slapping the woman's face or vagina with the penis; pulling on hair before and during sex; and deep thrusting in woman's throat, even if it provoked a gag reflex. Often the woman asked for this kind of treatment, telling men, for example, to "Spank me. Spank my ass." This kind of violence appeared in sex scenes between women as well; slapping and hair pulling were common in "lesbian" scenes.

Although the videos we analyzed were not advertised as sadomasochistic, S/M conventions were sometimes used. For example, in one scene in *Latex*, a woman was gagged with the man's tie, which he held to control her. Then he blindfolded her, and she performed fellatio on him. He slapped her buttocks during intercourse and later slapped her face with his penis.

The only scene in which violence was depicted as necessary to secure the woman's participation in sex came in *Buttman's Big Butt Backdoor Babes*, in a scene in which the director and one of his actors were being driven in a van in Brazil to a video store for a promotional appearance. The driver stopped to pick up a young female hitchhiker, who got in the back of the van with the actor. Flirtation turned into a fight, which led to sex. She fought back, and the slapping and wrestling in this scene did not seem likely to escalate into violence that would cause serious injury. Again, the role of the violence seemed to be to heighten the intensity of the sex that followed. However, he was clearly dominant; she didn't speak English and was depicted as being poor, needing to hitchhike. There were two other men in the front of the van, and it appeared that she had few choices.

Beyond that kind of overt violence, it is important to consider what the routine intercourse in videos likely feels like for the women. The sex often was a hard, repetitive pounding by the man into the woman for several minutes at a time. In scenes where the woman had intercourse with more than one man, that pounding often went on for more than 10 minutes (in edited video time; how long it lasted during taping is impossible to determine from viewing). That kind of routine sexual activity likely results in, at the very least, soreness if not more severe pain. This applies even more so to the anal sex, which also was routinely carried out with that same kind of pounding.

An example of this routine violence was seen in one of the scenes in *Buttman's Big Butt Backdoor Babes* in which Kristi Lynn, one of Buttman's stable of women performers, "takes a meeting" with a male pornography actor at the director's backyard pool. After running through the standard sequence of positions, the man was ready to penetrate her anally. His first attempts to enter her anally failed, partly because of the size of his penis, and as he pushed in harder the camera showed her face with what seemed clearly to be an expression of real pain. Her "fuck me" talk gave way to a guttural sound of pain that, again, sounded authentic. After a few minutes of anal sex, the man resumed vaginal intercourse before ejaculating onto her buttocks, slapping her buttocks with his penis, and spanking her. In the background, an ambulance siren on the street happened to be passing by, and the producer/cameraman joked, "Well, the ambulance is coming for you, Ms. Kristi Lynn. I know that was pretty rough." She then displayed her anus and vagina for the camera, and as the cameraman panned her body, he commented, "Yea, you've been worked over kid, pretty good." In this scene, not only did no one stop the action when it appeared that Kristi Lynn was in pain, but the director displayed the physical evidence of that pain and joked about it.

While not present in every video, this theme of men taking pleasure in female vulnerability and pain appeared routinely. An example of this was in the *New York Video Magazine Vol. 5* of Rick Savage, who encourages viewers to write in to suggest scenes or offer to be in a video. Mary Ann wrote in to say she liked a scene in which a woman wore a blindfold, and Savage invited her to appear. In the scene she put on a blindfold and Savage, who operated the camera, directed her to undress, touch herself, and expose her genitals to the camera. Mary Ann appeared to be scared throughout this, especially when the man with whom she would have sex (but whom she could not see) entered the room. Savage directed her: "He's going to put his cock in your mouth. So open your mouth big, so you can stoop to greet his cock." The man and woman moved to the bed as Savage said, "That's it. Lay there Mary and take it." During rear-entry vaginal intercourse with the man, who was physically large and heavy, Mary made sounds that indicated she was in pain, but the man did not stop penetrating her, methodically thrusting and eventually ejaculating on her buttocks. Part of the erotic charge of this scene was Mary Ann's fear and helplessness, her lack of control in a situation in which she could not even see the man.

Although it is important to focus on these routine acts of violence in pornography, it also is important to consider what Dworkin calls pornography's "psychic violence"—women's experiences of going numb before the images, the effect on women of knowing that "this is what men want, and this is what men have had, and this is what men will not give up" (1988, p. 23). If some women feel the violence looking at the image, we must wonder about the violence that the woman felt when the pornography was made with their bodies.

RACE

In a study that focused on racism and sexism in interracial pornography, Cowan and Campbell (1994) found support for the critique of sexism in previous studies. They also reported that the videos reinforced racial sexual stereotypes, particularly the notion of black men as sex machines and bestial in nature. Our analysis supports that finding.

Several patterns emerged in the construction of race in the videos. First, the overwhelming majority of the actors in videos that were not marked "interracial" were white. That is, consumers can assume that in renting or buying a typical pornographic video, there will be few, if any, non-white actors, male or female. The videos constructed whiteness as the norm, which while not surprising in the United States, always needs to be highlighted.

In our descriptions of the videos to this point, we have not identified the actors by race, because in the scenes we have discussed so far, race did not appear to signify any particular sexual traits. We are well aware that race will always be most likely read by many consumers as having sexual meaning. For example, no doubt some viewers always see a black woman as having a wild, bestial sexuality (see below). Our focus in this section is on videos in which these race-sex stereotypes were explicitly used by the pornographers.

In those videos that advertised themselves as using non-white actors, clear themes emerged. First, the interracial genre seemed to focus on various combinations of white and black women and men. In the two we viewed, *Afro Erotica #17* and *Black Pepper Vol. 13*, there was only one scene that involved someone of a race other than white (a black man and an Asian woman). Because the lighting in these videos was often poor, skin tones were difficult to determine; hence, there may have been Latina/os in some scenes, but if there were no other racial markers (names, explicit statements by the actors, cultural symbols, etc.) it was difficult to know.

Black men in these videos were portrayed in three basic ways. First, some struck the male pose described above, emotionally flat and mechanical. Second, some were portrayed as the black stud, the street-wise hustler who is both sexually more alluring and threatening. In both these kinds of scenes, which involved sexual activity with white women, frequent references were made to "that big black cock" and various permutations of that phrase. The videos in general contained constant references to men's "big cocks," but the difference in the interracial videos was the reference to color, the black cock. In none of the videos was there ever a reference to a "big white cock" or a "big brown cock." Only black cocks were noted, signifying some sort of extraordinary sexual size and prowess.

An extreme example of the portrayal of black men as wild, almost bestial, came in a scene in which a white woman was having sex with two black men who were wearing stereotypical voodoo/primitive costumes—painted markings on the face, nose rings, necklaces made of teeth, wild hair—with shrunken heads in the scene. The men traded off having sex with the woman and dancing in a wild style, before penetrating the woman at the same time (orally and vaginally, and then vaginally and anally). This encounter with the exotic primitive enhanced the woman's predictable orgasmic state, leading her to moan and request that they "put that big black cock in my ass," "fuck the shit out of me," and finally "fuck me to death."

The third type of depiction of black men was noticeable in the *Black Pepper* video, where in two scenes the men were more gentle and loving than the standard depiction of men. Their sex with the white women included more stroking of hair, caressing and kissing, including kissing during intercourse, which was extremely rare in the videos we analyzed. Also, the intercourse was gentler than the typical pounding in pornography. Another difference in these scenes was that the camera lingered on the black male body much more than it did on the white male body. That is, the black man was subject to the same scrutinization by the camera that women in pornography routinely receive.

It is not surprising that black men could be treated differently from white men and could to some degree become sexualized objects in the same way that women of all races can. To be female in the videos is to be subordinate; black men, who in a racist culture are categorized as naturally subordinate, also are candidates for being "feminized" in pornography. Again, it is important to note that the dominant portrayal of black men in our sample was black-man-as-stud, not this more feminized role. Also, no matter how much tenderness was shown between the man and woman, the sexual activity inevitably progressed through the regular script—oral, vaginal, anal—ending with the man ejaculating onto the woman.

The portrayal of black women was less varied. There were generally few differences between black and white women in terms of their use in the narrative or their reaction to the sexual activity. There was, however, a tendency for black women in the videos to ask for rougher sex from the men than white women. For example, in one scene in which a black woman and a Hispanic man had sex on a desk, the woman told him: "I like when you're macho like that. I like a mean man. I like a man who'll fuck me hard and treat me rough." This also constructed the Latino as a stereotypical "machismo" figure.

The depiction of black women as overtly primitive and exotic appeared once in the *Black Pepper* video, with the woman dressed in a grass skirt in the role of the daughter of a tribal chief. She danced for, and then had sex with, a black man dressed in a stereotypical explorer costume (a role that one would expect to be taken by a white man). The explorer had brought Western dresses and shoes to trade with the chief, apparently for the sexual services of the daughter. Calling her a "sweet native girl," the man asked "Do you like the way Bwana treats you?" The girl's response, predictably, was yes.

In the two videos marked as Asian (*3 Men and a Geisha*, and *Girls of the Bamboo Palace*), the depictions conformed to the stereotype of the compliant Asian woman who lives to serve men sexually. Asian men did not appear in these videos; the labeling of a video as Asian appeared to mean that the women will be Asian. Both stories took place in Asian brothels in the United States, where the special feature of the prostitutes was total subservience. While the sexual activity in these videos was not significantly different from any of the others, the framing of the sex was always with that construction of Asian women. The plot of *Girls of the Bamboo Palace* concerned a television reporter's investigation into a conspiracy by Asian business interests to take over the United States by undermining the morals of Americans in brothels using Asian women. The reporter eventually succumbed to the seductive powers of these women, concluding that it was natural for Asian women to perform sexual services:

Reporter: "You know, growing up I always heard about the mystery of the Orient. There's no mystery, at least about Oriental women. Obviously they are brought up to please the man."

Prostitute: "I promise I will please you as much as possible."

The plot of *3 Men and a Geisha* also was based on this premise. The brothel in the video serviced only Asian men. In his will, an Asian man left to his three Anglo friends disguises, credit cards, and identification with Asian names so that they could sneak into the brothel and enjoy "the Asian arts of pleasing men." The women of the brothel were said to provide sexual services that no non-Asian woman could. In addition to this stereotype, the Anglo men performed racist imitations, with accents, mispronunciations and a shuffling walk meant to depict Asian mannerisms and speech.

AGE

A subgenre of pornography sexualizes differences in age. Because of strict laws banning child pornography, actual children are almost never used in commercial pornography sold above ground. But videos are available that highlight the differences in ages between adults (such as women in their 20s and men over 50) or that use such markers as clothing and hair styles to portray adult women as children.

First, there were clear gender differences in how sex between young people and older partners was portrayed in the two videos we rented. When the sex was between an older woman and a younger man, the script was not considerably different from other pornography. In two scenes from *Senior Stimulation*, the young men, who appeared to be in their late teens or early 20s, were a bit more wide-eyed at first than older men in pornography, but the sex progressed through the usual sequence of positions. The older women, who appeared to be in their 40s or 50s, exerted no more control than women in the typical script; there was no sense that the woman's age gave her any additional power or control over the younger man. Also, in these two scenes the men and women were not depicted as having any formal relationship with each other, such as student and teacher; they simply met on the street and had sex.

When the scene involved an older man and younger woman, however, the situation was much different. In one scene in *Senior Stimulation*, the older man was the girl's teacher, and he made it clear that she would pass the test in his class if they had sex. The man appeared to be in his 40s, the woman in her 20s, and he was clearly in control of the situation. The scene ended with the standard ejaculation, onto the woman's face and in her mouth.

Another scene in *Senior Stimulation* involved a man who appeared to be in his 50s coming into the bedroom of a woman who appeared to be in her 20s, but was dressed as a teenager in a child's dress, saddle shoes, and hair barrettes. When the man determined that the book she was reading is about fish, he began a conversation about checking her vagina, which he called her "fish tank." He moved from penetrating her with his fingers to performing oral sex on her to intercourse; the scene ended with her on her knees and him ejaculating into her mouth.

The woman in that scene was clearly an adult, but the intent was the sexualization of an adult-child relationship. This strategy was the basis for the video *Cherry Poppers Vol. 10*. Four of the five scenes were sex between different women who appeared to be in their 20s and "Max," who appeared to be in his 40s (see comments of Max Hardcore above). The fifth scene used a different man who looked to be in his 30s. Each of the women dressed in a child's uniform: some combination of bows in the hair, pigtails, either short socks or knee socks, saddle shoes, frilly dresses, or school uniforms. These women also had smaller breasts and were more slightly built than is typical in pornography. The scenarios had Max providing the woman/girl with her first sexual experience. A detailed description of one of the vignettes shows how this video not only depicted child-adult sex, but offered realistic, detailed instructions on how to initiate a child into sex, a manual for how to perpetrate a sexual assault on a child.

In this scene, the girl went into a house, where she called out for her older sister. Max entered the house shortly after her, also looking for the sister. After he found the girl in her sister's bedroom snooping into her sister's possessions, Max said that if the girl was good to him, he would not tell the sister about her snooping. Acting confused, as one would expect a child to be in such a situation, the girl is told by Max that he would "show you what boys like" but that they would have to be careful because if the sister found them, "She'll get mad."

Max then showed the girl how to fondle his penis, instructing her to "give it a little kiss, don't be afraid, suck it. Just like a sucker, just like a lollipop." He continued to instruct her in a soft, gentle voice. She removed her clothes and continued to perform fellatio on him; "take a deep breath," he told her, taking his penis out of her mouth at times to let her breathe. He also showed her how to produce enough saliva to make the oral sex pleasurable for him.

After he put her up on the sink and basin and shaved her pubic hair, Max penetrated her with his fingers before vaginal intercourse, something rapists of girls often find necessary in order to stretch the child's vagina so that it can accept the penis. He then penetrated her anus with his fingers before anal intercourse. Although her facial expression suggested she was in pain, she said, "This is fun, mister." She then returned to the floor on her knees to perform fellatio on him, and he ejaculated onto her face.

Throughout the sexual activity Max alternated gentle talk of her being a "good girl" with rougher reminders that she was a cunt. "Say it," he demanded. "'I'm a little cunt.' Can you say 'teenage fuckmate'? Say it. Repeat it." He told her how fun it was but reminded her not to tell her sister. He treated her as if she was his special friend, yet also spit in her mouth at one point. These are the standard strategies of a pedophile: alternating affection and abuse to leave the child confused, and telling the child that the sex is special but must be kept a secret from others.

In addition to the cues to age in the women's appearance, they also "acted" like girls in these scenes. They were more passive than other women in pornography and had to be explicitly directed through sexual acts. The men in these scenes were more overtly controlling, moving the women's heads and bodies to position them as they desire. The women were generally more quiet, not vocalizing moans of pleasure; they were more likely to giggle in a childish voice or be silent.

This kind of portrayal is not limited only to videos that market themselves as age-related. In *Rick Savage's New York Video Magazine Vol. 5*, one of the scenes involved an 18-year-old woman who said she was a senior in high school. She said she had never been in a pornographic video but wanted to start working in them. Savage brought in a man who appeared to be in his late 30s or 40s. As she performed fellatio on him, he told her: "You suck cock good for a little girl.... Take it all in, you little tramp.... Have you ever sucked cock on a school bus?" The clear intent was to sexualize the age difference, to point how the erotic charge of having a teenager satisfy an adult's sexual desire. Throughout the video the girl was quiet and passive as the men directed her action, talking or making sounds of pleasure only when prompted by Savage.

Our analysis of this sample of pornography (again, defined as the material that is sold as pornography for the sexual stimulation of consumers) points at some of the ways in which pornography is pornographic (in the critical feminist sense of being a site of the social subordination of women). The elements of the pornographic discussed at the beginning of the chapter—hierarchy, objectification, submission, violence—were all present at various times in the material. In the remainder of this chapter, we apply that typology more directly to pornographic novels to further explore the ideology of pornography and assess the value of Dworkin's model.

THE NOVELS

Videos are currently the biggest sellers in pornographic stores, while pulp novels are likely one of the smallest segments of the contemporary market. An analysis of these books is revealing, however, because in them pornographers must set down in words exactly what provides the erotic charge in sex. Without pictures, still or moving, to arouse consumers, the authors and publishers must convey what is sex in written language, making it a useful place to investigate the ideology of pornography.

This is not to suggest that the "essential" meaning of literary texts is somehow easier to ascertain than the meaning of images. In both cases, acts of interpretation on the part of the reader/viewer create meaning in interaction with the text. But acknowledging the complexity of that process does not preclude one from identifying patterns and themes in a genre and interrogating the work for ideological content.

Another advantage of examining these novels is that we can reproduce portions of the text and allow readers of this book to have some direct contact with the material on which we base our analysis, which is not possible with videos.

At this point in the chapter, we switch from the plural to the singular, "we" to "I," because the analysis of the novels was carried out by Jensen alone.

THEMES OF PORNOGRAPHIC NOVELS

First, a few general observations. The twenty books I read were aimed at a heterosexual market. Only two scenes involved male homosexual sex, and the few lesbian scenes served (a) to loosen up frigid women; (b) to entertain male characters; or (c) as a substitute when men were not available. The one book that included a scene with what appeared to be "real" lesbians (*Taxi Tramps*) portrayed them and their sexual activity as repulsive to the male narrator.

In these novels almost every character, even those who appeared for a short time, became involved in sex, and the portrayals of sexuality fit into gendered categories. Men were portrayed as always sexually hungry, eager and willing to engage in sex without hesitation. Only young boys sometimes hesitated, usually only for the brief moment needed for them to get over the shock of being seduced by an older woman.

Depictions of women in the books were slightly more varied. There were several standard portrayals: (a) the "nymphomaniacs," either adult or teenage women who were similar to men in their constant desire for sex; (b) the "hesitant prudes," adult women who resisted sex at first but quickly were overcome by lust and developed voracious sexual appetites; and (c) the "uninitiated youths," who feared sex because of a lack of knowledge but became willing participants in sexual activity once their fears were overcome. No female characters rejected sex from any man, and the men viewed all women as being available for sex, unless another man had a stronger claim to a particular woman. The only difference between female characters was the amount of time it takes them to realize this hypersexuality and become willing participants.

What was the purpose of a woman in these novels? The key element was not that the female characters were always portrayed sexually; obviously male characters were as well. But these books suggested that for women there is no other defining characteristic. As one woman, a "nymphomaniac," told a teenager: "Whenever you aren't stuffed full of prick, you'll feel vacant. Hollow. You'll feel unfulfilled" (*Spreading It Around*, p. 72). Another woman, a doctor, overcame her reluctance to being forced to have sex, learning that in intercourse, "All she felt was a completion of her body as a woman, a fulfillment of her soul as a human being" (*The Lady Plays Doctor*, p. 23). Later, she told the doctor who employed her, "Come on and fuck me some more, dammit. I was made for it. Doctoring is just a sideline with me" (p. 139).

These pornographic novels constantly reminded the reader that, in the end, all women are the same in that all women are for sex. How is this hypersexuality of women portrayed? It is useful to turn to Dworkin's analysis of subordination.

HIERARCHY

The power imbalance in these pornographic novels was overwhelming, both in the ways in which characters were situated in the stories and in the descriptions of sexual activity. Men typically held the positions of power, as the executives, employers, supervisors, or doctors. The secretaries, students, and nurses—popular occupations for women in the books—were portrayed as being routinely sexually available to men. In one book, a nurse was approached for sex by two interns: "She hated it. Nevertheless, she knew that she was in no position to complain" (*Nurse's Secret Lust*, p. 87).

But men did not need formal authority to dictate the terms of sexual contact. When a female teacher tried to resist a fellow teacher's offer, he told her, "Look, I want to ball with you. And if you don't like it that's tough" (*Teacher's Passionate Urge*, p. 44). Often the man and woman engaging in sex were not described in terms of occupation or authority, but the power relationship was clear. In one such case involving a male car mechanic and a female customer, the man ordered the woman into a sexual position, telling her, "You just remember one thing. You're gonna have to listen to me at every step. I'm the one who's calling the shots. You got me?" (*Everybody's Virgin*, p. 141). Men often gained extra satisfaction from exercising that power: "He liked seeing her squirm. It gave him a feeling of power forcing her to suck his cock when he knew she hated every second of it" (*Easy Office Girl*, p. 17). Women in the books did not attempt to make such demands, nor were they described as gaining pleasure from control.

When women appeared in positions of authority, usually they were not allowed to exercise their power; sometimes they willingly gave it up. For example, male students routinely took charge over female teachers. In one book, a female teacher tried to reject a student's demand for anal sex. "'Maybe,' he laughed, 'I don't give a damn. I want to get my rocks off, Teach. I'm gonna do it the way I want to. Understand?'" (*Teacher's Passionate Urge*, p. 80). Even successful, assertive women who had achieved widespread fame gave up any power that fame brings when a man approached them for sex. A cabbie was at first nervous when he picked up a movie star, but after they began having sex, he relaxed. "Famous as she might be, she was just like any other woman when it came to loving. She wanted to be dominated by me" (*Taxi Tramps*, p. 154).

Occasionally, a woman was portrayed as having power that rivaled a man's. In *Power Trip*, the main female character's status comes from a large inheritance, something she did not create but merely received. With that power she was able to control a private detective who worked for her but who disliked taking orders from her. Eventually they fall in love (that is, what passes for love in these books, an extension of sexual desire) and married, and the power dynamic changed as the man took charge sexually. As he began to have sex with her, he reflected: "Total master of the situation, this was the first time he was feeling good since he had taken on [the woman as a client]" (*Power Trip*, p. 139). The message is not only that through sex a man assumes his natural dominant position, but that such dominance is the way to contentment for a man.

In general, the power that men held in these books came either from their position in society or simply from their being men. Any power that women held was almost always derived from their bodies, their ability to perform sexually—power that in the end was controlled by men. For example, in *Easy Office Girl*, an ambitious woman rose to the top job at a television station by having sex with men and then manipulating them. Her success was the result not of talent or hard work, but of sex.

Challenges to the male-dominant hierarchy were resolved quickly. In one book a man told the woman that he wanted her to get on her knees and that he didn't know why he liked that position. She told him:

> "Cause you are a male chauvinist pig," she exclaimed.
>
> "Honey, you've been liberated," he told her. "You'd better get on your knees fast and tell me you're sorry for talking to a man like that."
>
> For a second Susan wanted to slap his face. But she thought better of it. Reluctantly she dropped to her knees.
>
> "I apologize," she said as the man moved closer (*Secretary's Naked Lunch*, p. 77).

OBJECTIFICATION

In contemporary American media—indeed, throughout society—women are routinely presented as objects for the visual or sexual consumption of men; that these pornographic novels were no different is hardly surprising. The argument often is made, however, that pornography objectifies men as well, presenting them as sexual objects. While these books did present men as hypersexual beings, they did not present them as objects. Men in these novels were the sexual subjects, the beings with agency who controlled and directed the sexual activity.

One manifestation of this is the difference in the way in which male and female bodies were described. The physical descriptions of men were limited to a few words about the penis, which was invariably described as unusually large. There was almost no discussion of other male physical characteristics. But much attention was paid to describing the appearance of women, with special notice taken of the mouth, breasts, legs, and buttocks. Often, women were reduced to their genitalia: They didn't just have a vagina, they were a vagina. When teased by a male partner who was withholding sex, one woman cried out, "Yes, yes, whatever you say. I'm a cunt" (*Gal About Town*, p. 123). In another example, an attorney demanded sex from a woman, saying, "You owe me your cunt . . . and I'm going to collect" (*Power Trip*, p. 75).

Men in the novels had penises, but the men were never referred to as being a penis. The typical attitude toward the penis was one of reverence, of respect for its power. One man was described as "reveling in the wonderful sensation of his magnificent power as the great, rampaging cock continued to fill and refill her" (*Power Trip*, p. 80). The penis was treated almost as a religious symbol. In another book, a male student approached the teacher after class and said, "Why don't you get down on your knees and worship it?" (*Teacher's Passionate Urge*, p. 60).

In several instances in the novels, women embraced their own objectification by using and taking pleasure in pornography. In one novel, an older woman encouraged the boy she was seducing to show her pornographic magazines so they could reenact sexual positions from them:

> Molly laid the photo close to them so they could go on studying it. She arranged herself just like the lusty blonde, on her elbows and knees, with her cute little ass sticking out (*Balling, Sucking Widow*, p. 85).

In another book, a female doctor who had been coerced into sexual activity by her boss was blackmailed with photos taken during the coerced sex. But the woman found herself enjoying the photos, the record of her sexual enslavement: "Those photographs were their weapon over her, and they were also a source of joy to Joyce" (*The Lady Plays Doctor*, p. 147). As we shall see in the next two sections, this tactic of making women a party to their own subordination was central.

SUBMISSION

Occasionally in these novels, men had to rely on physical force to ensure women's submission. But an integral part of women's sexual submission in pornography, as Dworkin points out, is their willingness to comply with any request. This essential element generally took one of two forms. In some cases the woman was aware of her submissive nature and sought the degrading sex. These women came to the scenes ready for whatever the men wanted. For example, one woman considered leaving a husband who beat her and forced her to engage in strange sex. But, she concluded, "What's the use in kidding myself, Doctor? I love it as much as he loves punishing me, eh? Well, so be it!" (*Wives Who Will*, p. 125).

A more common scenario in pornographic novels involved women who were initially hesitant. The woman did not at first understand her need to submit and learned along the way to crave sex and domination. The man's job was to force the sex on the woman until she realized her proper role, a theme that will be discussed in the following section. This was perhaps the most pervasive theme; every book I analyzed included such descriptions of initial fear, revulsion, or anger on the part of women facing sexual situations. But the women quickly developed an unquenchable thirst for sex, often in ways that were painful or degrading. In it simplest form, the exchange works like this:

> "Ohhhh, don't fuck me. You can't fuck me!"
>
> [Man]: "You want it so bad, you don't even know what you're saying."

"I don't want it. I don't . . ."

"Fuck me! Ohhh, damn you, fuck me now!" (*What A Librarian!*, pp. 60–61).

Once converted, the woman was concerned with little but sex. In one book, a woman explained that although the man did not treat her with respect, she didn't mind. "He could degrade her any way he chose to, just as long as he didn't take that lovely hard meat out of her mouth" (*The Lady Plays Doctor*, pp. 63–64).

Sometimes the women remained ambivalent even after they have been "broken in," but that ambivalence always melted away. In a scene where an employee is forced to perform for her boss, the following thoughts went through her mind:

> She hated herself. She hated sucking on his prick. She discovered she hated herself worst of all—for enjoying this degradation. . . . This humiliating scene was sexually arousing her. . . . If she didn't get it, she would surely go crazy with lust (*Easy Office Girl*, p. 16).

Women in the books also sometimes wanted to submit to sex but pretended not to. In one book, a woman was set free to enjoy sex after the man put her dress over her head, concealing her reactions: "Now she would not be betrayed. Now she could be fucked and sucked without showing him how much she wanted to be fucked and sucked. Typical woman" (*The Town Sluts*, p. 93).

In all the books, any reservations that women had were eventually resolved, and they became willing sex partners, no matter how traumatic their past experiences may have been. For example, one book attributed an adult woman's resistance to sex to her ambivalent feelings over being sexually abused as a child. But, after finally giving in to her "natural" desire, she realized:

> God, what a fool she had been! What an insane fool! Just because several men used her the way a female should be used, she had spent most of her life without cock, wonderful cock (*Boy-Hungry Librarian*, p. 148).

This is one of the many instances in which the novels portrayed sexual submission as natural for young girls. In one book a woman described being picked up after school by a man when she was 12:

> And I might have been only twelve years old but I was willing to give him that blow-job too. Maybe that's why sexually I'm such a good wife today,

Doctor, because I had a lot of heavy sex when I was younger. I was just never afraid of it, you know what I mean? (*Wives Who Will*, p. 42).

Sexual assault of girls by stepfathers, fathers, or brothers also was portrayed sympathetically, usually with the girl as a willing participant.

VIOLENCE

The need for women to be shown their natural submissive role often was connected to violence. This took the form of everything from the use of mild force—"Candy was about to protest, but Daryl pulled her platinum blonde hair and shoved his cock into her wet mouth" (*Candy's Sweet Mouth*, p. 10)—to bondage, rape, and torture.

The language used to describe sex and the male organ was larded with violent images. The penis was consistently referred to as a type of weapon: "He continued sliding into her as he got off his gun" (*Secretary's Naked Lunch*, p. 159). This collection of descriptions is from *Everybody's Virgin*:

cock stabs (p. 19); his rifle-like penis (p. 20); his stirring, dagger-like rod (p. 27); his razor-sharp organ (p. 41); his jackhammer cock (p. 104); his steady spear (p. 105); my lover's quick, surging stabs (p. 142); his hurling dagger kept on slashing up between my buns (p. 157); I really want to slice with my cock (p. 170); just jackknife your prick inside me. Just stab it real nice (p. 176).

But beyond these uses of violent imagery were numerous descriptions of overtly violent acts committed by men against women. From the perspective of male characters in the novels, violence was an acceptable method of ensuring sexual cooperation from women. For example, in one book when a woman refused to participate in sadomasochistic sex, the man whipped her until she submitted. The man then told a friend, "Women, women ... they won't do what you want them to unless you use a little pressure" (*Teacher's Passionate Urge*, p. 101).

For men in these novels, the violence also was a source of pleasure once the woman's participation had been secured:

He slapped at her thighs several times, which caused Ray to feel an even greater measure of excitement as he kept on spiritedly thrusting his dick deep inside her pussy.... This time Ray asserted himself even more vigorously than before. He kept reaching out with his trembling hands, slapping at his lover's buttocks, enjoying the activity as he moved that much closer to climax (*The Hungry Hostess*, pp. 33–34).

Although it was always the men who committed the violent acts, violence and pain were typically described from the woman's point of view and came in two different forms. Some women who had eagerly agreed to sex found themselves enjoying pain that occurred in the course of sexual activity. In these cases, the violent act and resulting pain were not connected to coercion into the sex act. The second, and more common, description of violence and pain followed a standard rape-fantasy scenario, in which the woman initially resisted sexual contact, but eventually gave in to overwhelming pleasure. This scenario typically began with some level of force to overcome the woman's resistance and included varying levels of pain, which was described as adding to her pleasure.

In the 20 novels analyzed, 16 used the rape-fantasy scenario at least once, and most repeated it throughout the book. In four novels, the women were portrayed as nymphomaniacs who did not need to be coerced into sexual activity. The following examples show the different levels at which the portrayal of women enjoying this fusion of sex, pain, and violence were played out in the novels:

> His fingers cruelly cut into her soft flesh. . . . Oddly, this stimulated her to a fever pitch that she had missed. The pain in her rear end made the pleasure he was giving her asshole all the more apparent. . . . The pain actually heightened her senses, made her more aware of what was happening to her (*Easy Office Girl*, p. 127).

> As Susan felt the thick, long, slippery penis gliding up her asshole, she let out a small moan of pain. This pleased Larry. Having a streak of sadism in him added to his erotic pleasure. "Fuck my asshole," she told him. "Go ahead. I like it when it hurts, Larry'" (*Secretary's Naked Lunch*, p. 136).

> [*After a woman's father-in-law catches her masturbating and hits her on her buttocks with his belt*]:
> I was quite startled by the notion that he could beat me in one instant and make love to me in the next. My naked pink flesh shook with anticipation. . . . And soon my juices began to flow so plentifully that I could no longer deny how much I loved him even though he had only moments before strapped my buttocks. I gave way (*Wives Who Will*, pp. 33–34).

> [*A woman is tied up by several men for a gang rape*]:
> Sheila whimpered pitifully and tugged furiously at the ropes. She was no longer angry at Neil and Robbie. She merely wanted to free herself in order to play with the young man's prick and balls (*Sheila Spreads Wide*, p. 65).

She did not struggle. She had realized some time ago that she was having the time of her life. She merely wanted the men to get on with the gang-bang (*Sheila Spreads Wide*, p. 77).

In one book, rape is described as pleasurable for women, "one of those things in life that are disgusting when thought about, but downright fun when tried" (*Town Sluts*, p. 142). After the rape, Ramona berated the rapist for not satisfying her: "Hey! You can't leave me hanging! Christ, I'm hotter than hell! Come on, I wanta suck your cock!" (pp. 142–143). Later, in a typically absurd plot turn, Ramona met a boxing trainer who was angry because women were diverting his fighter from training. This man spontaneously hit her with a tree branch, sparking Ramona to cry out, "OH! THAT'S IT! BEAT THE SHIT OUT OF ME! HURT ME!" (p. 151). The trainer—whose visit to a prostitute was described earlier in the book—continued to beat her, hurt her, and finally kill her. The male violence here took on an aspect of retribution; men take sex from women, who were blamed for seducing men. The fitting punishment was death.

THE IDEOLOGY OF MALE SUPREMACY

The ideology of male supremacy appears throughout the nonstop descriptions of sexual activity in these pornographic novels, incorporating some or all of Dworkin's categories of sexual subordination. A final excerpt from one book shows how these elements can come together to present a picture of women as naturally powerless sexual objects who crave violence and sex at the direction of a man.

In the concluding chapter of *Easy Office Girl* (pp. 147–158), the woman who had used her sexual power over men to rise to the top at a television station approached the station owner to ask for the top management job. After owner Ed Morgan agreed to give Cheryl (who is never given a last name) the job, he took her into a sadomasochism chamber. She asked to leave, but he cut off her clothes and hit her with a paddle. Her resistance and fear of pain evaporated quickly:

Soon, the pain subsided and she found herself actually enjoying the scene. It was kinky. She couldn't explain why it was turning her on so. But it was. The pain had heightened her senses. She found herself totally alive now. But when was he going to get down and really fuck her?

Morgan then began a torture session that included Cheryl being bound, gagged, and whipped. He urinated on her and gave her a chemical enema. Cheryl reacted in standard pornographic fashion:

All she had gone through had turned her on! She had needed to be used, abused! He was such a forceful man, not like the namby-pamby men she had found before. He couldn't be pushed around. She couldn't use sex as a weapon against him.

He knew what he wanted—and took it. . . .

He knew women.

He knew what turned them on. . . . He could humiliate her and make her love every second of it.

She was humiliated, degraded, made to feel less than human.

He was using her.

Just like she had used all the other men to get to this point.

And the hell of it was, she enjoyed it!

She needed to be abused, to be humiliated. The pain heightened her senses all the way to where she could enjoy the pleasure. It gave her a good contrast of how good the pleasure actually was in comparison.

Most of all, she needed a man who was a man. Not the sniveling turds who could be wrapped around her little finger.

But when Morgan showed her that a man could make her do whatever he wanted, she found her true self. She needed to be used by this man in whatever fashion his mind could conjure up. It was necessary for her.

This was a man she could worship.

. . . [T]hen he used her again. All night long.

And she loved him for it.

CONCLUSION

We began this chapter by asking what makes pornography pornographic. Does pornography—defined loosely at the materials sold in pornography shops—promote the sexual and social subordination of women?

Our analysis of the videos and novels shows that the four elements of pornography that Dworkin has outlined (hierarchy, objectification, submission, and violence) are central to the representation of sexuality in pornography. We found that, as the feminist critique of pornography asserts, at the core of contemporary pornography is contempt for women. One need not look at the most violent or sadomasochistic pornography to reach this conclusion. Our analysis in this chapter is based on "normal" pornography, the material that is for sale in shops throughout the United States (as well as other parts of the world), the pornography that pervades our culture. An investigation into subgenres that are overtly sadistic and violent, also readily available in these shops, would reveal a more intense contempt. But one need not go beyond the "normal" to see the ideology.

If one asks the simple question, "What are women for in pornography?" this is made clear. As we watched these videos, we began referring to the women as "fuck-objects." That seemed to be the most succinct way to describe the construction of the female in everything we watched. Women exist to be fucked by men, in a way that fulfills men's desires. When the fucking is over, the woman's usefulness is over. This was stated clearly by Eddie, the producer/actor in *More Dirty Debutantes #37*. At the end of one sex scene, Eddie tells the woman, "You're officially done. Fuck the babe, get her out. That's how it's done in this house."

This analysis is not meant as the final word on the content of pornography, but as part of an ongoing conversation about content and meaning. It also is intended to be read in connection with narrative accounts of women and men about how pornography has affected their lives (see Chapter 5). Like all texts, of course, pornography does not offer a single meaning that will be decoded in the same fashion by all. As Stephen Prince (1990, p. 39) puts it, "To talk about the ideology of pornography, then, is to assume that pornography is one thing and plays one role."

Still, if our reading of pornography is not completely idiosyncratic, the consistent use of misogynistic themes indicates that there is an ideology that pornography can easily tap into. Whether it is possible in a culture structured by male dominance to create pornography that does not tap into this ideology is a more contentious question we will not address here.

conclusion

FIVE

Using Pornography

ROBERT JENSEN

How a question is asked has much to do with how it is answered. In investigating heterosexual men's use of pornography and the effects of that use, with a special concern about the possible links to sexual violence against women and children, should we ask, "Does pornography cause rape?" Or, should we ask, "Is pornography implicated in rape?" The form of the question suggests different research methods: The search for causation demands "science," while a concern for pornography's role in rape leaves us more open to listening to stories. Because science has no way to answer the question, predictably the search for causation and the use of science leads most everyone to conclude that we just don't know enough to say for sure. But a shift in emphasis and method offers a way to state not The Truth (or conclude we don't yet know The Truth), but a way to tell true stories and begin to make trustworthy moral and political decisions.

It is those stories I want to focus on in this chapter. I begin by critiquing contemporary culture's faith in science as the only valid route to knowledge about such issues and making a case for a narrative approach. I then present some of the available testimony of women about the role of pornography in their lives, followed by a report on my interviews with male pornography users and sex offenders. From those sources, I make some claims about the way in which pornography is implicated in the sexual abuse of women and children. The chapter concludes with my narrative about my use of pornography as a child and young man and some observations based on that story.

SCIENCE AND STORIES

We live in a culture that likes "science" answers provided by "experts," even when the questions are primarily about human values. Not surprisingly, experimental laboratory research has played an important role in the debate over pornography in the past three decades. Some advocates of regulation, both feminist and conservative, commonly cite studies showing links between pornography and violence, while opponents of regulation point to other studies that show no links or are inconclusive.

Experimental research on pornography looks at the effects of viewing or reading sexually explicit material. A typical study might expose groups of subjects to different types or levels of sexually explicit material for comparison to a control group that views nonsexual material. Researchers look for significant differences between the groups on a measure of, for example, male attitudes toward rape. One such measure could be subjects' assessments of the suffering experienced by sexual assault victims or subjects' judgments of the appropriate prison sentence for a rapist. From such controlled testing—measuring the effect of an experimental stimulus (exposure to pornography) on a dependent variable (attitudes toward women or sex) in randomly selected groups—researchers make claims, usually tentative, about causal relationships.

While there is disagreement among researchers about what has been "proved" by these studies (Zillmann, 1989; Linz, 1989), some researchers have drawn tentative conclusions. For example, Weaver (1992) reads the evidence to support the sexual callousness model, which suggests that exposure to pornography activates sexually callous perceptions of women and promotes sexually aggressive behavior by men (Zillman and Bryant, 1982; Zillman and Weaver, 1989). This appears to be the result of both pornography's promotion of a loss of respect for female sexual autonomy and the disinhibition of men's expression of aggression against women (Weaver, 1992, p. 307). A recent comprehensive meta-analysis of the experimental work found that (a) pictorial nudity reduces subsequent aggressive behavior, (b) material depicting nonviolent sexual activity increases aggressive behavior, and (c) depictions of violent sexual activity produce even more aggression (Allen, D'Alessio, and Brezgel, 1995). The researchers concluded that their analysis did not prove causality but made an argument for causality plausible.

Russell (1988, 1993b) makes such an argument. After reviewing the experimental research, she outlined four factors that link pornography to sexual violence. She argues that pornography (1) predisposes some males to desire rape or intensifies this desire; (2) undermines some males' internal inhibitions against acting out rape desires; (3) undermines some males' social inhibitions against acting out rape desires; and (4) undermines some potential victims' abilities to avoid or resist rape.

Taking a different approach, Donnerstein, Linz, and Penrod (1987) argue that only pornography that combines violence and sex has been shown to be harmful, and then only in the sense of immediate effects; they hesitate to speculate on the long term. They conclude there is not enough evidence to show that exposure to nonviolent pornography leads to increases in aggression against women under most circumstances, suggesting "some forms of pornography, under some conditions, promote certain antisocial attitudes and behavior" (Donnerstein, Linz, and Penrod, 1987, p. 171).

Although much of the experimental work supports that feminist critique, we need to be skeptical of the value of such studies, no matter what the results; the limits of the experimental approach should lead us to look elsewhere for answers.

The Limits of Experimental Research

In addition to a number of specific technical complaints over methodology and research design (summarized, but rejected, by Donnerstein, Linz, and Penrod, 1987, pp. 12–22), most of the critics of these studies suggest that any connection between pornography and sexual violence found in the lab is probably overstated; they warn of overgeneralizing from experimental studies because the effects found might evaporate outside the lab:

> It is a considerable leap from the laboratory to the corner store where men rifle the pages of magazines kept on the top shelf. It is a long step from the laboratory exposure to such stimuli and subsequent aggression to real world sexual and physical abuse (Brannigan and Goldenberg, 1987, p. 277).

Although it is possible that the research overreaches, we should be at least as concerned that lab studies underestimate pornography's role in promoting misogynistic attitudes and behavior (Dines-Levy, 1988a).

First, the measures of men's attitudes toward women, such as answers to questions about the appropriate punishment for rapists, do not necessarily tell us anything about men's willingness to rape. Men often do not view their sexually aggressive or violent behavior as aggression or violence; it's just sex. So, it is plausible that a man could endorse heavy penalties for rapists after viewing pornography because the sex in pornography, and in the man's life, doesn't appear to him to be rape. Also, paper-and-pencil surveys don't necessarily measure what we need to know. Sexual behavior is a complicated mix of cognitive, emotional, and physical responses, and the answers one gives to a survey may or may not accurately reflect that mix. Again, it is plausible that a man genuinely could endorse heavy penalties for rape and, when presented with an opportunity to rape, be sexually violent. In other words, it is not clear what the instruments that are used are actually measuring, and there is no way to devise an instrument to measure what we want to measure.

These lab studies also are incapable of measuring subtle effects that develop over time. If pornography works to develop attitudes and shape behavior after repeated exposure, there is no guarantee that studies exposing people to a small amount of pornography over a short time can accurately measure anything. For example, in one study, the group exposed to what the researchers called the "massive" category of pornography viewed six explicitly sexual eight-minute films per session for six sessions, or a total of four hours and 48 minutes of material (Zillmann and Bryant, 1982). The "intermediate" group saw half the number of sexual films. These categories are constructed, obviously, for comparative purposes, not to suggest that such an amount of viewing is massive. But even within the confines of a laboratory study, these amounts are likely to be inadequate to test anything.

In addition, as Brannigan and Goldenberg suggest, no lab can reproduce the natural setting of the behavior being studied. Brannigan and Goldenberg paint a rather harmless picture of men paging through magazines in the corner store, but there are other common settings for the consumption of pornography. How is watching a pornographic movie in a university video lab (the experience of experimental subjects) different from being one of a dozen men in a dark movie theater, frightened but excited by the illicit nature of the setting? How is the lab different from the living room of a fraternity house where a group of young men might watch a pornographic videotape, drinking beer and talking about how much they would like to have sex with the women on the screen? If the settings in which pornography is consumed affect the experience, then we must question the usefulness of lab research.

More specifically, and most importantly, how does the act of masturbating to pornography—a common male experience and perhaps the most important function of pornography for men—influence the way in which men interpret, and are affected by, pornography? The experience of viewing an image without sexually stimulating oneself is significantly different than viewing that same image while experiencing a sexual climax. Orgasm is a powerful physical and emotional experience that is central to understanding the pornographic experience, yet there is no ethical way that lab studies can take this into account. More than any other single factor, it is the inability of lab research to account for the effect of masturbation in pornography use that renders this work problematic, at best.

So, the lab experience is unreal in terms of both the physical and the psychological environments, and researchers have only the sketchiest notions of what they are measuring. If experimental data seems to suggest, for example, that exposure to depictions in which women appear to enjoy being raped can increase men's acceptance of sexual violence against women and increase men's endorsement of that rape myth (Malamuth and Check, 1981), can we assume those effects will be even more pronounced on a man who views that same sexual material in a real-world environment in which male aggression is often encouraged? Since it would be impossible, not to mention ethically unacceptable, to recreate such a situation in a lab, the value of lab data is questionable. Instead of assuming that the lab overstates the potential for aggression, we should consider how it could understate the effect.

Listening to Stories

So, if we resist the "grip of quantitative mysticism"—the idea that categorizing and quantifying experience lead to privileged knowledge (Berman, 1990, p. 117)—what can we do? Positivist social science considers the evidence that comes from people's narratives to be merely "anecdotal" and warns that generalizing from personal experience is problematic:

> Even if we were to observe a nearly one-to-one relationship between view-
> ing violent pornography and committing a sexual assault or rape in the
> real world, this finding is not as compelling in a causal sense as is an exper-
> iment (Donnerstein, Linz, and Penrod, 1987, p. 10).

Donnerstein, Linz, and Penrod have faith in the possibilities of lab research to answer these questions, although other researchers who share their loyalty to experimental methods are far less optimistic about proving causation. Zillmann, for example, warns that "research on pornography cannot be definitive. It cannot satisfy the demands for rigor and compelling-ness that have been placed on it" (Zillmann, 1989, p. 398). He believes that social science can, however, be of value in guiding policy and making final decisions. Although not definitive, this research is "far superior to hearsay, guessing, and unchecked common sense" (p. 399). But is guessing the only alternative to experimental research?

The work of feminist scholars who have challenged Western science's claims of objectivity and neutrality (e.g., Harding, 1991) and proposed alter-natives to traditional methods of social science research (e.g., Reinharz, 1992) makes it clear that human behavior and social patterns can be understood through research that takes seriously the stories people tell about their lives. To question the value of lab research is not to argue against the orderly investigation of the world or against all research that might be called social science. Rather than bemoan the loss of alleged objectivity and the hope of generalizability that comes with a shift to narrative method, I want to explore the possibilities opened up by a commitment to listening to people's stories.

In a sense, this is the epistemology of feminism—if there can be said to be an overarching epistemology of feminism—built on the model of consciousness-raising. As Marilyn Frye (1992, p. 63) writes, the worldview and the philosophy of feminism rest:

> on a most empirical base: staking your life on the trustworthiness of your own body as a source of knowledge. It rests equally fundamentally on intersubjective agreement, since some kind of agreement in perceptions and experience among women is what gives our sense data, our body data, the compelling cogency which made it possible to trust them.

From that kind of communal practice, attempts at generalizing can be made, even if they will always be tentative. While feminists are wary of enshrining any one method as the path to truth, the abandonment of any hope of generalization that connects people's experience is both intellectually and politically debilitating. As Frye acknowledges (1992, p. 64), "You have to have some sort of genuinely general generality to have theory, philosophy, politics." Her solution is in a less totalizing style of generalization that she calls "pattern perception":

> The experiences of each woman and of the women collectively generate a new web of meaning. Our process has been one of discovering, recognizing, and creating patterns—patterns within which experience made a new kind of sense, or, in many instances, for the first time made any sense at all. Instead of bringing a phase of enquiry to closure by summing up what is known, as other ways of generalizing do, pattern recognition/construction opens fields of meaning and generates new interpretive possibilities. Instead of drawing conclusions from observations, it generates observations (Frye, 1992, p. 65).

Frye (1992, p. 67) makes it clear that people's experiences are varied and that "not everything that is intelligibly located by a pattern fits the pattern." There are limits to patterns, and they are not immutable; in time, they may shift. As Frye suggests (1992, p. 69), "They work until they stop working. You find out where that is by working them until they dissolve."

People's experiences are reported in narratives, which Donald Polkinghorne describes as "the fundamental scheme for linking individual human actions and events into interrelated aspects of an understandable composite" (Polkinghorne, 1988, p. 13). Polkinghorne's sense of narrative is more specific than the everyday definition of the term, which often is used to describe any spoken or written presentation. He describes narratives as organizational schemes expressed in story form:

> [N]arrative is a meaning structure that organizes events and human actions into a whole, thereby attributing significance to individual actions and events according to their effect on the whole. Thus, narratives are to be differentiated from chronicles, which simply list events according to their place on a time line (Polkinghorne, 1988, p. 18).

For Polkinghorne, narratives do not force events to fit the patterns of existing laws or theories. Instead, narrative explanation is retroactive, in the sense that it explains by clarifying the significance of events on the basis of the outcome (p. 21).

In arguing for a central role for narratives, I don't claim that The Truth will emerge, a single account of reality that will answer all questions about pornography. The stories of some people will conflict with or contradict the stories of others; dealing with narrative accounts on a complex subject such as pornography is messy.

It follows that "there may be no facts of the matter in any absolute sense, either in science or in law, and . . . it really all amounts to telling plausible stories" (Code, 1986, p. 599). Like Lorraine Code, I believe that we can work toward knowing which stories are more plausible than others and that rejecting Truth need not involve rejecting the possibility of identifying true stories. The loss of the absolute, "big T" truth is not debilitating. Code writes:

> It is not as if we are left with nothing to put in place of the old, timeless truths. What we have instead is communal practice [based on communication]. . . . We need to make this practice as good, as responsible as we can, if the stories that grow out of it are to be stories we can live by (Code, 1986, p. 605–606).

What We Can Know

Three decades of experimental research on pornography's effects have not answered questions about pornography and sexual violence. Should we hold out hope that more experimental studies will provide answers? Should we privilege that research in the public policy debate over pornography? To do so marginalizes a type of knowledge that holds out much more promise for helping us understand pornography, sexuality, sexism, and violence.

Isolating with any certainty the effect of one particular manifestation of misogyny (pornography) in a culture that is generally misogynist, is hopeless. In fact, the danger of pornography is heightened exactly because it is only one part of a sexist system and because the message it carries about sexuality is reinforced elsewhere. What we learn from the testimony of women and men whose lives have been touched by pornography is how the material is implicated in violence against women and how it can perpetuate, reinforce, and be part of a wider system of woman-hating. Rather than discussing simple causation, we think of how various factors, in Frye's terms, make something inviting. In those terms, pornography does not cause rape but rather helps make rape inviting. Research can examine people's stories about their experiences with pornography and sexual violence to help us determine how close the relationship between the material and the actions is. The work of judging narratives can be difficult and sometimes messy; the process doesn't claim clear, objective standards that experimental research appears to offer. There are no experts to ask for authoritative answers; we all are responsible for building responsible and honest communal practices.

WOMEN'S NARRATIVES

As the stories of women about sexual violence have been taken more seriously, society has gained new understandings of stranger and acquaintance rape, the sexual abuse of children, and battering. That same honoring of women's and children's voices is crucial to understanding pornography. The following accounts, taken from scholarly publications and political hearings, have not been given the attention needed to understand pornography. Collecting these narratives in one place helps to overcome the criticism that such evidence is simply anecdotal and of limited value. Placing them next to the narratives of men who have used pornography in the next section brings the picture into clearer focus.

It is important to remember that the feminist anti-pornography critique grew out of these stories. The harms listed in the civil rights ordinance—women coerced into making pornography, forced to view pornography, sexually assaulted in ways connected to pornography, defamed by pornography, and trafficked in pornography—were identified not by experimental research but by taking seriously the lives of women. The following excerpts illustrate these harms.

Silbert and Pines Study

The first few accounts are taken from a study of the sexual abuse of street prostitutes. Of the 200 women interviewed, 73 percent reported being raped, and 24 percent of those women mentioned that their assailants made reference to pornography (Silbert and Pines, 1984). What makes that figure even more significant is that those comments were unsolicited; the research design did not include questions about pornography. Mimi Silbert and Ayala Pines reported that the women's comments about pornography followed a similar pattern: "the assailant referred to pornographic materials he had seen or read and then insisted that the victims not only enjoyed the rape but also the extreme violence" (p. 863).

In a typical comment reported by the victims, an assailant told the woman:

> I know all about you bitches, you're no different; you're like all of them. I seen it in all the movies. You love being beaten. (He then began punching the victim violently.) I just seen it again in that flick. He beat the shit out of her while he raped her and she told him she loved it; you know you love it; tell me you love it (p. 864).

Another woman reported this experience:

> After I told him I'd turn him a free trick if only he'd calm down and stop hurting me, then he just really blew his mind. He started calling me all kinds of names, and then started screaming and shrieking like nothing I'd ever heard. He sounded like a wailing animal. Instead of just slapping me to keep me quiet, he really went crazy and began punching me all over. Then he told me he had seen whores just like me in (three pornographic films mentioned by name), and told me he knew how to do it to whores like me. He knew what whores like me wanted ... After he finished raping me, he started beating me with his gun all over. Then he said, "You were in that movie. You were in that movie. You know you wanted to die after you were raped. That's what you want; you want me to kill you after this rape just like (specific pornographic film) did" (p. 865).

That woman suffered vaginal and anal penetration, and a variety of injuries, including broken bones. The rapist also held a loaded pistol at her vagina, threatening to shoot, insisting this was the way she had died in the film he had seen.

Silbert and Pines also summarized the experience of one woman:

[O]ne of the subjects in the study described a primitive movie projector her father had set up in the garage. He used to show himself and his friends pornographic movies to get them sexually aroused before they would rape her. (She was 9 at the time.) Her brother would also watch the movies when the father was gone; then he also abused her sexually (p. 865).

Russell Study

In her survey of more than 900 women about experiences with sexual violence, Diana E.H. Russell included the question, "Have you ever been upset by anyone trying to get you to do what they'd seen in pornographic pictures, movies, or books?" (Russell, 1980). Ten percent of the women reported at least one such experience. The following are some of the responses to that question (pp. 225–227):

I was staying at this guy's house. He tried to make me have oral sex with him. He said he'd seen far-out stuff in movies, and that it would be fun to mentally and physically torture a woman.

It was physical slapping and hitting. It wasn't a turn-on; it was more a feeling of being used as an object. What was most upsetting was that he thought it would be a turn-on.

My husband enjoys pornographic movies. He tries to get me to do things he finds exciting in movies. They include twosomes and threesomes. I always refuse. Also, I was always upset with his ideas about putting objects in my vagina, until I learned this is not as deviant as I used to think. He used to force me or put whatever he enjoyed into me.

He forced me to go down on him. He said he'd been going to porno movies. He'd seen this and wanted me to do it. He also wanted to pour champagne on my vagina. I got beat up because I didn't want to do it. He pulled my hair and slapped me around. After that I went ahead and did it, but there was no feeling in it.

This guy has seen a movie where a woman was being made love to by dogs. He suggested that some of his friends had a dog and we should have a party and set the dog loose on the women. He wanted me to put a muzzle on the dog and put some sort of stuff on my vagina so that the dog would lick there.

My old man and I went to a show that had lots of tying up and anal intercourse. We came home and proceeded to make love. He went out and got two belts. He tied my feet together with one, and with the other he kinda beat me. I was in the spirit, I went along with it. But when he tried to penetrate me anally, I couldn't take it, it was too painful. I managed to convey to him verbally to quit it. He did stop, but not soon enough to suit me.

My boyfriend and I saw a movie in which there was masochism. After that he wanted to gag me and tie me up. He was stoned. I was not. I was really shocked at his behavior. I was nervous and uptight. He literally tried to force me, after gagging me first. He snuck up behind me with a scarf. He was hurting me with it and I started getting upset. Then I realized it wasn't a joke. He grabbed me and shook me by my shoulders and brought out some ropes, and told me to relax, and that I would enjoy it. Then he started putting me down about my feelings about sex, and my inhibitedness. I started crying and struggling with him, got loose, and kicked him in the testicles, which forced him down on the couch. I ran out of the house. Next day he called and apologized, but that was the end of him.

Kelly Study

For a study on how women experience sexual violence, Liz Kelly (1988) conducted detailed interviews with 60 British women, some who identified themselves as sexual assault survivors and some who didn't. Kelly found that women reported that pornography often is a part of this continuum of violence:

> The many statements women made in their discussion of experiences of pressurized sex, coercive sex and sexual assault which implicated pornography cannot be ignored. Nor can the fact that many women also discussed feeling pressured or coerced into looking at pornography, either in magazines or on film and video. I was initially shocked at the extent to which porn videos had become integrated into social events; they seemed to be an automatic part of many parties. Whilst many feminists were engaging in academic debates about the definition and meaning of pornography, many of the heterosexual women I interviewed were having to cope with its unwelcome presence in their lives. Their feelings about this did not reflect a "prudery" about sex but were grounded in feeling upset at the objectification (and at times abuse) of the women appearing in porn, and by implication themselves, and the reality that their partner expected them to engage in the sexual practices represented (pp. 116–117).

Kelly reports that for the women she interviewed who objected to having pornography forced on them, this was not an abstract political issue; none seemed to be aware of feminist debates on the issue:

> They were reacting on the basis of how pornography made them feel. They were resisting attempts to make its presence acceptable within their homes and social life. In making these stands, women took a number of risks. For example, the possibility of being labelled "prudes" within their friendship network and the probability of a prolonged dispute with their male partner, which in some cases ended in violence (p. 169).

The following comments are from the women interviewed for Kelly's book:

> He was a photographer and he took lots of photos of me and they became pornographic. I wasn't aware of that at the time. He'd been giving me lots of drinks. I met him about a week later and he showed me these photos which really threw me. I was very upset and he refused to give them to me. I had to sleep with him to get them (pp. 113–114).
>
> I now see a lot of my relationship with him as being some kind of sexual assault. He used to use pornography at the same time as having sex with me—it was as if I became one of those pictures. (long pause) That's a much more subtle form of assault (p. 108).
>
> We used to watch films and he would want me to do what (long pause) He said that anything that turned you on and involved two people was alright, but I didn't feel it was alright (p. 110).
>
> He wanted to do everything they said in the book (p. 110).
>
> Whatever happened in this magazine we used to have to do it, it was like a manual. I'd think, "Oh god, I better read it to see what I've got to do tonight" (p. 111).

Minneapolis Hearings

The hearings before a committee of the Minneapolis City Council included the testimony of a number of women about how pornography was a part of sexual violence against them. As Catharine MacKinnon stated in her opening remarks at the hearing, "This hearing, this opportunity for our speech is precious and rare and unprecedented" (*Public Hearings*, 1983, p. 2). Opposition to the ordinance also was voiced at the hearings, but the following excerpts are a representative sample of the testimony of women who had been injured by pornography:

Ms. N was 21 years old at the time of the incident she described involving a man she was having a sexual relationship with:

> [My boyfriend] had gone to a stag party, this particular evening I was home alone in my apartment. He called me on the telephone and he said that he had seen several short pornographic films and that he felt very horny.... So he asked if he could come over specifically to have sex with me. I said yes because at that time I felt obligated as a girlfriend to satisfy him. I also felt that the refusal would be indicative of sexual, quote-unquote, hang-ups on my part and that I was not, quote-unquote, liberal enough. When he arrived he informed me that the other men at the party were envious that he had a girlfriend to fuck. They wanted to fuck too after watching the pornography. He informed me of this as he was taking his coat off. He then took off the rest of his clothes and had me perform fellatio on him. I did not do this of my own volition. He put his genitals in my face and he said, "Take it all." Then he fucked me on the couch in the living room. All this took about five minutes. And when he was finished, he dressed and went back to the party. I felt ashamed and numb and I also felt very used. This encounter differed from others previous. It was much quicker, it was somewhat rougher, and he was not aware of me as a person. There was no foreplay. It is my opinion that his viewing of the pornography served as foreplay for him (p. 41).

Ms. P described her husband's increasing interest in pornography as their marriage progressed. Out of a sense of duty, she accompanied him to pornographic movies and sex shows, but objected when he wanted to live out some of the pornography-based fantasies he had about group sex:

> He told me if I loved him I would do this. And that, as I could see from the things that he read me in the magazines initially, a lot of times women did-n't like it, but if I tried it enough I would probably like it and I would learn to like it. And he would read me stories where women learned to like it. [The husband then tried to initiate sex with a third person.] ... To prevent more of these group situations, which I found very humiliating and very destructive to my self-esteem and my feeling of self-worth as a person, to prevent these I agreed with him to act out in privacy a lot of those scenarios that he read to me. A lot of them depicting bondage and different sexual acts that I found very humiliating. About this time when things were getting really terrible and I was feeling suicidal and very worthless as a person,

at that time any dreams that I had of a career in medicine were just totally washed away. I could not think of myself anymore as a human being.... He would read from pornography like a textbook, like a journal. In fact, when he asked me to be bound, when he finally convinced me to do it, he read in the magazine how to tie the knots and how to bind me in a way that I couldn't get out. And most of the scenes that we—most of the scenes where I had to dress up or go through different fantasies were the exact scenes that he had read in the magazines. [After their divorce, her husband remarried.] ... And at the time I had seen him to finalize things on our divorce and get some of my last possessions, he showed me pictures of [his new wife] and said, "Do you want to see what she looks like?" They were pictures of her naked and in pornographic poses (pp. 43–46).

Ms. Q, a former prostitute, spoke about the ways in which pornography was part of her life and the lives of other prostitutes in a group to which she belonged. All of them had been introduced to prostitution through pornography. In her testimony, she related the experiences of one of those women:

Another story is a woman met a man in a hotel room in the 5th Ward. When she got there she was tied up while sitting on a chair nude. She was gagged and left alone in the dark for what she believed to be an hour. The man returned with two other men. They burned her with cigarettes and attached nipple clips to her breasts. They had many S-and-M magazines with them and showed her many pictures of women appearing to consent, enjoy, and encourage this abuse. She was held for 12 hours, continuously raped and beaten (p. 49).

Ms. Q also read from a letter written by a former prostitute who did not want to be publicly identified:

When I went into that room, the trick said that I was almost too old, but he was pleased with me because I looked young. He stripped me, tied me up, spread-eagled on the bed so that I could not move and then began to caress me very gently. Then, when he thought that I was relaxed, he squeezed my nipple really hard. I did not react. He held up a porn magazine with a picture of a beaten woman and said, "I want you to look like that. I want you to hurt." He then began beating me, and when I didn't cry fast enough, he lit a cigarette and held it right above my breast for a long time before he burned me. I told him that as God was my witness, he had better kill me or untie me right now, because if he didn't, I would turn him in to the police and that I would call his wife and tell his family about him. He believed me and let me go. But I know that this house continued to provide that service for those who could pay (p. 48).

Ms. W described the sexual abuse of a woman she lived with for many years. The woman's ex-husband also lived there, refusing to leave and threatening to kill his ex-wife if she took legal action to evict him:

Over a period of 18 years the woman was regularly raped by this man. He would bring pornographic magazines, books, and paraphernalia into the bedroom with him and tell her that if she did not perform the sexual acts that were being done in the "dirty" books and magazines he would beat and kill her. I know about this because my bedroom was right next to hers. I could hear everything they said. I could hear her screams and cries. In addition, since I did most of the cleaning in the house, I would often come across the books, magazines, and paraphernalia that were in the bedroom and other rooms of the house. The magazines had pictures of mostly women and children and some men. Eventually, the woman admitted to me that her ex-husband did in fact use pornographic materials to terrorize and rape her. [She also described how the man abused her during this time.] . . . I believe that part of the psychological abuse I suffered from was from the pornographic materials that the man used in his terrorization of us. I knew that if he wanted to, he could do more of the things that were being done in those magazines to me. When he looked at the magazines, he could make hateful obscene, violent remarks about women in general and about me. I was told that because I am female I am here to be used and abused by him and that because he is male he is the master and I am his slave (pp. 65–66).

Ms. X, a Native American woman, described how she was raped by two white men who made reference to a pornographic video game called "Custer's Revenge" in which a white Army officer scores points by raping Indian women:

They held me down and as one was running the tip of his knife across my face and throat he said, "Do you want to play Custer's Last Stand? It's great. You lose but you don't care, do you? You like a little pain, don't you, squaw?" They both laughed and then he said, "There is a lot of cock in Custer's Last Stand. You should be grateful, squaw, that All-American boys like us want you. Maybe we will tie you to a tree and start a fire around you." They made other comments, "The only good Indian is a dead Indian." "A squaw out alone deserves to be raped." Words that still terrorize me today. It may surprise you to hear stories that connect pornography and white men raping women of color. It doesn't surprise me. I think pornography, racism, and rape are perfect partners. They all rely on hate. They all reduce a living person to an object. A society that sells books, movies, and video games like "Custer's Last Stand" on its street corners gives white men permission to do what they did to me. Like they said, I'm scum. It is a game to track me down, rape and torture me (pp. 66–67).

Attorney General's Commission

No matter what one thinks of the politics of the Attorney General's Commission on Pornography (1986) and the recommendations of its report, the commission was a forum for women to tell about their experiences with pornography. The following excerpts are from the report of the group, which became known as the Meese Commission.

The report contains numerous accounts of how pornography is used to break down the resistance of children, especially girls, to sexual activity with adults. Among those accounts are:

This father took a *Playboy* magazine and wrote her name across the centerfold. Then he placed it under the covers so she would find it when she went to bed. He joined her in bed that night and taught her about sex (p. 775, from letter to the commission from Oklahomans Against Pornography).

A five year old child told her foster mother, "We have movies at home. Daddy shows them when mother is gone. The people do not wear clothes, and Daddy and I take our clothes off and do the same thing the people in the movies do" (p. 775, from letter to the commission from Oklahomans Against Pornography).

I was sexually abused by my foster father from the time I was seven until I was thirteen. He had stacks and stacks of *Playboys*. He would take me to his bedroom or his workshop, show me the pictures, and say, "This is what big girls do. If you want to be a big girl, you have to do this, but you can never tell anybody." Then I would have to pose like the women in the pictures. I also remember being shown a *Playboy* cartoon of a man having sex with a child (p. 783, from anonymous letter to Women Against Pornography submitted to the commission).

The incest started at the age of eight. I did not understand any of it and did not feel that it was right. My dad would try to convince me that it was ok. He would find magazines with articles and/or pictures that would show fathers and daughters and/or mothers, brother and sisters having sexual intercourse. (Mostly fathers and daughters.) He would say that if it was published in magazines that it had to be all right because magazines could not publish lies.

He would show me these magazines and tell me to look at them or read them and I would turn my head and say no. He would leave them with me and tell me to look later. I was afraid not to look or read them because I did not know what he would do. He would ask me later if I had read them and what they said or if I looked real close at the pictures. He would say, "See it's okay to do because it's published in magazines" (p. 786, from letter to the commission).

In testimony and letters to the commission, a number of women described how they had been expected to perform specific acts in pornography.

When I first met my husband, it was in early 1975, and he was all the time talking about *Deep Throat*. After we were married, he on several occasions referred to her performances and suggested I try to imitate her actions. . . . Last January . . . my husband raped me. . . . He made me strip and lie on our bed. He cut our clothesline up . . . and tied my hands and feet to the four corners of the bedframe. (All this was done while our nine month old son watched.) While he held a butcher knife on me threatening to kill me he fed me three strong tranquilizers. I started crying and because the baby got scared and also began crying, he beat my face and my body. I later had welts and bruises. He attempted to smother me with a pillow. . . . Then, he had sex with me vaginally, and then forced me to give oral sex to him (p. 775, anonymous letter to the Pornography Resource Center forwarded to the commission).

I had not realized the extent of the harm that pornography had done to me until a year and a half ago when I was working on a photo montage of the kinds of pornography for an educational forum. I came across a picture of a position that my ex-husband had insisted we try. When we did, I found the position painful, yet he was determined that we have intercourse that way. I hemorrhaged for three days. I finally went to my doctor and I recall the shame I felt as I explained to him what had caused the bleeding.

Once we saw an X-rated film that showed anal intercourse. After that he insisted that I try anal intercourse. I agreed to do so, trying to be the available, willing creature that I thought I was supposed to be. I found the experience very painful, and I told him so. But he kept insisting that we try it again and again (p. 778, from commission hearing in Chicago, Vol. II, p. 241F3).

[My husband] had a large collection of bizarre S&M and bondage pornography that he kept in the nightstand drawer in our bedroom. On one occasion [he] tied me to our bed and sodomized me. This occurred after I refused to agree to be bound and tied as the models appeared in some of [his] pornographic magazines.

Also, the girls told me that [he] sometimes played a game with them in which their feet were tied up tightly with a rope. The molestation included "bad touching" and exhibitionism by [him], but did not involve actual penetration (p. 791, from Washington, DC, hearing, Vol. I, p. 126–127).

A number of women also testified about how pornography was made without their consent or under duress. Many of them were young girls at the time, and some were prostitutes, including this woman:

There was an apartment that I was sent to often. There were usually two to three men there. After I had sex with them, they would take pictures of me in various pornographic poses. When I was a young girl I didn't have the vocabulary to call them pornographers. I used to refer to them as "the photographers."

On another occasion another young girl and myself were taken to an apartment to meet some men. We were told that they were gangsters and that we should be nice to them. When we arrived we were taken into a room that had a large bed at its center surrounded by lighting and film equipment. We were told to act out a "lesbian scene." After about fifteen minutes we were told to get dressed, that they couldn't use us. We were returned to [our city] unpaid. Again, it was only in retrospect as an adult that I realized I had been used in a commercial pornographic film loop (p. 781, from Washington, D.C., hearing, Vol. I, p. 180).

These are excerpts from the narratives of women who have been hurt by pornography. To acknowledge and believe them does not mean we have to pretend there aren't women who see pornography as a positive force in their lives (McElroy, 1995). To point out that some women have pornography forced on them is not to argue that no woman ever choose to look at pornography. There is no need to pretend the women speak with one voice. We desperately need, however, to listen to these women, to acknowledge that their experiences are real, to acknowledge that they are real, and that they matter.

MEN'S NARRATIVES

This section reports on 24 interviews I conducted with men about their pornography use. (I refer to men's "use" of pornography rather than their "viewing" of it, to make it more clear that men routinely use pornography as an aid in masturbation.) When analyzed in conjunction with narrative accounts of women's experiences presented in the previous section, these interviews illuminate and provide support for the feminist anti-pornography critique. These narratives give specific examples of how pornography can (1) be an important factor in shaping a male-dominant view of sexuality; (2) contribute to a user's difficulty in separating sexual fantasy and reality; (3) be used to initiate victims and break down their resistance to sexual activity; and (4) provide a training manual for abusers.

Again, it is important to be clear about what narratives can tell us. Such accounts do not prove that pornography causes sexual violence. They do, however, show how pornography is implicated in the abusive behavior of some men. That does not mean that all sex abusers use pornography or that all pornography users will become sex abusers; proponents of the feminist anti-pornography critique have never made such simplistic assertions. But the narratives do suggest that for some sex abusers, pornography is an integral part of their abuse (see also Wyre, 1992).

Pornography Users and Sex Offenders

This project included two sets of interviews. In both cases, subjects were not asked their names, though some wanted me to know their names (all names in this chapter are pseudonyms), and the interviews were tape recorded. The first 11 interviews (the "pornography users" group) were with men who responded to a classified ad in the personals section of the two Minneapolis-St. Paul entertainment weeklies seeking male interview subjects who "read or view any sexually explicit material."

The second set of interviews (the "sex offenders" group) was with 13 residents of the Alpha Human Services sex offender treatment program in Minneapolis. Those subjects volunteered after my project was explained to them by a staff member. Both the Alpha staff and I made it clear that their participation was voluntary, that I had no connection to the program, and that their responses would not affect their status in the program. All the interviews were conducted in an office in the Alpha residence facility.

After some general observations about the interviews, I will focus on several cases in which the links between pornography use and abuse were most clear.

The subjects in both groups were white and came from a variety of class backgrounds and occupations, including students, blue-collar workers, and professionals. The average age of the pornography users group was 34, with a range from 23 to 52. The average age of the sex offenders group was 36, with a range from 21 to 50. In a qualitative study with a small sample, the demographics of the group are not crucial. In general, however, both groups included a fairly even mix of Western religions (Protestant, Catholic, Jewish, and none), political affiliations (conservative, liberal, and no-interest), and marital status (single, married, separated, and divorced). The user group included two gay-identified men and one preoperative male-to-female transsexual, and the offender group included one gay-identified man. The other subjects identified themselves as heterosexual.

Members of the two groups had similar general experiences with pornography. The average age of first viewing for the pornography users group was 10, with a range of 3 to 18. The average age for the sex offenders was 12, with a range from 8 to 19. In the users group, all but one of the men had seen pornography before graduating from high school; in the offenders group, that was true for all but two. As adults, all the men in both groups had viewed the kind of material that is commonly called "hard-core" or "X-rated" pornography: oral, vaginal, and anal sex presented in graphic detail.

For the most part, there were few differences in the history of pornography consumption between the users and offenders. The men told similar stories about their entry into the world of pornography, most often through magazines found at home or supplied by friends. The stolen copy of *Playboy* secreted away in a clubhouse or retrieved from dad's drawer was common for men in both groups. The progression from *Playboy* to *Hustler* and more explicit material was also much the same in both groups. The only noticeable difference is that several of the men in the offenders group said they had used overtly violent pornography or child pornography, while none of the men in the users group said they were interested in such material. But in terms of explicitness and frequency of use, both groups had similar ranges of experiences.

One important difference between the two groups is that the stories told by the sex offenders had been filtered through extensive group and individual therapy in the Alpha program. Of specific interest is the program's policy on pornography. Residents are not allowed to keep or use pornography, and such material is confiscated when they arrive. Use of it could result in expulsion from the program, which is a serious sanction; for most of the residents, expulsion would mean a return to jail or prison. In general, pornography is treated as part of a resident's problem in developing a healthy sex life. On rare occasions, counselors present pictures of nude people to residents who are unable to get beyond fantasizing about children. Such material is intended to illustrate more appropriate sex partners and "age their fantasies." These pictures show full nudity but do not depict sexual activity.

Also, acknowledging the harm done to victims and taking responsibility for it are key elements of Alpha treatment. One aspect of that is known as "running a process": When residents begin to fantasize about abusive behavior, they are asked to take those actions to their logical conclusion and think about the harm that individuals will suffer because of it.

Does this therapy "taint" the interviews with the sex offenders? Of course the therapy affected how they understood their pornography use, just as any framework for understanding our experience affects how we report our experience. However, it is crucial to remember that both sets of interview subjects were working from a well-defined ideology that might "taint" their narratives. With the sex offenders, it was a view of pornography shaped by, among other things, therapy. For the pornography users, it was a view shaped by the general cultural ideology of sexual and expressive freedom, the idea that any sexual activity is, by definition, liberating. (This ideology of sexual liberation obviously exists alongside an ideology of repression that views sex as appropriate only in the context of a culturally sanctioned relationship, such as a heterosexual marriage, and the relative power of each ideology on any individual depends on a variety of factors.) The sex offenders were willing to consider the connections between pornography and their behavior. The pornography users generally didn't consider that as a possibility. If one considers it likely that the sex offenders have been led to certain conclusions by an ideology acquired in therapy, it is at least equally likely that the pornography users were led to their conclusions by a different ideology acquired from contemporary culture. In short, no one has access to an account of their behavior that has not been refracted through ideology. My job as a researcher is to make judgments about which subjects seemed to be making an honest effort to tell their truth as they understand it.

Before concentrating on the stories of several of the men for whom pornography was an important influence on their sexual behavior, it is important to note that most of the pornography users who reported heavy consumption also reported no abusive sexual behavior and that some of the sex offenders reported relatively light consumption and did not see a connection between the pornography and their offenses.

In the pornography user group, only one of the men reported behavior that clearly was abusive, which will be described later. More typical was "Bill," a 39-year-old heterosexual lawyer. He said he began using *Playboy* as a teenager, became a regular viewer of sexually explicit pornographic movies, and used pornographic videos or magazines an average of three times a week. He said his sexual relationships were with consenting adults and that while some of his sexual activity mirrored acts he had seen in pornography, he never purposefully tried to act on fantasies he had about bondage. In Bill's view:

> [T]here's a lot of people like myself who go in with coat and tie, very respectable people who use pornography. If our fantasies are carried out they're carried out only with consenting adults. And we harm no one.

"Pete," a 40-year-old predominantly heterosexual (he reported some sex with men in his past and a continued interested in homosexuality but said he no longer acted on it) office manager, also reported early exposure to pornographic magazines and a long-standing interest in pornographic movies. He said the movies don't spark actual sexual desire in him: "I [have] never sat and watched a movie and thought, God, I got to go jump in bed with a woman."

In the sex offender group, "Brian," a 50-year-old heterosexual insurance salesman who had sexually abused his stepdaughter when she was 10–15 years old, saw *Playboy* as a teenager and continued to occasionally look at pornographic magazines throughout his adult life. His only experience with explicit pornography—renting a half-dozen videos that he watched by himself—came after he had stopped having sex with his stepdaughter. Brian said those videos shaped his fantasies, increased the frequency of masturbation, and reduced the frequency of sexual contact with his wife, but he saw no connection between his earlier sporadic use of pornography and his abusive behavior.

Similarly, "Jack," a 43-year-old heterosexual electronics technician, saw *Playboy* in high school and continued to buy similar magazines as an adult. He reported seeing about a dozen explicit movies in his adult life, usually at the urging of a friend. "After you've seen one or two, you've seen all of them," he said, explaining his lack of interest. Jack said that he didn't want to ignore the possibility that his use of pornography played some role in his sexual abuse of his daughter but that he did not see direct connections.

The other men from the sex offenders group, however, saw some connection between pornography use and abusive acts, even when their use of pornography was not regular or extensive. What follows are more extensive descriptions of, and excerpts from, my interviews with four of the sex offenders and one of the pornography users. These were cases in which it was most clear that their use of pornography and real-life sexual behavior were linked in some fashion.

Craig

"Craig" was a 34-year-old heterosexual lumber worker who had never been married. He grew up in a small town in a rural area and had completed the 10th grade. He was raised Catholic but no longer considered himself a religious person and had no interest in political issues. Craig reported the most violent and abusive sexual history of the men I talked with. He said he had beaten and raped prostitutes, raped other women, used drugs and coercion to have sex with teenage girls, and sexually abused young girls.

Craig's first exposure to pornography came at age 7 or 8 when he found a box of *Playboy*, *Penthouse*, and *Hustler* magazines in a hayloft of an abandoned farm. From that point, he continually used those and other magazines that he shoplifted from stores. In his early teens, he began sneaking into an adult bookstore to watch videos. In his later teens, he continued to use magazines, sometimes masturbating to them in his parked car while he watched girls on the street.

At age 18, Craig joined the Marines and at about the same time began heavy consumption of explicit pornography, including violent pornography. He compared the "rush" of violent pornography to taking drugs. Shortly after that, he also began using prostitutes, sometimes paying a higher price to be allowed to tie the women up and whip them. He later repeated that behavior with women who weren't prostitutes, beating them up "because towards the last [before his arrest], that was the only way I could get aroused." He said the pornography use and visits to prostitutes were roughly at the same time: "When I got into it heavy, the pornography and the prostitutes kind of fell into together. I believe the pornography came first."

From about age 21 on, Craig's pornography use centered on explicit videotapes he watched at home. He said he liked a variety of sexual acts on the screen but preferred that the men in the movies always be in control, fast-forwarding past scenes of women in control: "It was like it was a threat to me, to have a woman [in control]." He said that was also a factor in his use of bondage pornography: "The control you had, to put the women in any position you wanted, to force her to do anything."

Craig recently had been involved in a long-term relationship, but the woman left him because of his violent behavior. He said he thought some of his ideas for sexual activity, such as his constant desire for women to perform oral sex on him, were sparked at least in part by the pornography he used:

> There was a lot of oral sex that I wanted her to perform on me. There were, like, ways that would entice it in the movies, and I tried to use that on her, and it wouldn't work. Sometimes I'd get frustrated, and that's when I started hitting her.... I used a lot of force, a lot of direct demands, that in the movies women would just cooperate. And I would demand stuff from her. And if she didn't I'd start slapping her around.

While in his 20s, Craig also began using child pornography obtained from underground sources. His sexual activity also began to focus more on children, usually girls in their early teens. Eventually, he abused girls as young as 7. At some point, he began to use pornography and women together:

> Towards the end it was so exhilarating to me to have the pornography and the child at the same time, or the woman at the same time ... and sometimes I have a longing for that feeling, the complete exhilaration, my whole body goes numb I'm so excited.

Craig described his view of women before his arrest as "that they were made for sex, and that's all. I grew up with that attitude.... [My older brother] kept saying over and over, that women are for sex. Use them and throw them away. I thrived on that."

Craig was reluctant to blame his behavior on pornography, but he emphasized its importance in shaping his sexuality as a child and its continuing influence on him as an adult.

> It's like it all stemmed from when I was growing up, watching the movies, pornography.... Once I saw the materials it's like I got new ideas. It's like it reinforced my thinking.... But it was my choice to react to it. I don't think the pornography made me do what I did. I made the decision to do it. I could have talked to people and let them know what my thinking

was, and I possibly could have got help a lot sooner. But I had to keep this a big secret. I could control this, I'm this super-being.

Larry

"Larry" was a 41-year-old heterosexual man who had been divorced twice and had two children he had fathered and one stepdaughter. He was a biomedical technician and had two associate degrees. Larry grew up outside a large city and said that as a child he was sexually and emotionally abused by his mother and older sister. He was raised Catholic but had been a member of Lutheran and Baptist churches since then and considered himself Christian. He served in Vietnam as a Marine for two years and called himself an independent-leaning Democrat. Larry was convicted of sexually abusing his stepdaughter. He also said that much of what he considered to be consensual sex when he was a young adult involved force and the use of women who were drunk or stoned.

Larry's first exposure to sexual material came at age 9, when he found his father's *True Detective* magazine with a picture of a woman bound in bra and panties. He saw *Playboy* and other similar magazines sporadically through his teenage years. He saw his first sexually explicit pornographic movies while in the Marines after high school but did not start using pornography heavily until he was out of the service and working. A foreman at his shop introduced him to pornographic novels, especially ones involving bestiality. "And that's when it seemed like my appetite really got out of hand. And it never seemed to be enough," Larry said, describing an escalating use of pornography and an increase of what he called a desire for "deviant sex."

That phase of his life ended temporarily when he married for a second time, but after losing a job and a lot of his self-esteem, Larry said he returned to more heavy pornography use. In this period he began renting and copying sexually explicit videos, amassing a collection of about 15 movies. He said that his wife refused to watch them but that he could manipulate his stepdaughter into watching them, which was part of the process of grooming her for abuse that began when she was 8 years old. He used the tapes to break down her resistance, and he played them while he was abusing her:

[The movies] played a big role, because I was fantasizing that I was, that my stepdaughter and myself were actually engaging in the same behavior that was on the tape. So, it was more like I was having my own private orgy right there, with the tape, too. And also, it was something for my daughter to concentrate on. It made it more exciting for me.

Elaborating on his use of pornography with his stepdaughter, Larry said the boundaries between the world of pornography and the real world became hazy:

> In fact, when I'd be abusing my daughter, I'd be thinking about some women I saw in a video. Because if I was to open my eyes and see my stepdaughter laying there while I was abusing her, you know, that wouldn't have been very exciting for me. You know, that would bring me back to the painful reality that I'm a child molester, where I'm in this reality of I'm making love or having intercourse with this beautiful woman from the video. The video didn't even come into my mind. It was just this beautiful person who had a beautiful body, and she was willing to do anything I asked.

Larry resisted putting sole, or even primary, blame for his abusive behavior on pornography. But he did see it as contributing to that abuse. He rejected the possibility that pornography could have been a catharsis:

> The pornography actually helped me work into my abuse, I feel. It accelerated that appetite for more. That's what I feel about it. Because, if I wouldn't have been introduced to a lot of this, and got my appetite whetted, then I don't think I'd thought of half the deviant things I've done.

Kevin

"Kevin" was a 24-year-old single heterosexual man who had most recently worked as a school bus driver. He had attended one year of college and one year of vo-tech school after graduating from high school in the Minneapolis suburb where he grew up. He was raised Catholic but did not consider himself religious any longer, and he described himself as a conservative Republican. Kevin was convicted of the sexual abuse of two 6-year-old girls, and he said he had committed several other rapes and acts of sexual abuse.

Kevin had the most extensive and most constant use of pornography of the men interviewed. His first viewing of pornographic material was at age 11, when he and a friend found the friend's father's collection of *Playboy* magazines. From an ad in *Playboy*, he sent away to a mail-order company for 8-millimeter movies, using his name and his friend's address. When he ordered movies, Kevin said he signed a form stating he was 18 years old, and because his friend's parents were divorced and the mother was often not home, they could use that address for orders and watch the movies there. By the time he was 14 or 15, he looked old enough to buy magazines, including

Hustler, in stores. During his high school years he also began buying explicit videotapes, which he watched both alone and with groups of male friends.

After high school, Kevin began buying sexually explicit magazines and patronizing the 25-cent movie booths at adult bookstores. In recent years he also had begun calling phone sex lines. At the time of his arrest, he had 50 to 75 magazines, about a dozen videotapes, and a handful of 8-millimeter movies in his closet. He had looked at the magazines every day and had watched a movie at least twice a week. The movies consisted of explicit depictions of sex, including group and woman-woman sex scenes. He described the interaction between men and women in these videotaped movies:

> The man would be the boss, and the woman would just do exactly what he said. And it was more of a subtle violence. . . . On the movies it gives you the impression that if the woman hadn't agreed to what the man said, then he was capable of being very violent. There'd be some slapping and hair pulling and stuff. But not like the ones in 8-millimeter, where they really got some really violent things on there, like smack them over the head.

Kevin said the typical women were:

> portrayed like they were just sex dolls, or whatever, just laying there on the bed. . . . the man would walk up and the woman would just kind of be brain-dead, do whatever the man said. Either they would just do it, and she would, like it was a reflex. Or he would boss her around, or whatever, and say, "You do this, you do that, bend over, roll over," whatever the case may be.

Kevin said he sometimes bought movies and magazines in discount packs without knowing anything about the content. Although he said he didn't seek out violent pornography, he occasionally received such material in those packs and watched it. Those movies included scenes with women tied to beds, with men using whips and handcuffs on them and penetrating them with objects such as soda bottles, "[s]tuff I thought was kind of sick in a way, at the time, but as I got more into it, I got more . . . into it." He described one of those movies:

> One that sticks out in my mind right now was really violent. There was pistol whipping and [a man] chained this woman up to a, had her in a dog-

house, chained up like a dog in a doghouse, and this guy would come out and stick her head in the dog bowl and then have sex with her from behind.... At first, I thought it was disgusting, but then as time wore on I did get into it more. I got excited by it more.

In his own sex life in his late teens and early 20s, Kevin said he relied on manipulative techniques with teenage girls, trading drugs for sex on several occasions each with four or five girls ranging in age from 10 to 16. He also raped a junior-high girl who had passed out at a party. When he could afford it, he also used prostitutes at a local massage parlor. During this time he also began looking at younger girls in his neighborhood and fantasizing about them.

Kevin described pornography as his introduction to, and main source of information about, sex:

I think the main thing I got out of it was that sex was good.... I also got out of it that women were objects. Women, or girls or any female was an object. As long as you got what you wanted everything was OK.... If I got what I wanted, that was fine. Whatever they did or whatever they felt was their own business. At the time I didn't really care, as long as I got what I wanted out of it, got my jollies out of it.

Kevin said that when the pornography started to bore him, he began his abusive behavior. He described the progression of his thinking:

When I was masturbating to these pornography things, I would think about certain girls I had seen on the bus or ones I had sold drugs to, and I would think as I was looking at these pictures in these books, what would it be like to have this girl or whoever doing this, what I'm thinking about.... Just masturbating to the thought wasn't getting it for me anymore. I actually had to be a part of it, or actually had to do something about it....

I think a lot of it had to do with just, the pictures are pictures. They're not real. And a fantasy is a wish for reality. You're wishing this would be real. And I got to the point where I wanted it, I was so ingrained, I wanted it to be real, that I would start to associate what I was seeing on the picture with someone I knew or had seen or associated with. And then I think it turned from that, I would start to actually really think about, you know, like with the girls I committed the crime with, or other ones I'd see on the bus. Like sometimes after I'd see like a certain load of kids would get off the bus, I'd pick out a couple and I'd watch them or stop and look at the mirror and stare at them and stuff like that. I would think, later on in the day, I'd masturbate to some pornography, I'd just use that picture kind of as a mental, it's kind of a scenery or whatever, and I'd put in my mind I'd put myself and whoever at the time I was thinking about, in that picture. . . .

And sometimes, even with the pornography and the young girls, I wouldn't be satisfied and I'd go over to the prostitution place and get a woman, and I'd pay her and she'd do whatever I wanted, and I wouldn't get in trouble or wouldn't get caught or she wouldn't say no, or whatever. I could just do whatever I wanted, I could do.

Kevin said he may have become a sex abuser even without his heavy use of pornography but that the pornography was "the straw that broke the camel's back."

Brad

"Brad" was a 34-year-old heterosexual heating-and-refrigeration service person who attended a vo-tech after high school. He grew up in a rural area, had no religious or political ties, and was separated from his second wife at the time of the interview. Brad said he met his first wife, a Korean woman who was working as a prostitute, while stationed overseas. She came to the United States to continue to work as a prostitute and divorced him. Brad was in the pornography-user group, but in many ways seemed more dangerous to himself and others than most of the men in the sex offender group. He was extremely volatile and seemed capable of violence; this was the only interview during which I felt concerned about my safety.

Brad first saw pornographic magazines at age 3 or 4 with his brothers, who also engaged in sex with him. Although he was not clear about some details, he seemed to have continued to use such magazines through his childhood, and as an adult he has been a regular customer of adult bookstores, using the 25-cent movie booths, renting and buying sexually explicit movies and magazines, calling phone-sex lines, and using prostitutes. He also said that he had videotaped sexual acts with his second wife and that he continued to look at those tapes.

Brad said he had been a shy teenager and avoided women. When he left high school and joined the Army, he began using pornography, from which he said he got most of his sexual education:

I didn't know nothing about the world, or women, or, just what I read or saw. I was pretty deluded about women, that's for sure. I'm still fucked up about them. Didn't know how to talk to them or nothing, thought I just knew everything from reading everything.

These excerpts from my interview with Brad reflect the erratic nature of his comments. He alternately seemed to enjoy and detest his life, sometimes referring to himself as a "sex addict" and other times mocking therapists he had seen. Pornography was a source of both pleasure and shame for him.

Brad said he had grown to prefer things that were rougher and more unusual. He liked pornography to "[s]how some nasty bitches. Be a little more vulgar about it." But after viewing such material, he said he felt ashamed: "As soon as the big excitement's over, I just come down."

Brad described his fantasies as more intense than actual sex with women and said he often had trouble controlling his fantasy life. Often that took the form of thinking of his own life in terms of pornographic scenes and then becoming upset with the resulting fantasy. He described how this affected his relationship with his second wife:

> I just freaked her out a few times, with some of the stuff I'd dream up, or whatever. I'd fantasize stuff that wasn't true, and I'd get myself so hyped up into believing it and calling up phone sex or reading in magazines or something, reading stories or watching stories or hearing stories about somebody's wife screwing around on him, and I'd think, "Yep, she's doing it to me too." Just my imagination.

Although he has thought about stopping his use of pornography, Brad said he often felt helpless. In the course of discussing that question, he often was unclear about whether he thought his actions were harmful to himself or others, again expressing his ambivalence about his sex practices. He described his use of pornography as "pretty much uncontrollable":

> It's like a fucking bee-line to the [adult bookstore]. I'll be thinking about something else and driving along, and all of a sudden there the fuck I am, sitting in front of the place. I've felt like, you know, why control it. Just fucking do what you want to do, and whatever. Pretty much constant my whole life. I think sex is fun and sex is good, stuff like that. I don't see anything wrong with that at all.

Brad put much of the blame for his sexual problems on women, suggesting that they flaunt their sexuality and use it against men: "And these women blame men for pornography and all this, and it's the women out there showing us their pussies, you know, taking all our money like fucking fools." Brad's misogyny was evident throughout the interview, as seen in this exchange:

> Q: Generally, what are the strongest emotions you feel connected with pornographic material? Just the real gut-level feelings you have.
> A: Hate.
> Q: Hate for?
> A: Women.

When asked what he usually did after a trip to an adult bookstore, Brad replied, "Just go home and terrorize my wife, maybe," and laughed.

Brad said the attitude toward women in pornography—which he described as "Fucking bitch, man, that's all they're good for"—mirrored his own feelings toward women:

> Pretty much a general attitude against women. [Sex] is about all they're really good for. That's what the movies and books and pornography tries to put across: The fucking woman is shit. That's what I see. See women screwing a couple different guys. And they have little skits, like, you know, the husband is gone and these guys come over and fuck the shit out of her for a few hours, and you know, stuff like that. I have a hard time with my own imagination without looking at all these other weirdoes' ideas about things.

Brad said he had never raped a woman but once tried to force a female hitchhiker he picked up to have sex with him. But when she screamed, he let her go. I asked him twice if he thought he was capable of rape. The first time he replied, "I wouldn't do it, but my mind would say, 'Yea, that sounds exciting.'" The second time he said, "Not unless I was in the wrong mind. In my normal mind, I'm fine, you know.... Yea, I could see myself actually doing something like that."

Brad expressed conflicting opinions and emotions about his sex life and pornography use. But it was clear from his statements that pornography had been a part of his own sexual victimization as well as his sexual abuse of women. He had difficulty disengaging from the fantasy world of pornography and often imposed the narratives of pornography on his own life. The anger he felt toward women because of events in his life has been reinforced by the misogyny in pornography. These are particularly tentative conclusions that are hard to feel completely confident about because of Brad's erratic comments. But, I include his story because of the unrestrained way in which he talked about his experiences and my feeling that woven through that story were important illustrations of how pornography can influence a person.

David

"David" was a 37-year-old man who was married but since his arrest had come out as gay. He was divorced, had a daughter and son, and had been convicted of abusing the son from infancy. He had worked in sales and marketing and had completed about three years of college. He grew up in a large city. He said that after his arrest he was reevaluating his former commitment to Catholicism and to "ultra-conservative" political beliefs.

At age 12, David saw his first sexual material, a nudist magazine. He also began using *Playboy* magazines that friends had obtained. David said this was about the time he began playing cruel sexual games with his younger brother and sister. Shortly after that time, he saw explicit pornographic magazines that older boys in the neighborhood had. Those magazines were part of the manipulation and coercion that these 17- and 18-year-old boys used to get David to perform oral sex on them: "I remember looking at the magazines and seeing women perform orally on these men, and that's what gave them the idea to have me do that to them." Several years after that, David began molesting male friends while on camping trips, fondling them while they slept in ways that left the friends feeling taken advantage of.

In his early 20s, when he was first married, David stopped using pornography. At about age 24 he started buying gay pornographic magazines, as his fantasy life became completely centered on sex with men. He rejected violent and sadomasochistic pornography, preferring magazines with no overt violence. By not allowing himself to use the material that depicted force:

> that was the way that I gave myself permission, because it didn't involve hurting people. It's part of the denial system I had. Both people wanted to do it, and nobody looked like they were getting hurt. So it was like the gateway into a tremendously hurtful kind of situation.

David said that his fantasizing eventually became focused on the son his wife was carrying and that his use of pornography was fuel for those fantasies:

Prior to [my wife] giving birth to our son, I had masturbated to fantasies of sexually abusing him. So by the time he was born, I had rehearsed over and over in my mind, what I wanted to do. And eventually I acted that out. And intermittently I used pornography to keep my sexual thing going. So, by the time he was born, he was a ready-made victim. In my mind, I had done it many times.

Like the other men in the sex offender group, David was reluctant to place blame for his actions on anything or anyone. But he described pornography as "the primary stepping stone that I took to sexually acting out." He used the concept of boundary violations to explain how he thought pornography had functioned in his life. This way of framing the question of pornography's effects was not part of his therapy at Alpha. David said he had been thinking of this on his own and had not discussed it at length with staff members:

I think what this really is for me, was pornography was a way to begin violating people's boundaries. And it kind of went from there. Where, like when you look at somebody engaging in sex, I think it's a violation of boundaries. That's something that should be private. So, it's like I gave myself permission to voyeur on them. And the more I did that, the more liberties I took to actually act that stuff out. . . . It's a subtle thing. . . . I mean, I didn't realize I was, I didn't even know what boundaries were. I never had any idea of what that was. . . . Well, I brought things into the pornography. There was things in me, that, you know, it's like pornography and I [slapping his hands together], we got bound somehow. And I ended up taking permission over a long period of time to violate boundaries, and I think pornography was the beginning of that violation.

In David's case, his early use of pornography was connected both to his own abuse of his siblings and his abuse at the hands of older boys. In adulthood, pornography was a link in the chain of events that led to his abuse of his son.

Seeing Patterns

The purpose of these narratives is not to suggest that one interview can identify the causes of a person's history of sexual violence. My goal is not to focus on the individual and attempt a psychological profile to explain their actions. Obviously, many of these men experienced abuse as children that played a role in their own abusing, and countless other factors—including the culture's institutionalized misogyny—may have been crucial in leading them to abuse.

However, these interviews can help us identify ways in which pornography is an important actor in the construction of sexuality and gender relations—what men come to see as acceptable, exciting, or necessary sex. Pornography is not the only force in our society constructing sex and gender in these ways, but the use of it is a common experience in the lives of the men interviewed. These interviews identified specific ways in which the use of pornography can be linked to sexual violence. For these men, pornography was an important factor in shaping a male-dominant view of sexuality, and in several cases the material contributed to the men's difficulty in separating fantasy and reality. Pornography also was used by at least one of the men to initiate a victim and break down a young girl's resistance to sexual activity. For several others it was used as a training manual for abuse, as sexual acts and ideas from pornography were incorporated into their sex lives.

In the next section I will reflect on my own use of pornography as a child and young adult to pursue some of these issues in more detail.

MY NARRATIVE

History gets written with the mind holding the pen. What would it look like, what would it read like, if it got written with the body holding the pen? (Berman, 1990, p. 110).

In this section of the chapter, I want to let my body hold the pen.

First, the potentially relevant facts about who "I" am include, in no particular order: white and of northern European ancestry, born in 1958, Midwestern born and currently living in the south, raised in the lower-middle to middle class and now residing in the middle class, married for six years until a recent divorce, father of a 5-year-old boy, living as a heterosexual most of my life until recently coming out (more on that later), anti-sexist/pro-feminist, anti-racist, anti-capitalist, the third of four children from a typically dysfunctional American family with one alcoholic parent.

I have spent much time in the past decade trying to be in my body as I have researched and written about pornography. In conjunction with many other sources of information presented in this chapter, I-in-my-body have insights into the role of pornography in the construction of male sexuality in contemporary U.S. culture.

Part of the authority for that claim comes from a simple observation: I get erections from pornography. I take that to be epistemologically significant; my body understands the charge of pornography. Because I was raised in a sexist culture with few (if any) influences that mitigated that sexism, I am in a position to explore how that sexual charge is connected to the ideology of male dominance and female submission that structures contemporary commercial pornography.

I focus on this embodied, personal approach partly in reaction to the scholarly literature on pornography, so much of which is written by men and is distinctly disembodied (for exceptions, see Abbott, 1990; Baker, 1992; and Kimmel, 1990). Political tracts, law review articles, and reports of social science studies written by men rarely include any acknowledgment of the position of the author in a pornographic world, let alone an examination of what it means for how one comes to know about pornography. That kind of embodied exploration is rare because, as feminist theorists have long pointed out, in all those areas—philosophy, law, social science—emotional detachment and objectivity are seen as virtues. But that stance actually has repressed much of what we might know about pornography. As Morris Berman (1990, p. 110) puts it, "[T]o leave your body and believe that you can still know anything at all is quite literally a form of madness." In that sense, many of the scholarly works on pornography are quite mad—misguided attempts to sever mind and body, reason and emotion—that lead to less, not more, trustworthy knowledge.

In the remainder of this chapter I will say a bit more about the value of embodied narratives, describe my own pornography use, and offer observations on pornography's effects on me and men.

Embodied Narratives

Consciousness-raising for men is loaded with potential problems if done in isolation from women, a problem that can be seen in various parts of the contemporary men's movement, especially the mythopoetic wing, where a focus on the personal often impedes social analysis and liberatory politics (Jensen, 1995a; Kimmel & Kaufman, 1994). For men, the process must include women; that is, we have to pay attention to feminist criticism to help us make sense of our experience. Men must acknowledge that women have some epistemic privilege—the idea that "members of an oppressed group have a more immediate, subtle and critical knowledge about the nature of their oppression than people who are nonmembers of the oppressed group" (Narayan, 1988, p. 35). My goal is to examine my life and compare it with the narratives of other men, using feminist insights to make sense of it all. Of course, there is never a unified feminist or women's stance on any question. My job is not simply to listen to women and do what they say, since "they" do not speak with one voice and I have to remain responsible for my choices. In my work in feminist theory, I have tried to listen to the many voices speaking on the issue of pornography and have made commitments to a radical feminist position (and to particular women in feminism) that I think best explains the world as I understand it. This process is always ongoing; at the same time, one must make choices between conflicting accounts of the world and act on those choices (Jensen, 1997b).

So, this writing is an attempt at the "critical story-telling" that Jeff Hearn (1987, p. 182) calls for in the project of "collective self-reflective theorising." To reiterate points made earlier in this chapter, I do not assert that my experience with pornography can be generalized to all men. Instead, I view this as a contribution to an ongoing conversation about pornography. Such work is difficult to do with integrity, but my hope is, following Joseph Boone, that:

> if the male critic can discover a position from which to speak that neither elides the importance of feminism to his work nor ignores the specificity of his gender, he may also find that his voice no longer exists as an abstraction, but that it in fact inhabits a body: its own sexual/textual body (Boone, 1990, p. 12).

As introduction to my story, I need to explain my own journey to this position. My early work on legal aspects of the pornography debate used traditional methods, which allowed me to distance myself from my personal experience with pornography. But a growing sense of dissatisfaction with that work led me to a project designed to confront the content of pornography in 20 pornographic paperback novels analyzed in the previous chapter. I read the books, taking detailed notes about scenes, themes, portrayals, and language used. In the role of detached investigator, I tried to move through the books using my "rational" faculties, but I found that my body kept making its presence known; I kept getting erections.

Before I started that project I was aware that pornography still could produce intense sexual reactions in me, even though at that time it had been several years since my last contact with pornography (I stopped using pornography after returning to graduate school and coming into contact with the feminist critique). Yet, in my pursuit of intellectual knowledge I had detached from the emotional, embodied knowledge of my past experience with pornography; the scholarly endeavor insulated me from those other ways of knowing about pornography. The deeper I got into the scholarly work, the further I got from that embodied knowledge until, finally, I was forced to confront it through the reaction of my body. As I read the books, intellectually I was able to identify and analyze the misogynistic images and messages, but physically, my body responded the way it had been trained.

That reaction threw into question assumptions that I had been smugly comfortable with. This had, and continues to have, an important effect on my sexuality and my personal life. My concern here, however, is with the equally important effect that experience has had on my scholarly work. I realized that I could no longer deny that part of what I knew about pornography was personal and embodied, and that I would have to explore those issues if I wanted to be an competent and ethical researcher. As I planned the interviews with pornography users, I knew I would have to write my own story as well as theirs.

A Personal History of Pornography Use

I begin this account with the understanding that my interpretation of my experiences can be challenged. Clearly, I have a kind of access to my emotions and sexual reactions that others do not. But in invoking the personal, I don't claim I am exempt from critique; experience is not a guarantee of insightful interpretation. This is my narrative, my reconstruction of experience. At various points in my life there will be varying personal and political factors that shape my understanding of self. There is no experience of self unmediated by culture, no pretheoretical knowledge of the self. My interpretations have changed over time, and what I offer is the best reading I have of them at this time, a reading that others may have grounds to challenge.

From my research and informal discussions with men, I believe that my use of pornography is fairly typical for a United States male born after World War II, what I call the *Playboy* generation. My exposure to pornography began around second grade. I have hazy memories of a soft-core motorcycle magazine, which included pictures of women naked from the waist up, that a friend had found and hid in his backyard. Using the magazine was always a group project; we would pass it around and comment on the women's bodies. After that, someone in my circle of friends almost always had a copy of *Playboy*, *Penthouse*, or some similar magazine that had been found, stolen from a store, or taken from dad. One friend had a hiding place in his attic, where we occasionally would go to look at them.

In my first year of high school, I had a friend who had perfected the art of getting into movie theaters through exit doors. Usually we went into mainstream films, but when we felt bold we made a run at X-rated movies. I also remember having access to pornographic novels in my high school years and finding them as intense an experience as the visual material.

In college I saw a few X-rated movies with friends (both all-male and mixed-gender groups), who treated the outings as campy fun, and I went to a couple of those movies on my own. When I would go with friends from our small-town college to Minneapolis, we often would stop at pornography shops to see what the big city had to offer. In my 20s, my use of pornography was episodic. At various times I would feel drawn to pornographic movies, and in a six- or seven-year period, I probably saw 10 to 15 of them, once or twice with someone else, but usually alone. I saw some of these movies at mainstream theaters, but more typically at adult theaters and bookstores, where I would browse among other material. The movies were what is most often called hard-core pornography: graphic sex scenes built around a contrived story line. I typically stayed for no more than 15 to 30 minutes; after the initial excitement wore off, feelings of guilt and shame made it uncomfortable to be in those theaters.

I typically did not purchase pornography to use at home, although through the years I occasionally bought magazines such as *Playboy* and *Penthouse*. I never showed pornography to women with whom I was involved, with the exception of one trip to an adult theater with a girlfriend in college. I never made homemade pornography or recorded sexual activity.

Although I did not actively use pornography with partners, pornography was central to my sex life at various times. From grade school on, I masturbated to pornographic images, either those in front of me or those retained in my mind from earlier consumption. I focused on certain kinds of images (women performing oral sex on men, men penetrating women anally, group sex involving a woman and more than one man), and I could summon up those images easily.

This brief summary of my past pornography use leaves out some details that are too painful to recount in a public forum. Even though I no longer use pornography, this still was difficult to write. In my anxiety and fear is a lesson about pornography. At the macro level, pornography works to create, maintain, and reinforce a system of male control. But for each individual who uses pornography, the story is more complicated and not just an expression of the desire to control women. I feel a kind of residual guilt and shame over my use of pornography, even though I realize most men have had similar experiences. Some of the pornography users I interviewed expressed the same feelings. Others expressed no regrets over their use and were proud of what they saw as a transcendence of sexual inhibitions. While it is difficult to generalize about these emotions, I believe that, like me, most men who use pornography struggle with the mixed messages from society. On the one hand, pornography is widely accepted and can be used for male bonding; in other situations, a man's use of it can be turned against him with the charge that he can't get a "real woman." Men who were raised in sexually or emotionally repressed families, again like me, may use pornography but then confront those early internalized proscriptions.

Although I have been arguing for the importance of narratives, these differences in men's reactions to their own pornography use highlight how important it is to remember that no single narrative is the whole story. That does not mean that no coherent account of pornography in this society can be constructed. It need not be shown that all men use pornography in exactly the same way for pornography to be a key component of a system of male dominance. In this case, for instance, whether a pornography user feels guilt and shame or is proud of his use, the result is generally the same: The use of pornography continues.

Pornography and I

I focus now on the effects pornography had on me. In my experience:

1. Pornography was an important means of sex education.
2. Pornography constructed women as objects, which encouraged me to see women in real life in that same way.
3. Pornography created or reinforced desires for specific acts, most of which focused on male pleasure and can cause female pain.
4. Rather than unlocking sexual creativity, pornography shaped and constrained my sexual imagination with its standardized scripts.
5. Race was an important aspect of pornography, reinforcing my view of women of color as the "exotic primitive."
6. Viewing a large amount of overtly violent pornography was not necessary for pornography to have the effect of eroticizing violence for me.
7. That eroticization of violence had a tangible effect on my sex life.
8. Pornography is most centrally about control, and I was attracted to it by my need for a sense of control over women and their sexuality.

Sex Education

Sex was not openly discussed in my home and at the time I was growing up sex education in the schools was limited or nonexistent. So, most of my sexual education came on the streets with peers and was rooted in pornography. It was in that material that I first saw nude adult women and figured out the mechanics of sex.

There is nothing inherently problematic about learning about sexuality from a publication. The problem is when those publications construct sexuality in a male-dominant framework and present women as sexual objects. These images were incredibly powerful for me and my childhood friends. They helped plant in me some basic assumptions about sex: that a certain kind of female appearance was most desirable, that women could be used for sex in ways portrayed in the magazines and movies (as well as through my use of those materials), that women's resistance to certain kinds of sexual activity was the result of prudish inhibitions that could, and should, be overcome. Those messages were transmitted by other cultural products and institutions as well, but it was in pornography that I found them most explicitly expressed.

Objectification of Women

Women are objectified not only in pornography, of course, but in numerous other sites in the culture. For me, pornography intensified that tendency to see women first and foremost not so much as sexual beings but as sexual objects for men to view and use. For me, the immediate "sizing up" of a woman is institutionalized; that is, it takes active effort on my part to interrupt the process and refuse to objectify. The reality is, of course, that I often let the process continue, even though I am aware of what I am doing. That is one of the most basic privileges of being a man; I always have the option of ignoring my own convictions and using a woman for my own fantasy.

Is this really an act of male supremacy, or simply an appreciation of female beauty or an acknowledgment of human sexuality? I do not mean to suggest that sexual attraction is inherently corrupt; to raise these issues is not to advocate a prudish repression of sexuality. But it is crucial to examine the power at work in sexual situations. Heterosexual men's sexuality in this culture is constructed around the domination of women. In some other world, one not structured by sexism, my concerns perhaps could be minimized. But in a culture that for centuries has defined woman as object, it is essential that men be aware of, and honest about, the way in which we see women.

Again, pornography is not the only element in this construction of women. But my use of pornography was a central component of it. In my case, I have seen women on the street and created sexual scenes with them that were taken directly from pornography I had seen. That has not happened in some time; it's one thing I no longer allow myself. But the fact that it was once a routine part of my sexual imagination tells me something about how pornography has affected my view of women.

Although some commentators have suggested that such objectification is unavoidable, even natural, I believe that resisting it is a fundamental step for men trying to avoid sexist behavior. As Susanne Kappeler (1986, p. 61) writes:

> The fundamental problem at the root of men's behavior in the world, including sexual assault, rape, wife battering, sexual harassment, keeping women in the home and in unequal opportunities and conditions, treating them as objects for conquest and protection—the root problem behind the reality of men's relations with women, is the way men see women, is Seeing.

Desire

As the testimony of women has pointed out, men's desire for certain kinds of sexual activity can be taken directly from pornography. The question of the causal chain likely cannot be answered definitively: Do the desires exist independently and then get represented in pornography, or does pornography help create the desires? One convention of pornography that we discussed in the previous chapter leads me to think that in some ways, pornography can construct desire. Since the mid-1970s, the cum shot—showing the man ejaculating onto the woman's body—has been a standard of explicit pornography to provide visual proof of men's pleasure (Williams, 1989). As a veteran pornographic movie actor put it, "The cum shot in the face is the stock-in-trade of orgasms. It's the ejaculation into a woman's waiting face that gets the audience off more than anything else" (Bill Margold, quoted in Hebditch and Anning, 1988, p. 31).

Some of the men I interviewed said they enjoyed that type of climax, and I can recall similar desires in the past. Consider this comment from a man's response to a sex survey:

> Nude pictures from men's magazines turn me on, and when I finally ejaculate, I aim right at the girl's breasts, pubic hair, or buttocks, whichever pleases me most. The more copious my output of sperm, the more satisfied I am (Hite, 1982, p. 781).

Did that desire arise from some "natural" source? From a social construction view of sexuality, the concept of authentic sexual desire is problematic; there is no pure, natural sexuality that isn't mediated by culture. Here I simply contend that pornography is a force that can shape desire and that we should be concerned with how men may be conditioned to desire sexual acts that are humiliating, degrading, or painful for women.

Scripting Sex

Several men I interviewed argued that sexually explicit material helped open up their sexual horizons. For me, pornography constricted, not expanded, my sexual imagination. Looking back on my experiences, I see no evidence that pornography fueled sexual creativity or sparked creative fantasies. Fantasy, in this sense, implies a flight of imagination, a letting go of oneself, the possibility of transcending the ordinary. For me, pornography did none of those things. It constrained my imagination, helped keep me focused on sexual activity that was rooted in male dominance, and hindered me from moving beyond the ordinary misogyny of the culture. Instead of my imagination running wild, my imagination was locked into a film loop, reproducing scripts and scenes from pornography. Pornographic sexuality— as reproduced in pornography and throughout our culture—crippled my erotic imagination, and I have only recently begun the long project of recovering the erotic, in the expanded sense the term is used by such writers as Carter Heyward (1989) and Audre Lorde (1984).

A validation of this view comes, ironically, from the pornographic actor Bill Margold, who saw no harm in pornography but understood the way it restricts the erotic. In discussing why people need pornographic films, he said: "We're drowning in our own sexual quicksand because there's a lack of imagination" (quoted in Hebditch and Anning, 1988, p. 27).

Race

For me, racial differences had erotic potential. Some of the men I interviewed, all of whom were white, said that they did not like pornography that used women of color and fast-forwarded past it in videotapes or passed over it in magazines. There was no pattern to these judgments; some men liked Asian women but not black women, while for others the opposite was true. Some men only wanted to watch white women. In the pornography market, there are publications and films that cater to all these tastes.

Those two responses—fascination with, or distaste for, women of color—are flip sides of the same racist coin. For white consumers, women of color can be even more sexually stimulating. For some, such as me, that connected to the stereotype of the "exotic primitive" and conjured up images of a wild sexuality. So, I found pornography that used women of color especially attractive and have specific memories of pornographic magazines that featured black women and Asian women. That reaction, of course, is hardly progressive. The pornography that highlighted nonwhite women played on stereotypes of the subservient Asian woman, the hot-blooded Latina, and the sexually promiscuous black woman. Although I did not consider myself racist at the time, my interest in such material grew out of the racism I had learned (and continue to struggle to unlearn), just expressed in a manner less overtly racist than those men who told me they found women of color in pornography to be unattractive to them.

Violence and Pornography

As in the previous chapter, I use the terms "violent" and "nonviolent" hesitantly, because there is no clear line between the two categories in a misogynistic culture. But in the common use of those terms, violent pornography is usually taken to mean depictions of sexual activity that include overt violence, such as physical abuse, the use of restraints, the presence of weapons, or strong verbal coercion. Nonviolent pornography usually describes depictions of sexual activity without those elements. The feminist claim that pornography fuses sex and violence is often rejected by men who say they do not use or enjoy violent pornography. But pornography does not need to be overtly violent to be part of a process by which violence is eroticized. I was never interested in overtly violent pornography, yet I was conditioned, in part by "nonviolent" pornography, to accept violence as erotic. Again, this is one of those claims that is difficult to prove because we live in a culture that, in general, sexualizes violence; no one can say for sure what specific images or influences create an appetite for sexualized violence. But my sense from my life is that pornography played an important role.

I realized that violence had been eroticized for me when reading the novels previously mentioned. At the time, I would have vigorously denied any claim that I found sexual violence erotic. But as I read those books, I was aroused by descriptions of sexual violence, such as a description of a man's sexual torture of a woman with whips and other paraphernalia. No matter what I thought about sexual violence, the eroticization of violence had taken place in my body; it worked on me. I responded sexually not only to the descriptions of sex, but also to those portions that used explicit violence and coercion. I found myself becoming sexually aroused by material that violated what I thought was my own sense of what was appropriate and healthy sex. I wanted to reject any experience of pleasure from those images, but my body accepted them.

What I had learned to find arousing was a basic power dynamic of male dominance and female subordination, which is much the same in violent and nonviolent pornography. Once male dominance is eroticized, male violence becomes at least potentially erotic. I could have denied that, as I think many men do, but my sexual reaction to the novels uncovered the reality of my erotic imagination.

Sex and Violence in the World

In defense of pornography, F. M. Christensen (1990, p. 41) argues that "the existence of violent sex in no way impugns nonviolent sex or its portrayal." I disagree. When the sex depicted in pornography is conditioned by male dominance, the line between the violent and nonviolent isn't nearly as crucial as many would like to believe. The hierarchical structure of nonviolent pornography trained my body to understand the erotic potential that this culture has assigned to rape. During my study of pornography I learned that rape was sexy to me. That reality had been living in my body for some time, but it was disturbing to admit. It led to the inescapable conclusion that I am capable of rape, even if I can't imagine ever committing such an act. The simple truth is that in this culture, men have to make a conscious decision not to rape, because rape is so readily available to us and so rarely results in sanctions of any kind.

If that claim about violence I just made is true—that both the sex offenders and I learned to eroticize violence—then why have I never committed a sex crime? First, to repeat earlier assertions, it is not my contention, nor the contention of anyone in the feminist anti-pornography movement, that pornography alone causes rape or that all pornography users commit rape. A complex network of factors lead a man to rape, and while pornography can be an important component, it obviously is not the only one.

But it also is important to remember that while I say I have never committed a sex crime, all I can really say is that I have not committed a sex crime under the male-defined sexual standards of this culture, which are similar to the standards set out in pornography. My own sexual definitions were framed by my use of pornography, and according to those definitions I have not raped. Yet, I do not know if that is an opinion that would be shared by every woman I have known (Jensen, 1995a). After trying to examine my sexual history from a nonpornographic perspective, I still come to the conclusion that I never crossed the line into coerced sex. But the final answer to that question would have to come from those women.

Control

The single most important thing I have learned from analyzing my own history and from the interviews is how central the concept of control—of women by men—is to pornography. In my life, that is most clear from the period in which I used pornography the most heavily. It came in my mid-20s after the break-up of an intense relationship with a woman. One reason I found the relationship, and its unraveling, so troublesome was that I was not in control. In most of my intimate relationships before and after, I retained most of the power to make basic decisions about the nature of the relationship. But in that situation, for a variety of reasons, I gave up control to the woman. That left me in a particularly volatile emotional state after the break-up, which I believe made pornography even more attractive.

In pornography, control remains in male hands in two ways. First, the magazines and movies that I can recall seeing depicted sexual encounters in which men were in control, guiding women's actions to produce male pleasure. The images that stay with me from that period are those in which the woman was completely subordinate, performing sexual acts on, and for, the man. Second, by making female sexuality a commodity, pornography allowed me to control when and where I used it, and therefore used the women in it. Barry Brummett makes this point in his analysis of pornographic movies viewed on a home VCR, pointing out how the control offered by the text is reinforced by the control offered by the medium (the ability to fast-forward and rewind to play back):

> VCRs never say no to their users; neither do characters in pornographic films. People agree to requests for sex with the same instant and uncritical willingness shown by the television and the VCR (Brummett, 1988, p. 209).

Technological advances continue to offer consumers even more control. In a story about the growing market in pornographic CD-ROMs, a sex shop manager explained, "They're good for releasing a little tension. CD-ROMs are great because you can control everything, all the action" (quoted in Marriott, 1995, B7). But all pornography offers that control to the consumer at some level. For me, retreating to a pornographic world allowed me to regain a sense of control over female sexuality that I had lost in real life.

A FOOTNOTE

This book is about pornography marketed to heterosexual men, and at the time I did much of the research and writing for this portion of this chapter, I lived and identified myself as heterosexual. I now identify myself and live as a gay man. I still at times find myself attracted to women, and some people might suggest I am bisexual, even if I do not act on such feelings. I have no need, and no way, to fix my sexual orientation in stone; perhaps I never will.

While this is not the place for an extended discussion of the extent to which sexuality is determined by socialization and/or biology, certainly my own life is an example of how one's behavior is shaped by social norms and expectations. My use of heterosexual pornography was one way in which I, with the help of a heterosexist culture, made myself heterosexual. No matter what kind of desire I felt for men during that time (and I did at times feel that desire), I "was" heterosexual in a very real sense. This change in my life is, of course, relevant to an autobiographical paper, but I have left a discussion of it until the end because the change does not undermine my analysis of heterosexual pornography.

SIX

"Feeding People in All Their Hungers"*

One Woman's Attempt to Link the Struggle against
Violence with the Struggle for Sexual Freedom

ANN RUSSO

For all the women for whom the answers don't come easy—

because of sexism, because of racism, because of sex, because of violence, because of family loyalty, because of sexual shame and stigma, because of denial, because of class exploitation, because of child rape, because of ethnic and racial loyalty, because of homophobia, because of self-hatred, because of sexual coercion, because of sexual repression, because of fear, because of rape and battering, because of compulsory heterosexuality, because of alcoholism and drug addiction, because of lack of choices, because of misogyny, because of low self-esteem, because of sexual degradation and humiliation, because of self-blame, because of sexual violence, because of repetition, and finally, because life is hard.

For all the women for whom the answers don't come easy, but for whom the search for hope, and love, and social justice, and sexual desire, and respect, and self-determination, and family, and intellectual and emotional freedom, and community, and sexual autonomy, and mutuality, and choices, and sexual pleasure, and dignity, and confidence, and bodily integrity, and hope, and vision is absolutely essential, necessary, and urgent.

For years I have sought to reconcile myself to one side or the other in the polarized "sex war" debates over sexuality, violence, and pornography. In my work I've placed myself among "the women for whom the answers don't come easy." For every attempt to ground myself solely in the anti-pornography movement, I would return to the recognition that neither "side" speaks to the full complexities and contradictions in women's lives. I define

*(Moraga, 1983).

the positions as, on the one hand, the struggle against violence and, on the other hand, the struggle toward sexual freedom. The either/or framework in which most feminist and lesbian feminist debates over sexuality and violence get lodged is limited, counterproductive, and, for the most part, destructive. Many women have been sexually victimized and oppressed through sexualized mistreatment, coercion, abuse, and violence, and simultaneously their sexual identities, desires, and practices also have been restricted and repressed through stigmatization and punishment. I disagree with those feminists who defend the multibillion-dollar pornography industry under the guise of individual rights and sexual freedom, and who refuse to recognize how gender and racial inequalities and violence are intricately connected with social constructions of sexual identities and practices. But, I also disagree with feminist work against sexual violence and pornography which does not recognize the impact of the stigmatization of women's sexual identities and practices nor value the quest for sexual freedom. To create a more inclusive movement for change that might speak to the complexities of women's lives and hopes for the future, it seems important to combine the struggle for sexual freedom and autonomy with the struggle for freedom from sexual and physical coercion and violence. As Dorothy Allison expresses about her own life, "As deeply as I wanted safety or freedom, I wanted desire, hope, and joy. What, after all, was the worth of one without the other?" (Allison, 1994, p. 112).

As a survivor and resister of both sexual violence and sexual stigmatization, I need the wisdom and passion of a variety of perspectives in the struggles for equality, mutual respect and dignity, and social justice. Writers and theorists on both sides of the sexuality debates have had a significant impact on my personal, social, and political life. The books of Andrea Dworkin (1974, 1976, 1988, 1989), Dorothy Allison (1994, 1995), Chrystos (1991, 1993), Audre Lorde (1984, 1988), Cherríe Moraga (1983, 1993), Kathleen Barry (1979), bell hooks (1984, 1989), Catharine MacKinnon (1987), and Joan Nestle (1987, 1992), sit side by side on my bookshelf. Each writer has had a deep impact on my thinking about endemic sexual violence and sexual repression. It is my belief that pervasive sexual violence cannot be addressed fully without considering the impact of stigma, shame, and the sexual double standard, particularly in terms of the personal, social, and institutional responses to that violence. Moreover, the struggle to address the sexualized violence in women's lives cannot be separated out and/or opposed to the struggle of women themselves to gain a sense of sexual integrity and to work toward the goal of sexual self-determination.

SEXUAL VIOLENCE/SEXUAL STIGMA

The feminist movement against violence, and the critical analysis of pornography's production and consumption of inequalities, share the commitment to end the violence and suffering in women's lives—to support women in their efforts to resist sexualized domination and subordination in all of its many forms; to recognize and validate women's stories of harassment, abuse, and violence within and outside of the pornography industry; to advocate for women discriminated against in the criminal (in)justice system and in other social institutions (employment, medicine, education); to confront, challenge, and stop the mistreatment, abuse, and violence in women's lives; to create more personal, social, economic, and political options for women; and to create alternative visions of personal and social life so that women might imagine and work toward a future without endemic discrimination and violence. What feminists against violence and pornography have sought to do is to show the connections between the sexualized objectification and abuse of women in the pornography industry and through the processes of production, consumption, and distribution and the structural inequalities of gender, race, class, and sexuality. The immediate goal has not been to prove a monocausal and unidirectional link between pornography and violence, but to show the interconnectedness of pornography's subordinating practices with structures and practices of inequality evident throughout the society. The ultimate goals are to recognize and stop abuse and violence, to challenge the sexual stigmatization and punishment of women, and to create the possibilities for mutual respect, dignity, and social justice.

The feminist theories and politics against sexual abuse and violence saved my life, particularly the words of Andrea Dworkin. They gave me a language and an analysis that helped me make sense of my life experiences. They helped me to understand that what had been and was happening to me wasn't "just life." As Dworkin (1988, p. 134) so eloquently writes: "It is politics; it is history; it is power; it is economics; it is institutional modes of social organization: it is not 'just life.'" Dworkin's writings provided me with a clarity that made drugs, alcohol, and depression much less necessary in the routines of my everyday life. Her analysis gave me a framework not only to make sense of the mistreatment, abuse, and violence, but the will to change the social conditions of the life I was leading. Dworkin speaks to the anger as well as to the grief of sexual abuse and exploitation, and she offers a road map to change through political analysis and activism. Her analysis of pornography made clear how sexualized and racialized mistreatment, abuse, and violence become legitimized and perpetuated in this culture, but also pointed to the ways in which women who are made into sexualized objects are stigmatized and treated as inferior human beings. She showed how the process of stigmatization was not separate from the violence, but integrally related. I was able to use her analysis to decode similar ideological constructions in social, sexual, and political discourses that are connected, not separate, from the discourses of pornography.

In the movement against sexual violence, women's quest for sexual desire, sexual pleasure, and sexual freedom often is framed solely in terms of freedom from violence. In the face of the concrete destruction of violence in women's lives, including that legitimated and perpetuated by the practices of the pornography industry, it has seemed less than urgent to explore women's conflicts and contradictions with regard to sexual desire and practice, including pornography, or to focus on women's sexual exploration, pleasure, and freedom in response to sexual restrictions and stigma. The feminist debates over pornography created a false polarization between stopping violence and challenging sexual repression and stigmatization. The anti-pornography feminists focused on sexual violence and the sexual liberals focused on sexual restrictions and punishments. Within the feminist anti-pornography movement, the stakes are very high given the levels of sexual violence in the society. Many have felt it important to focus primarily on violence because women are being brutalized, terrorized, and killed on a daily basis. The life-and-death realities are paramount in our minds and hearts.

The result of an exclusive focus on gender-based violence and the minimization of the contradictions women may experience in relation to desire and sexual practices, particularly sexualized power dynamics, however, has been the development of an implicit ideology around sexual issues. For instance, in my work among anti-pornography feminists, I have run up against a fairly rigid, though often unspoken, orthodoxy around sexual behavior and attitudes. Challenges to this orthodoxy are not welcome, especially within the context of the polarized debates. I, myself an activist involved in feminist anti-pornography politics, have been accused of siding with "the enemy" simply for raising questions, for wanting to have an open dialogue about the complexities of sexual desire, for wanting to discuss the contradictions between feminist analysis and individual practice, and for being influenced by the writings of those on the "other side." The atmosphere created in some parts of the movement remind me of the staunch and unrelenting catholicism of my childhood—a dogma that had extraordinarily narrow and rigid boundaries about thought and action and that rarely gave human beings room for complexity or contradiction. It's a dogma set up for transgression and failure, because no one can live up to it. In some parts of the women's movement, the struggle for change has been translated into demands for conformity where strict standards of analysis and behavior are used to judge and exclude people. As Dworkin suggests:

> People become slaves to theory because people are used to meeting expectations they have not originated—to doing what they are told, to having everything mapped out, to having reality prepackaged. The deepest struggle is to root out of us and the institutions in which we participate the requirement that we slavishly conform (Dworkin, 1988, p. 127).

The sexual orthodoxy that seems implicit in much of the anti-pornography analysis does not address the complexities and contradictions in women's lives. Such contradictions are inevitable in a society rife with sexual discrimination and repression. The anti-pornography analysis has not, for the most part, addressed the confusions, ambivalences, or fears of many women who are seeking to address the sexual violence and repression within their own lives and the lives of others. One of the effects of sexual abuse in sexually repressive atmospheres is an intense confusion, as well as fear and terror, around sexuality. Again, the integral relationships between sexuality and violence need more exploration, rather than simplistic answers that exclusively focus on the gendered aspects of violence and ignore or minimize the complexities of sex, ethnicity, class, and race. The exclusive focus has been justified on the grounds that the issue is power and violence, not the complexities of sexual desire. However, if our goal is to create a broad-based movement for social justice, it is incumbent upon all of us to listen to women and to recognize the differences in our experiences and responses to sexual experiences. We must explore the contradictions between our feelings, political beliefs, and actions that are inevitable for people who live in a society based on sexual, racial, and economic bigotry, inequality, exploitation, and abuse. In this way the voices and experiences of many women would make up the movement, not only those women who have the same perspective or who experience oppression in the same way.

The lesbian and feminist theorists and writers who I have been drawn to who are associated with the sexual liberal position are those who are committed to the fight against sexual exploitation in all of its economic, racial, and gendered manifestations, as well as to the exploration of sexual passion and desire that such exploitation seeks to rob and destroy. Allison, Chrystos, Moraga, and Nestle speak to the centrality of sexual shame, stigma, and the criminalization of difference in women's lives. They each challenge their audiences to consider the intersections of sexual stigma with racial, ethnic, class, and gender identities in the construction and experience of discrimination and violence.

Allison eloquently asks us to consider:

> how our lives might be different if we were not constantly subjected to the fear and contempt of being sexually different, sexually dangerous, sexually endangered. What kind of women might we be if we did not have to worry about being too sexual, or not sexual enough, or the wrong kind of sexual for the company we keep, the convictions we hold? . . . Not addressing the basic issues of sexual fear, stereotyping, and stigmatization reinforces the rage and terror we all hide, while maintaining the status quo in a new guise (Allison, 1994, p. 117–118).

Her recognition of the fear and contempt toward sexual difference speak to the heart of the polarized debates. The way to move beyond such polarization is to open up the discussion in a way that allows women to speak about the full complexity of their experiences.

In my own life, the experience of sexual abuse and violence was intertwined with the experience of stigmatization and punishment. A major obstacle to recognizing the violence and abuse in my family is attributable to having grown up in a staunchly Roman Catholic context with very strict standards of sexual behavior for women that, in my case, were continually transgressed within and outside of the family. Being raised in a rigid catholicism that restricted and stigmatized women's sexual desire and autonomy confounded the experience of sexual abuse and violence. While the anti-pornography movement helped me to understand the sexualization of the violence, the writings of Allison, Chrystos, and Moraga spoke to the issues of stigmatization and shame and answered the yearning for sexual autonomy and sexual self-determination.

As a lesbian, feminist, outspoken survivor of sexual violence, I have not succumbed to the rigidity of the catholicism that I grew up with, nor to the rigid tenets of the radical feminism that helped change my life; and, I have not been destroyed by the violence that seemed so much a part of my life for so many years. I resist efforts to control my desire for sexual integrity and self-determination. For me the goal of the women's movement is not to enforce conformity, nor to construct sameness across our many differences, nor to create monolithic standards to be used to judge everyone's attitudes and behaviors. As Allison writes:

Throughout my life somebody has always tried to set the boundaries of who and what I will be allowed to be. . . . What is common to these boundary lines is that their most destructive power lies in what I can be persuaded to do to myself—the walls of fear, shame, and guilt I can be encouraged to build in my mind. . . . I have learned through great sorrow that all systems of oppression feed on public silence and private terrorization (Allison, 1994, p. 116–117).

This does not mean that I do not expect to be challenged; it means that I expect dialogue, discussion, and recognition of contradictions and complexities. Both "sides" of the debate have challenged public silences. The anti-pornography movement has created a public discussion of the endemic sexualized violence in women's lives, and some of the sex radicals mentioned in this essay have created a public discussion of women's sexual identities, desires, and yearnings. It is time that feminists break the silences implicit within each of the two positions. Women's lives are complex; they are not simple cut-outs to be fit into ideological boxes. As Dworkin (1988, p. 127) writes, "The struggle for freedom has to be a struggle toward integrity defined in every possible sphere of reality—sexual integrity, economic integrity, psychological integrity, integrity of expression, integrity of faith and loyalty and heart." In speaking of the individual who struggles for integrity, she writes: "The mind struggling towards integrity does not accept someone else's version of the story of life: this mind demands that life itself must be confronted, over and over, by all who live it. The mind struggling toward integrity confronts the evidence and respects experience" (Dworkin, 1988, p. 129).

Thus, in our continually evolving analyses and politics, as feminists we must struggle towards integrity. In this struggle, we would refuse analyses which exclude either the questions of structural inequalities and violence or the questions of individual sexual autonomy and self-determination. As Cherríe Moraga suggests in *Loving in the War Years* (1983), we must strive to feed people in all of our hungers; for me, this would include the hungers for freedom from bigotry, hatred, and violence, for bodily and sexual integrity, for sexual passion and connection, and for social and economic justice.

SEVEN

The Pain of Pornography

ROBERT JENSEN

The most successful conversations I have had with people who take a pro-pornography position have happened when I have talked honestly about my life and my emotional and physical reactions to the pornographic world. To do that, I have to talk about pain. I believe that pain is a thread that connects people in the pornographic world—the pain that exists all around us which makes a mass-marketed pornography industry possible, and the pain that pornography creates and feeds on. It is a pain of varying intensity felt to varying degrees by different people in different social locations. But I believe that we all have some connection to that pain and that it is a route to common ground and understanding.

This pain can at times feel so overwhelming that connecting to it seems too much to handle. I have felt that at various times working on this book. As I watched the pornographic videos described in Chapter 4, I could not avoid the pain it took to make them. As I read the stories of women and talked to the men discussed in Chapter 5, I could not avoid the pain that results from the use of pornography. And the more I felt that pain, the more it connected to the pain that fueled my use of pornography as a child and young adult that I described in Chapter 5. As difficult as it is to face that pain, connecting all these elements deepens my understanding of the industry, the videos, the use of pornography.

The pornographers hope we don't make these connections, that we don't talk about the pain so that we don't critique them and their work. I believe that if everyone acknowledged the pain it takes to make pornography on the scale it is produced today—if we refused to turn away from the broken bodies and broken spirits—the pornography industry would collapse. A friend told me she thought this was too optimistic a hope. Many people with power often understand that their privilege and pleasure require that others endure pain, and they simply don't care, she said. I think her assessment of the world is accurate, and that there certainly are people who, as a practical matter, seem to be beyond compassion and unconcerned with justice.

But I also think that acknowledging that pain can force us to stop and ask why we live in a world in which the bodies and spirits of people (primarily women and children) can be bought, sold, and broken with such callousness and contempt. People have the capacity for compassion that can make justice possible, even when systems of power, and the rewards those systems offer some of us, make it easy to turn away from compassion. Even when we have learned to take pleasure in pornography, as so many of us have, confronting the pain can change how we see that pleasure.

Connecting to the pain made it possible for me to struggle to disconnect from the pornographic world. Rather than avoid the pain, I try to find ways to work through and with it, both by myself and with others. The connection to others and to politics is crucial. If we focus this kind of emotional exploration inwardly only, if we psychologize the pain and care only about our personal recovery, we give up the power we have collectively to change the world. It is crucial not only for me to engage my own pain, but also to remember that no matter how much I may hurt at times, there are people in the world (again, primarily women and children) who live with pain that is beyond my experience, maybe even beyond my knowing. Not turning away from that pain is, for me, one way I both heal myself and stay connected to my capacity for compassion, to my hope for justice.

PLAYING BY THE RULES

So, I have come to believe that in addition to knowing more about pornography, we also need to feel more. Or, put another way, we need to realize that there is never thinking without feeling, and that when we suppress discussion of emotion, we know less. The rules of scholarship say that I am not supposed to talk like this. If I discuss this pain, I am supposed to wall it off from my research and theory; it can be a personal footnote perhaps, something mentioned in passing, not part of the "real" intellectual work. The conventional wisdom, as summarized by Lorraine Code (1991, p. 47), suggests that "emotional response is ineluctably whimsical and unstable, erratic, idiosyncratic, and irrational: that uncontrolled hysteria is the paradigmatic emotion." In a similar vein, Naomi Scheman (1993, p. 25) argues that sexism has inhibited women's ability to interpret feelings and behavior in political perspective, partly through "the myth about the emotions, women's emotions in particular, that tells us they are irrational or non-rational storms.

They sweep over us and are wholly personal, quite possibly hormonal. . . . They don't, in any event, mean anything."

But our emotional reactions do mean something. Reason and emotion are not wholly separate but intertwined, and fragmenting them and devaluing emotion impedes our ability to understand the world. To acknowledge the role of emotion is not to reduce the answer to every question to emotion. As Sarah Hoagland suggests, our interpretations of emotions can be questioned and challenged, but they are a source of knowledge: "Feelings are not isolated, private events. They do not arise in a vacuum, nor are they expressed in a vacuum. They exist in a context, are a perception of events" (Hoagland, 1988, p. 192). The empathy and understanding that come through engagement with our own pain and the pain of others is crucial not only for sorting out our personal emotional lives, but also for understanding the world and its oppressive structures. We must be honest about the pain if we are to understand the systems that are responsible for it.

The moment I begin talking about this, however, I risk being dismissed as overly emotional, too subjective, not properly detached. This gives people who disagree with me an easy out, a way to dismiss what I say as the product not of careful scholarship but quite possibly of irrationality. Not objective. Unscientific. Politically motivated. That is the risk in discussing the pain here. But perhaps the greater risk is ignoring the pain and not speaking of it. What would it mean to detach from pain in a world in which the sexualized violence and violation celebrated in pornography are so common? Would I be more objective, scientific, and credible if I were to detach emotionally from that reality? When I listen to what seems like an endless string of stories about sexual abuse and violence, should I be detached? Would I be a better researcher? Would I be a better person? Who would I be?

PAIN AND GENDER

Pain is felt by everyone. But pain also is gendered. An example:

Gail Dines and I sit in front of a television and VCR, pornographic videos stacked on the floor. We're on the third tape, and a woman is being penetrated by three men (vaginally, anally, orally) at the same time. Gail says she wonders how this must have felt for the woman. How could this not be physically painful? Gail empathizes with the woman, tries to sort out what this video might have meant in the woman's life. As the scene progresses, the woman is unable to continue to make sounds of pleasure. She seems to be concentrating on surviving the penetration. Gail winces. Through all this, I understand what Gail is saying. And I have an erection.

Later, Gail and I talked about our reactions to the videos. Gail talked about the pain of watching women's bodies violated so routinely, so incessantly, so casually. She talked about her anger at the men, those in the scenes and behind the camera, and the consumers. I talked about the sexual arousal the videos produced. I acknowledged that I identified with the men and had to struggle to empathize with the women. Through most of the viewing, I dealt with the conflicting feelings by emotionally dissociating.

Women sometimes report that pornography, including pornography that depicts violence against women, is sexually arousing, just as men often do. That is not surprising in a world that not only trains men to be sexual aggressors but trains women to be victims. Such emotions and sexual reactions are complicated, the intersection of socialization and personal history that can be difficult to unpack. But it was clear in that situation that Gail's connection to the women on the screen was different than mine; she lives as a woman in a culture in which she is at risk for the same kind of treatment as the women in the videos. I live, for the most part, free of that fear. That made it possible for me, in the short term, to cut myself off from the women's pain on the screen, one of the many privileges of being male.

But there was more for me to explore in my reaction. While the videos forced Gail to confront the fact that she is defined by the culture as a fuck-object, I had to confront the fact that I was trained by that culture to be the one who fucks. Being honest about my reaction and what it says about me, while difficult, opens up space for me to think about how that training has really served me in my life. Has pornographic fucking made me happy? Is there some way in which the women's pain can connect to my own?

VICTIMS AND PAIN

To talk about pain in this way implies that there are victims in the world. When one looks at sexual violence statistics, this seems like a banal statement. Yet focusing on the way men who live in a patriarchal system routinely hurt women through sex and violence leaves one open to the charge that one is turning women into victims. One popular writer argues that such "victim feminism" needs to be replaced with "power feminism" (Wolf, 1993). Another claims that radical feminists, or "gender feminists," have hijacked the women's movement and betrayed the real interests of women (Sommers, 1994). In an odd twist of responsibility, feminists who critique and analyze sexual violence somehow are told they have turned women into victims. The men who commit the violations and the social structure that allows that violence to happen so routinely tend to fade from view. But what does it mean to be a victim? Andrea Dworkin has spoken eloquently on this point:

It's a true word. If you were raped, you were victimized. You damned well were. You were a victim. It doesn't mean that you are a victim in the metaphysical sense, in your state of being, as an intrinsic part of your essence and existence. It means somebody hurt you. They injured you. . . . And if it happens to you systematically because you are born a woman, it means that you live in a political system that uses pain and humiliation to control and to hurt you (Dworkin, 1990, p. 38).

Understanding one's victimization is not the same as playing the victim or being permanently relegated to helplessness. Acknowledging that women often are victimized is not an admission of weakness or a retreat from responsibility. Instead, it makes possible organized and sustained resistance to the powers that cause the injuries. Again, following Dworkin (1990, p. 39), "[T]he first step in resisting exploitation is recognizing it, seeing it, and knowing it, and not lying about where it is sitting on you."

VICTIMIZERS AND PAIN

Men in patriarchy who are committed to gender justice have to struggle to understand the pain of women as well as their own pain. Both tasks can be difficult, depending on one's history and social location. It requires sophisticated analysis and honesty. Men need to acknowledge both the ways in which we are victimizers, complicit to varying degrees in patriarchy's oppression of women, and the ways that our own lives are impoverished by patriarchy even as we are reaping material rewards (again, to varying degrees depending on history and social location).

I have never had sex with a woman in a manner that would be called violent or described as rape. Yet at various times in my history I have talked with other men about women in a sexually denigrating fashion. I have used women sexually in ways that, in retrospect, were degrading and disrespectful. When I began to read feminist theory and critiques of male sexuality, my first reaction was typical: I thought these women needed to lighten up and enjoy life a bit more. I saw them as prudes, scared of the power of sex, manhaters—the common litany of insults and lies necessary for men to remain willfully ignorant about their own misogyny and that of their culture. But something made me keep reading. I think the motive was my own discomfort with masculinity and sexuality, my growing sense that no matter how much power and privilege I was accorded as a man in patriarchy (and specifically as a white man in a white supremacist patriarchy), that power left me feeling unfulfilled, disconnected from myself and others, and fearful. I was in pain, and the source of the pain was patriarchy. I could not achieve what the hegemonic masculinity (Connell, 1995, pp. 76–81) asked of me, and exercising the power that I had under that system could not fill the void. I was looking for a way out.

I have been lucky to have a job that allows me to devote a substantial amount of time to reading and research on these subjects. I also am fortunate to have a close friend, Jim Koplin, who had been struggling with these issues for years. I remember a conversation with Jim over coffee one morning in which he said, "I think that when men get past the bravado, we know deep down that getting our sexual kicks at the expense of someone else just doesn't feel good." I believe he is right. When one is in a dominant position, it is easy to obtain sexual gratification by dominating. But after the sexual stimulation is over, what are we left with?

ESSENTIALISM AND EMPATHY

In certain scholarly circles, much of what I have said here would be dismissed as "essentialist," which is one of the quickest ways to label an idea unworthy of consideration. At times it feels as if any attempt to talk about patterns of behavior in a society or notions of what it means to be human has been boxed out by the fear of being accused of making indefensible generalizations or totalizing assertions that deny the wide range of human experience. So, if a man argues that it is in men's interests to resist socialization into sexualizing domination, he can be critiqued for not having an appropriately sophisticated understanding of the psychology of sexuality. If a woman acknowledges what while watching a pornographic movie she is thinking "it hurts to watch this" or "I wish that woman didn't have to go through this," she can be accused of imposing her interpretation of an event on the woman in the scene, of not honoring the woman's right to choose to participate in pornography.

In other words, when one speaks honestly about the experience of being human and feeling such emotions, one is not supposed to connect those emotions to anyone else. These reactions are supposed to be taken as nothing more than individual, subjective experiences. To suggest that we need to discuss the feelings and search for common ground is deemed essentialist and, therefore, unacceptable. As Sheila Jeffreys (1993, p. 83) points out, "A quite new meaning of the word essentialist has been invented so that it can be used against all those who maintain some belief in the possibility of social action to create social change."

There is wide agreement in contemporary feminism that simplistic notions of the category "woman" that deny the differences between women (race, class, sexual orientation, etc.) are naive and dangerous. While it is absurd to assume that all members of a group should feel the same way about something because they belong to the group, to cut oneself off from discussion out of such fear is politically and personally debilitating. One can publicly discuss these issues, making it clear where one stands, without being essentialist, totalizing, or patronizing.

When did such attempts to connect and understand become dangerous to speak about openly? When did the postmodern deconstruction of the concept "woman" become so complete that no woman could say, "I wouldn't want that to happen to me, and I worry about the world in which that woman lives"? When did empathy become politically suspect?

FROM HERE

The pornography debate has split communities that are in solidarity on other issues of justice. Our hope is that this book can be read by people on all sides without being automatically dismissed or uncritically accepted. Carter Heyward suggests that it is:

> more critical than ever that folks who honestly desire a more just and compassionate world be clear with one another how we do, and do not, envision the justice and compassion that we seek. Only insofar as we are clear in this way, thereby allowing differences with our friends to emerge, publicly and unapologetically, can we stay in the struggle together, holding and working out our differences relationally, in community, over time; in faith that what we cannot resolve will be taken up in new ways by those who come after us (Heyward, 1995, pp. ix–x).

The point of this conclusion, and this book, is not to suggest that everyone's experiences with pornography are exactly the same. Pornography has not been a positive force in my life, yet I accept that others will have a different view of its role in their lives. Our goal has been to look beyond debates about individual tastes and pleasures to explore an industry, its products, and the effect of those products in the world. Whatever one's personal preferences concerning pornography, we all have an obligation to confront how pornography is made, what it says about gender and sexuality, and how it is used. And we have an obligation to those with the least power, to those who are hurt in this pornographic world. We have a political and moral obligation to "reconsider our appetite for sexual entertainment in light of its costs" (Clarke, 1993, p. 117).

One of the costs of pornography is an incredible amount of pain. Yes, some women choose to work in pornography, aware of what is involved.

But what about those for whom economic deprivation and histories of sexual abuse leave them feeling they have no choice? Yes, some women choose to incorporate pornography into their sex lives. But what about those who find themselves being forced to reproduce pornographic scenes against their will? Yes, some men believe that pornography is transgressive and liberating. But what if, every time a man bought and used pornography, he thought about the women and children for whom pornography is not liberation but bondage, not transgression of social norms but a bodily and spiritual violation? What would it be like if we struggled to empathize and connected it to political and social analysis, if we all reconsidered such entertainment in light of the costs, of the pain?

It may be that some of these disagreements will not be resolved in our lifetimes, but "by those who come after us." Even if that is the case, we have the responsibility to keep talking, as honestly as possible, about just what is at stake.

EIGHT

Living in Two Worlds

An Activist in the Academy

GAIL DINES

For the last ten years, as an academic and an anti-pornography activist, I have lived and moved between two worlds. Much of the scholarly work on pornography published in the last five years has taken a pro-pornography position, arguing that pornography is a form of sexual fantasy that has little to do with the rape, battery, torture, and murder of women in the real world (see for example, Assiter and Carol, 1993; Carol, 1994; Strossen, 1995; Kipnis, 1996). Yet, as an activist, I have met hundreds of women and men who have stories to tell about pornography and the devastating impact it has had on their lives. Managing these two worlds has not been made any easier by the so-called "porn wars," which have put anti-pornography scholars outside of much of the academic community. The battles that have raged within the feminist movement have left many of us exhausted, drained, and alienated from academic feminism.

My main form of activism has been focused on developing and giving slide/lecture presentations on pornography and its effects. I have lectured across the country at colleges and community forums and have done numerous television and radio shows on both the pornography industry and the feminist anti-pornography civil rights legislation. My travels have put me in contact with people from every corner of this vast country, and many have similar stories to tell. After my lecture, there is always a long line of women who want to tell me their story, often telling it for the first time. I have heard about what it is like to be coerced into making pornography by parents, brothers, uncles, boyfriends, husbands, and pimps. I have listened to women tell me about being raped and brutalized by men who wanted to re-enact their favorite porn scene, and I have spent time with women who were ganged-raped by their male "friends" after watching pornography. The women who tell their stories speak of the lasting effects that pornography has had on their lives. For them, pornography is not a polysemic text, a fantasy to be savored, a form of sexual liberation, or a discourse. It is an event that forever changed their life and has to be dealt with every day.

In the world of scholarly discourse, these stories are contemptuously referred to as "anecdotal evidence," first-person accounts that may make for interesting reading, but are not comparable with real scholarship. In a world cleansed of pain and passion, the realities of these people's lives are lost in the maze of postmodern terminology and intellectual games. Academics who choose to make their daily bread from lecturing and writing, speak about women in pornography as "choosing" to fuck men, dogs, bottles, and hair dryers in a way that suggests some form of equality of choice.

The women who have told me their stories did not make a choice to be in pornography. Being raped as a child and sold to the highest bidder does not constitute a life of choices. Running away from a sexually abusive home and being "saved" by a pimp who then turns you into one of his "girls" is sexual slavery, not choice. These women form part of the pornography industry and rather than telling their stories, many of the pro-pornography books give us detailed accounts of those few women—such as Annie Sprinkle or Candida Royalle—who have managed to switch sides of the camera. The Horatio Alger story of pornography tells us much about the endurance of mythology in America, but little about the lives of the majority of women in pornography.

To read many of the scholarly books on pornography, one would think that men who use pornography have this uncanny ability to compartmentalize their lives. It seems that just as they put their penis away after using the stuff, so too they put the images away in that part of their brain that is marked fantasy, never to leak out into actual life. This is a ridiculous assertion that does not hold up in the lived experiences of men and women. Men may differ in how pornography leaks into their sexual relationships, but leak it does. Women have talked about being forced by their partners to watch the pornography so they can learn how to dress, suck, fuck, moan, talk, gasp, lick, cry, or scream like the woman in the pornography. And many of these men get very upset if their partners don't react the same way as the women in the pornography. The carefully constructed images on the screen or on the page are read as "ideal types," and should his partner fail to live up to the ideal, then there is often hell to pay. Some women have talked about their partners beating them or raping them for failing to smile the right way; others talk about the more mundane punishments of being ignored or ridiculed for failure to meet the pornography standard. These women's stories are testimony to the myriad ways in which pornography lives in the lives of real women in the world.

Working on the civil rights legislation in the Massachusetts Legislature in 1992 provided me with a firsthand view of how power works within capitalist patriarchy. As a sociologist who was and is interested in macro structures of oppression, I was well aware of how the legislative system works to protect the rights of the elite, at the expense of the non-property owning classes. What I was not aware of, however, was just how efficiently and swiftly these protective mechanisms can be activated. Within a couple of days of filing the legislation, the media began an anti-ordinance blitz that continued throughout the campaign. Apart from the local Feminists Against Censorship Taskforce, we encountered no organized opposition until the day of the hearings. Suddenly, Massachusetts was invaded by East and West coast lawyers representing the pornography industry and the media industry. Our side of the room was filled with women who had come to tell their stories while the other side was awash in dark blue suits and starched white shirts. We found that within 24 hours of the hearings, most of the influential members of the Judiciary Committee had been lobbied by these lawyers, and we could not get our elected representatives to even return our phone calls. Some months later we found that the bill had died in committee. The aide to the chief sponsor of the bill said that in all his years at the state house, he had never seen such as orchestrated campaign to destroy a piece of legislation.

For an industry that is meant to be about fantasy, the owners are incredibly adept at marshaling material resources to fight their battles. This is no small-time operation, existing at the margins. This is an extremely powerful industry that will unmercifully destroy any potential opposition to its power. It has friends in high places and can count on employing the most seasoned and expensive of lawyers to defend their economic interests. In retrospect, we did not stand a chance against the forces of capitalism and patriarchy. We had no money, no lawyers lobbying the committee, and few friends in high places. This imbalance of power is never discussed in the pro-pornography books; indeed, we are the ones who are characterized as powerful while the pornographers are represented as marginalized defenders of the First Amendment working to protect the rights of the powerless.

My experiences as an activist have shown me the enormous gap that exists between those who work in academe and those who live in the real world of economic and sexual exploitation. The academic discussions over the nature of the pornographic text, the problems of definition, the polysemic qualities of pornography, the work of Annie Sprinkle, and so on, are utterly removed from the lives of the women who are the casualties of this multibillion dollar a year industry. By refusing to deal with the realities of pornography, the pro-pornography academics have chosen to defend a multibillion-dollar-a-year industry and to ignore the ways in which pornography is implicated in the oppression of women. Now that's a real choice.

Appendix

VIDEOS ANALYZED

Chug-a-Lug Girls #6. (1995). Production Video Team.
Buttman's Big Butt Backdoor Babes. (1995). Evil Angel Productions.
Taboo VIII. (1990).
The Nympho Files. (1995). Nitro Productions.
Latex. (1994). VCA Pictures.
Rick Savage's New York Video Magazine Vol. 5. (1995). Outlaw Productions.
More Dirty Debutantes #37. (nd). Nasty Brothers Productions.
Senior Stimulation. (1995). Coast to Coast Video.
Cherry Poppers Vol. 10. (1995).
Slave on Loan. (nd). B&D Pleasures.
Afro Erotica #17. (1990). Wet Video.
Black Pepper Vol. 13. (1994).
3 Men and a Geisha. (1990).
Girls of the Bamboo Palace. (nd).

NOVELS ANALYZED

Balling, Sucking Widow. (1985). By Nick Eastwood. San Diego: Greenleaf Classics. 152 pp.
Boy-Hungry Librarian. (1978). By Randy Howard. San Diego: Greenleaf Classics. 150 pp.
Candy's Sweet Mouth. (1990). By R. K. Kopp. 1974. Reprint, Sun Valley, CA: American Art Enterprises. 159 pp.
Easy Office Girl. (1976). By Robert Vickers. San Diego: Greenleaf Classics. 158 pp.
Everybody's Virgin. (1989). By Debbie Ray. 1977. Reprint, North Hollywood: American Art Enterprises. 191 pp.
Gal About Town. (1981). By Jack O'Latern. Published in one volume with *Spreading It Around.* New York: Carlyle Communications. 180 pp.
The Hungry Hostess. (1989). By Marsha Mead. 1975. Reprint, North Hollywood: American Art Enterprises. 192 pp.

The Lady Plays Doctor. (1975). By Jerry Milner. San Diego: Greenleaf Classics. 155 pp.

Nurse's Secret Lust. (1989). By John Crowley. 1977. Reprint, North Hollywood: American Art Enterprises. 192 pp.

Power Trip. (1989). By Rod Strong. North Hollywood: American Art Enterprises. 154 pp.

Secretary in Heat. (1976). By Ray Manning. San Diego: Greenleaf Classics. 158 pp.

Secretary's Naked Lunch. (1989). By Tanya Mazuk. 1976. Reprint, North Hollywood: American Art Enterprises. 190 pp.

She Blew Her Oral Exam. (1986). By Tom Allison. San Diego: Greenleaf Classics. 148 pp.

Sheila Spreads Wide. (1976). By David Brown. San Diego: Greenleaf Classics. 158 pp.

Spreading It Around. (1981). By Bea Linder. Published in one volume with *Gal About Town*. New York: Carlyle Communications. 163 pp.

Taxi Tramps. (1975). By Chris Harrison. New York: Midwood Publications. 187 pp.

Teacher's Passionate Urge. (1989). By Carol Davis. North Hollywood: American Art Enterprises. 191 pp.

The Town Sluts. (1976). By J. H. Long. San Diego: Greenleaf Classics. 158 pp.

What a Librarian! (1986). By John Kellerman. San Diego: Greenleaf Classics. 153 pp.

Wives Who Will. (1990). By Roger Crowell. 1976. Reprint, Sun Valley, CA: American Art Enterprises. 160 pp.

References

Abbott, Franklin (Ed.). (1990). *Men and Intimacy: Personal Accounts of Exploring the Dilemmas of Modern Male Sexuality.* Freedom, CA: Crossing Press.

Alexander, Priscilla. (1987). Prostitution: a difficult issue for feminists. In Frédérique Delacoste and Priscilla Alexander (Eds.), *Sex Work: Writings by Women in the Sex Industry* (pp. 184–214). San Francisco: Cleis Press.

Allen, Mike, Dave D'Alessio, and Keri Brezgel. (1995). A meta-analysis summarizing the effects of pornography II. *Human Communication Research,* 22(2), 258–283.

Allison, Dorothy. (1995). *Two or Three Things I Know for Sure.* New York: Penguin.

Allison, Dorothy. (1994). *Skin: Talking About Sex, Class and Literature.* Ithaca, NY: Firebrand Books.

Andrea Dworkin fights back. (1985). *New Directions for Women* (November/December), 1.

Anzaldúa, Gloria (Ed.). (1990). *Making Face, Making Soul: Creative and Critical Perspectives by Women of Color.* San Francisco: Aunt Lute Press.

Armstrong, Louise (Ed.). (1978). *Kiss Daddy Goodnight: A Speak-Out on Incest.* New York: Hawthorn Books.

Assiter, Alison, and Avedon Carol. (1993). *Bad Girls and Dirty Pictures: The Challenge to Reclaim Feminism.* London: Pluto Press.

Attorney General's Commission on Pornography. (1986). *Final Report.* Washington, DC: U.S. Department of Justice. [The report was published commercially as *Final Report of the Attorney General's Commission on Pornography.* (1986). Nashville, TN: Rutledge Hill Press, introduction by Michael J. McManus. Excerpts from the testimony before the commission were published in Phyllis Schlafly (Ed.). (1987). *Pornography's Victims.* Westchester, IL: Crossway Books.]

Baker, Peter. (1992). Maintaining male power: why heterosexual men use pornography. In Catherine Itzin (Ed.), *Pornography: Women, Violence and Civil Liberties* (pp. 124–144). Oxford: Oxford University Press.

Baldwin, Margaret. (1984). The sexuality of inequality: the Minneapolis pornography ordinance. *Law and Inequality,* 2, 635–670.

Barko, Naomi. (1953). A woman looks at men's magazines. *Reporter* (July 7), 29—32.

Barry, Kathleen. (1995). *The Prostitution of Sexuality*. New York: New York University Press.

Barry, Kathleen. (1979). *Female Sexual Slavery*. New York: Prentice-Hall.

Barry, Kathleen, Charlotte Bunch, and Shirley Castley (Eds.). (1984). *International Feminism: Networking Against Female Sexual Slavery*. New York: International Women's Tribune Center.

Bell, Laurie (Ed.). (1987). *Good Girls/Bad Girls: Feminists and Sex Trade Workers Face to Face*. Seattle: Seal Press.

Beneke, Tim. (1981). *Men on Rape*. New York: St. Martin's Press.

Benn, Melissa. (1987). Adventures in the Soho skin trade. *New Statesman* (December 11), 21—23.

Bergen, Raquel Kennedy. (1995). Surviving wife rape: how women define and cope with the violence. *Violence Against Women*, 1(2), 117—138.

Berman, Morris. (1990). *Coming to Our Senses: Body and Spirit in the Hidden History of the West*. New York: Bantam.

Betterton, R. (1987). *Looking On: Images of Femininity in the Visual Arts and Media*. London: Pandora.

Bogaert, Anthony F., Deborah A. Turkovich, and Carolyn L. Hafer. (1993). A content analysis of *Playboy* centrefolds from 1952 through 1990: changes in explicitness, objectification, and model's age. *Journal of Sex Research*, 30(2), 135—139.

Bogdanovich, Peter. (1984). *The Killing of the Unicorn: Dorothy Stratten (1960–1980)*. New York: William Morrow.

Boone, Joseph A. (1990). Of me(n) and feminism: Who(se) is the sex that writes? In Joseph A. Boone and Michael Cadden (Eds.), *Engendering Men: The Question of Male Feminist Criticism* (pp. 11—25). New York: Routledge.

Brady, Frank. (1974). *Hefner*. New York: Macmillan.

Brannigan, Augustine, and Sheldon Goldenberg. (1987). The study of aggressive pornography: the vicissitudes of relevance. *Critical Studies in Mass Communication*, 4(3), 262—283.

Bronski, Michael. (1984). Spirits in the material world: gay publishing, pornography and the gay male. *Radical America*, 18(4), 21—29.

Brosius, Hans-Bernd, James B. Weaver III, and Joachim F. Staab. (1993). Exploring the social and sexual "reality" of contemporary pornography. *Journal of Sex Research*, 30(2), 161—170.

Brown, Dan, and Jennings Bryant. (1989). The manifest content of pornography. In Dolf Zillman and Jennings Bryant (Eds.), *Pornography: Research Advances and Policy Considerations* (pp. 3—24). Hillsdale, NJ: Erlbaum.

Brummett, Barry. (1988). The homology hypothesis: pornography on the VCR. *Critical Studies in Mass Communication,* 5(3), 202–216.

Buchwald, Emilie, Pamela R. Fletcher, and Martha Roth (Eds.). (1993). *Transforming a Rape Culture.* Minneapolis: Milkweed Editions.

Burger, John R. (1995). *One-Handed Histories: The Eroto-Politics of Gay Male Video Pornography.* New York: Harrington Park Press.

Burgess, Ann. (1984). *Child Pornography and Sex Rings.* Lexington, MA: D.C. Heath.

Burstyn, Varda (Ed.). (1985). *Women Against Censorship.* Vancouver: Douglas and McIntyre.

Califia, Pat. (1986). Among us, against us: the new puritans. In FACT Book Committee (Ed.), *Caught Looking* (pp. 20–25). New York: Caught Looking.

Carol, Avedon. (1994). *Nudes, Prudes and Attitudes: Pornography and Censorship.* London: New Clarion Press.

Castañeda, Antonia I. (1993). Sexual violence in the politics and policies of conquest. In Adela de la Torre and Beatríz M. Pesquera (Eds.), *Building with Our Hands: New Directions in Chicana Studies* (pp. 15–33). Berkeley: University of California Press.

Charles, Beth. (1985). The pornography explosion. *Ladies Home Journal* (October), 104.

Christensen, F. M. (1990). *Pornography: The Other Side.* New York: Praeger.

Chrystos. (1993). *In Her I Am.* Vancouver: Press Gang Publishers.

Chrystos. (1991). *Dream On.* Vancouver: Press Gang Publishers.

Clarke, D. A. (1993). Consuming passions: some thoughts on history, sex, and free enterprise. In Irene Reti (Ed.), *Unleashing Feminism: Critiquing Lesbian Sadomasochism in the Gay Nineties* (pp. 106–153). Santa Cruz, CA: HerBooks.

Code, Lorraine. (1991). *What Can She Know? Feminist Theory and the Construction of Knowledge.* Ithaca, NY: Cornell University Press.

Code, Lorraine. (1986). Stories people tell. *New Mexico Law Review,* 16(3), 599–606.

Cole, Susan. (1989). *Pornography and the Sex Crisis.* Toronto: Amanita.

Collins, Patricia Hill. (1990). *Black Feminist Thought.* New York: Routledge.

Connell, R. W. (1995). *Masculinities.* Cambridge: Polity Press.

Coontz, Stephanie. (1992). *The Way We Never Were: American Families and the Nostalgia Trap.* New York: Basic Books

Cowan, Gloria, Carole Lee, Daniella Levy, and Debra Snyder. (1988). Dominance and inequality in X-rated videocassettes. *Psychology of Women Quarterly,* 12(3), 299–311.

Cowan, Gloria, and Robin R. Campbell. (1994). Racism and sexism in interracial pornography. *Psychology of Women Quarterly,* 18(3), 323–338.

Crenshaw, Kimberlé. (1994). Mapping the margins: intersectionality, identity, politics, and violence. In Martha Albertson Fineman and Roxanne Mykitiuk (Eds.), *The Public Nature of Private Violence* (pp. 93–120). New York: Routledge.

Davis, Angela. (1981). Rape, racism, and the myth of the black male rapist. In *Women, Race and Class* (pp. 172–201). New York: Random House.

Delacoste, Frédérique, and Priscilla Alexander (Eds.). (1987). *Sex Work: Writings by Women in the Sex Industry*. San Francisco: Cleis Press.

Delacoste, Frédérique, and Felice Newman (Eds.). (1981). *Fight Back: Feminist Resistance to Male Violence*. Minneapolis: Cleis Press.

Dietz, Park E., and Alan E. Sears. (1987–88). Pornography and obscenity sold in adult bookstores: a survey of 5132 books, magazines, and films in four American cities. *University of Michigan Journal of Law Reform*, 21(1–2), 7–46.

Dines, Gail, and Jean M. Humez (Eds.). (1995). *Gender, Race and Class in Media: A Text-Reader*. Thousand Oaks, CA: Sage.

Dines-Levy, Gail. (1988a). An analysis of pornography research. In Ann Wolbert Burgess (Ed.), *Rape and Sexual Assault II* (pp. 317–323). New York: Garland.

Dines-Levy, Gail. (1988b). Pornography: the propaganda of misogyny—III. *The Community Church News* (May). Community Church of Boston.

Donnerstein, Edward, Daniel Linz, and Steven Penrod. (1987). *The Question of Pornography*. New York: The Free Press.

Duggan, Lisa. (1984). Censorship in the name of feminism. *Village Voice* (October 16), 11–22.

Duggan, Lisa, Nan Hunter, and Carole Vance. (1985). False promises: feminist antipornography legislation in the U.S. In Varda Burstyn (Ed.), *Women Against Censorship* (pp. 130–151). Vancouver: Douglas and McIntyre.

Dworkin, Andrea. (1990). Woman-hating right and left. In Dorchen Leidholdt and Janice G. Raymond (Eds.), *The Sexual Liberals and the Attack on Feminism* (pp. 28–40). New York: Pergamon.

Dworkin, Andrea. (1989). *Pornography: Men Possessing Women*. New York: Dutton. (Reissued with a new introduction)

Dworkin, Andrea. (1988). *Letters from a War Zone*. New York: Dutton.

Dworkin, Andrea. (1987). *Intercourse*. New York: Free Press.

Dworkin, Andrea. (1981). *Pornography: Men Possessing Women*. New York: Perigee.

Dworkin, Andrea. (1976). *Our Blood: Prophecies and Discourses on Sexual Politics*. New York: Harper and Row.

Dworkin, Andrea. (1974). *Woman-Hating*. New York: Dutton.

Dworkin, Andrea, and Catharine A. MacKinnon. (1988). *Pornography and Civil Rights: A New Day for Women's Equality*. Minneapolis: Organizing Against Pornography.

Ehrenreich, Barbara. (1983). *Hearts of Men*. New York: Anchor Books

Elshtain, Jean Bethke. (1982). The victim syndrome. *The Progressive* (June), 42–47.

English, Deirdre. (1980). The politics of pornography. *Mother Jones* (April) 20–23, 43–50.

Estrich, Susan. (1987). *Real Rape*. Cambridge: Harvard University Press.

Faludi, Susan. (1991). *Backlash: The Undeclared War Against American Women*. New York: Anchor Books.

Farnham, Marynia, and Ferdinand Lundberg. (1947). *Modern Woman: The Lost Sex*. New York: Harper and Brothers.

Feminist Anti-Censorship Task Force Book Committee (Ed.). (1986). *Caught Looking: Feminism, Pornography, and Censorship*. New York: Caught Looking.

Fletcher, Pamela R. (1993). Whose body is it, anyway? In Emilie Buchwald, Pamela R. Fletcher, and Martha Roth (Eds.), *Transforming a Rape Culture* (pp. 427–442). Minneapolis: Milkweed Editions.

Flynt, Larry. (1984). Ten great years. *Hustler* (July), 7.

Flynt, Larry. (1983). Politics of porn. *Hustler* (November), 5.

Forna, Aminatta. (1992). Pornography and racism: sexualizing oppression and inciting hatred. In Catherine Itzin (Ed.), *Pornography: Women, Violence and Civil Liberties* (pp. 102–113). Oxford: Oxford University Press.

Friedan, Betty. (1974/1963). *The Feminine Mystique*. New York: Dell.

Frye, Marilyn. (1992). *Willful Virgin*. Freedom, CA: Crossing Press.

Frye, Marilyn. (1983). *The Politics of Reality*. Freedom, CA: Crossing Press.

Fullerton, Kim. (1982). An interview with Andrea Dworkin. *City Limits*, 1(11) (August), 5.

Gaines, Judith. (1992). Home-video sex sells; unwilling stars cry foul. *Boston Globe* (May 17), 1, 26.

Gardner, Tracey. (1980). Racism in pornography and the women's movement. In Laura Lederer (Ed.), *Take Back the Night: Women on Pornography* (pp. 105–114). New York: William Morrow.

Geertz, Clifford. (1973). *The Interpretation of Cultures*. New York: Basic Books.

Gerbner, George. (1990). Epilogue: advancing on the path of righteousness (maybe). In Nancy Signorielli and Michael Morgan (Eds.), *Cultivation Analysis: New Directions in Media Effects Research* (pp. 249–262). Newbury Park, CA: Sage.

Gibson, Pamela Church, and Roma Gibson (Eds.). (1993). *Dirty Looks: Women, Pornography, Power*. London: BFI Publishing.

Giobbe, Evelina. (1995). Surviving commercial sexual exploitation. In Gail Dines and Jean Humez (Eds.), *Gender, Race and Class in Media: A Text-Reader* (pp. 314–318). Thousand Oaks, CA: Sage.

Giobbe, Evelina. (1993). Connections between prostitution and pornography. *Whisper* VII (No. 1), 3, 9.

Giobbe, Evelina. (1991). Prostitution: buying the right to rape. In Ann Wolbert Burgess (Ed.), *Rape and Sexual Assault III* (pp. 143–160). New York: Garland.

Gordon, Linda. (1988). *Heroes of Their Own Lives: The Politics and History of Family Violence*. New York: Viking Press.

Griffin, Susan. (1986). *Rape: The Politics of Consciousness*. San Francisco: Harper and Row.

Hall, Stuart. (1989). Ideology and communication theory. In Brenda Dervin, Lawrence Grossberg, Barbara J. O'Keefe, and Ellen Wartella (Eds.), *Rethinking Communication: Volume 1, Paradigm Issues* (pp. 40–52). Newbury Park, CA: Sage.

Hall, Stuart. (1986). On postmodernism and articulation. *Journal of Communication Inquiry*, 10(2), 45–60.

Haralovich, Mary Beth. (1989). Sitcoms and suburbs: positioning the 1950s homemaker. *Quarterly Review of Film and Video*, 11, 61–83.

Harding, Sandra. (1991). *Whose Science? Whose Knowledge?* Ithaca, NY: Cornell University Press.

Hearn, Jeff (1987). *The Gender of Oppression: Men, Masculinity, and the Critique of Marxism*. New York: St. Martin's Press.

Hebditch, David, and Nick Anning. (1988). *Porn Gold: Inside the Pornography Business*. London: Faber and Faber.

Herek, Gregory M., and Kevin T. Berrill (Eds.). (1992). *Hate Crimes: Confronting Violence Against Lesbians and Gay Men*. Newbury Park, CA: Sage.

Herman, Judith Lewis. (1992). *Trauma and Recovery: The Aftermath of Violence from Domestic Abuse to Political Terror*. New York: Basic Books.

Herman, Judith Lewis. (1981). *Father-Daughter Incest*. Cambridge: Harvard University Press.

Hernandez-Avila, Inés. (1993). In praise of insubordination, or, what makes a good woman go bad? In Emilie Buchwald, Pamela R. Fletcher, and Martha Roth (Eds.), *Transforming a Rape Culture* (pp. 375–392). Minneapolis: Milkweed Editions.

Heyward, Carter. (1995). *Staying Power: Reflections on Gender, Justice, and Compassion*. Cleveland: Pilgrim Press.

Heyward, Carter. (1989). *Touching our Strength: The Erotic as Power and The Love of God*. San Francisco: Harper and Row.

Hite, Shere. (1982). *The Hite Report on Male Sexuality*. New York: Ballantine Books.

Hoagland, Sarah Lucia. (1988). *Lesbian Ethics: Toward New Value*. Palo Alto, CA: Institute of Lesbian Studies.

hooks, bell. (1993). Seduced by violence no more. In Emilie Buchwald, Pamela R. Fletcher, and Martha Roth (Eds.), *Transforming a Rape Culture* (pp. 351–358). Minneapolis: Milkweed Editions.

hooks, bell. (1992). *Black Looks: Race and Representation*. Boston: South End Press.

hooks, bell. (1990). *Yearning: Race, Gender and Cultural Politics*. Boston: South End Press.

hooks, bell. (1989). *Talking Back: Thinking Feminist, Thinking Black*. Boston: South End Press.

hooks, bell. (1984). *Feminist Theory: From Margin to Center*. Boston: South End Press.

hooks, bell. (1981). *Ain't I a Woman*. Boston: South End Press.

I Spy Productions. (1992). Pornography and capitalism: the UK pornography industry. In Catherine Itzin (Ed.), *Pornography: Women, Violence and Civil Liberties* (pp. 76–87). Oxford: Oxford University Press.

Itzin, Catherine (Ed.). (1992). *Pornography: Women, Violence and Civil Liberties*. Oxford: Oxford University Press.

Jeffreys, Sheila. (1993). *The Lesbian Heresy*. North Melbourne, Australia: Spinifex Press.

Jeffreys, Sheila. (1990). *Anticlimax: A Feminist Perspective on the Sexual Revolution*. New York: New York University Press.

Jensen, Robert. (1997a). Patriarchal sex. *International Journal of Sociology and Social Policy*, 17(1–2), 91–115.

Jensen, Robert. (1997b). Privilege, power, and politics in research: a response to "Crossing sexual orientations." *Qualitative Studies in Education*, 10(1), 25–30.

Jensen, Robert. (1996). Knowing pornography. *Violence Against Women*, 2(1), 82–102.

Jensen, Robert. (1995a). Feminist theory and men's lives. *Race, Gender and Class*, 2(2), 111–125.

Jensen, Robert. (1995b). Pornographic lives. *Violence Against Women*, 1(1), 32–54.

Jensen, Robert. (1995c). Pornography and affirmative conceptions of freedom. *Women and Politics*, 15(1), 1–18.

Jensen, Robert. (1994a). Pornographic novels and the ideology of male supremacy. *Howard Journal of Communications*, 5(1–2), 92–107.

Jensen, Robert. (1994b). Pornography and the limits of experimental research. In Gail Dines and Jean M. Humez (Eds.), *Gender, Race and Class in Media: A Text-Reader* (pp. 298–306). Thousand Oaks, CA: Sage.

Jones, Ann. (1994). *Next Time She'll Be Dead: Battering and How to Stop It*. Boston: Beacon Press.

Kaite, Berkeley. (1995). *Pornography and Difference*. Bloomington: Indiana University Press.

Kaplan, Ann. (1987). Pornography and/as representation. *Enclitic*, 19, 8–19.

Kappeler, Susanne. (1986). *The Pornography of Representation*. Minneapolis: University of Minnesota Press.

Kellner, Douglas. (1995). *Media Culture: Cultural Studies, Identity and Politics Between the Modern and the Postmodern*. London: Routledge.

Kelly, Liz. (1988). *Surviving Sexual Violence*. Minneapolis: University of Minnesota Press.

Kendall, Christopher N. (1993). "Real dominant, real fun!": gay male pornography and the pursuit of masculinity. *Saskatchewan Law Review*, 57(1), 21–58.

Kimmel, Michael S. (1996). *Manhood in America: A Cultural History*. New York: Free Press.

Kimmel, Michael S. (Ed.). (1990). *Men Confront Pornography*. New York: Crown.

Kimmel, Michael S., and Kaufman, Michael. (1994). Weekend warriors: the new men's movement. In Harry Brod and Michael Kaufman (Eds.), *Theorizing Masculinities* (pp. 259–288). Thousand Oaks, CA: Sage.

Kipnis, Laura. (1996). *Bound and Gagged: Pornography and the Politics of Fantasy in America*. New York: Grove Press.

Kipnis, Laura. (1992). (Male) desire and (female) disgust: reading *Hustler*. In Larry Grossberg, Cary Nelson, and Paula Treichler (Eds.), *Cultural Studies* (pp. 373–391). New York: Routledge.

Kornack, Marie. (1989a). New Bedford serial murderer targets women used in prostitution. *WHISPER* III. 2 (Winter/Spring), 8

Kornack, Marie. (1989b). Porn and murder: new evidence in serial killings. *WHISPER* III. 3 (Summer), 5.

Kuhn, Annette. (1985). *The Power of the Image: Essays on Representation and Sexuality*. London: Routledge.

Langelan, Marty. (1981). The political economy of pornography. *Aegis*, 5 (Autumn), 5–17.

Lau, Grace. (1993). Confessions of a complete scopophiliac. In Pamela Church Gibson and Roma Gibson (Eds.), *Dirty Looks: Women, Pornography, Power* (pp. 207–232). London: BFI Publishing.

Lawrence, D. H. (1955). *Sex, Literature and Censorship*. Melbourne: William Heinemann.

Lederer, Laura (Ed). (1980). *Take Back the Night: Women on Pornography*. New York: William Morrow.

Lederer, Laura, and Richard Delgado (Eds.). (1995). *The Price We Pay: The Case Against Racist Speech, Hate Propaganda, and Pornography*. New York: Hill and Wang.

Leidholdt, Dorchen. (1987). In memoriam Althea Flynt 1955–1987. *WAP Newsreport* IX.I (Fall), 8.

Leidholdt, Dorchen, and Janice G. Raymond (Eds.). (1990). *The Sexual Liberals and the Attack on Feminism*. New York: Pergamon.

Linz, Daniel. (1989). Exposure to sexually explicit materials and attitudes toward rape: a comparison of study results. *Journal of Sex Research*, 26(1), 50–84.

Lipsitz, George. (1990). *Time Passages: Collective Memory and American Popular Culture*. Minneapolis: University of Minnesota Press.

Lobel, Kerry (Ed.). (1986). *Naming the Violence: Speaking Out About Lesbian Battering.* Seattle: Seal Press.

Lorde, Audre. (1988). *A Burst of Light.* Ithaca, NY: Firebrand Books.

Lorde, Audre. (1984). *Sister Outsider.* Freedom, CA: Crossing Press.

Lovelace [Marciano], Linda, with Mike McGrady. (1986). *Out of Bondage.* New York: Berkley.

Lovelace [Marciano], Linda, with Mike McGrady. (1980). *Ordeal.* New York: Berkley.

MacKinnon, Catharine A. (1993). *Only Words.* Cambridge: Harvard University Press.

MacKinnon, Catharine A. (1989). *Toward a Feminist Theory of the State.* Cambridge: Harvard University Press.

MacKinnon, Catharine A. (1987). *Feminism Unmodified: Discourses on Life and Law.* Cambridge: Harvard University Press.

MacKinnon, Catharine A. (1985). An open letter to Adrienne Rich. *Off Our Backs* (October), 18.

MacKinnon, Catharine A. (1984). Not a moral issue. *Yale Law and Policy Review,* 2(2), 321–345.

MacKinnon, Catharine A. (1979). *Sexual Harassment of Working Women: A Case of Sex Discrimination.* New Haven: Yale University Press.

Madigan, Lee, and Nancy Gamble. (1991). *The Second Rape: Society's Continual Betrayal of the Victim.* New York: Lexington Books.

Malamuth, Neil, and Barry Spinner. (1980). Longitudinal content analysis of sexual violence in the best-selling erotica magazines. *Journal of Sex Research,* 16(3), 226–237.

Malamuth, Neil, and J. V. P. Check. (1981). The effects of mass media exposure on acceptance of violence against women: a field experiment. *Journal of Research in Personality,* 15, 436–446.

Maltz, Wendy, and Beverly Holman. (1987). *Incest and Sexuality: A Guide to Understanding and Healing.* Lexington, MA: Lexington Books.

Marriott, Michel. (1995). Virtual porn: ultimate tease. *New York Times* (October 4), B1, B7.

Marshall, W. L. (1988). The use of sexually explicit stimuli by rapists, child molesters, and nonoffenders. *Journal of Sex Research,* 25(2), 267–288.

Martin, Del. (1976). *Battered Wives.* New York: Pocket Books.

Matacin, Mala L., and Jerry M. Burger. (1987). A content analysis of sexual themes in *Playboy* cartoons. *Sex Roles,* 17(3–4), 179–186.

Matsuda, Mari J., Charles Lawrence III, Richard Delgado, and Kimberlé Crenshaw. (1992). *Words That Wound: Critical Race Theory, Assaultive Speech, and the First Amendment.* Boulder, CO: Westview.

May, Elaine Taylor. (1988). *Homeward Bound: American Families in the Cold War Era.* New York: Basic Books.

Mayall, Alice, and Diana E. H. Russell. (1993). Racism in pornography. In Diana E. H. Russell (Ed.), *Making Violence Sexy: Feminist Views on Pornography* (pp. 167–178). New York: Teachers College Press.

McClintock, Anne. (1993). Sex workers and sex work. *Social Text*, 37 (Winter), 1–10.

McCracken, Ellen. (1993). *Decoding Women's Magazines: From Mademoiselle to Ms.* New York: St. Martin's Press.

McElroy, Wendy. (1995). *XXX: A Woman's Right to Pornography.* New York: St. Martin's Press.

McNaron, Toni, and Yarrow Morgan (Eds.). (1982). *Voices in the Night: Writings by Women Survivors of Child Sexual Abuse.* Minneapolis: Cleis Press.

Miller, Douglas, and Marion Nowak. (1977). *The Fifties: The Way We Really Were.* Garden City, NY: Doubleday.

Miller, Russell. (1984). *Bunny: The Real Story of* Playboy. London: Michael Joseph.

Millett, Kate. (1971). *Sexual Politics.* New York: Avon.

Mills, C. Wright. (1953). *White Collar.* New York: Oxford University Press

Moraga, Cherríe. (1993). *The Last Generation.* Boston: South End Press.

Moraga, Cherríe. (1983). *Loving in the War Years.* Boston: South End Press.

Moraga, Cherríe, and Gloria Anzaldúa (Eds.). (1983). *This Bridge Called My Back.* New York: Kitchen Table: Women of Color Press.

Morgan, Robin. (1980). Theory and practice: pornography and rape. In Laura Lederer (Ed.), *Take Back the Night: Women on Pornography* (pp. 134–140). New York: William Morrow.

Morrison, Toni (Ed.). (1992). *Race-ing, Justice, En-gendering Power: Essays on Anita Hill, Clarence Thomas, and the Construction of Social Reality.* New York: Pantheon.

Narayan, Uma. (1988). Working together across difference: some considerations on emotions and political practice. *Hypatia*, 3(2), 31–47.

Nelson, Vednita. (1992). Black women and prostitution. *WHISPER* VI 3–4 (Summer/Fall), 1.

Nestle, Joan. (1992). *Persistent Desire: A Femme-Butch Reader.* Boston: Alyson.

Nestle, Joan. (1987). *A Restricted Country.* Ithaca, NY: Firebrand Books.

New York Radical Feminists (Eds). (1974). *Rape: The First Sourcebook for Women.* New York: New American Library.

Omolade, Barbara. (1994). *The Rising Song of African American Women.* New York: Routledge.

Orlando, Lisa. (1982). Bad girls and "good" politics. *Voice Literary Supplement* (December), 1+.

Osanka, Franklin, and Sara Lee Johann. (1989). *Sourcebook on Pornography.* Lexington, MA: Lexington Books.

Palys, T. S. (1986). Testing the common wisdom: the social content of video pornography. *Canadian Psychology,* 27(1), 22—35.

Parsons, Talcott. (1963). *Essays in Sociological Theory.* New York: Free Press.

Pheterson, Gail. (1993). The whore stigma: female dishonor and male unworthiness. *Social Text,* 37 (Winter), 39—64.

Polkinghorne, Donald E. (1988). *Narrative Knowing and the Human Sciences.* Albany: State University of New York Press.

Porn: liberation or oppression? (1983). *Off Our Backs* (May), 14.

Porn's Horatio Algers. (1980). *Mother Jones* (April), 32.

Pornography and Sexual Violence: Evidence of the Links. (1988). London: Everywoman Press. Reprint of *Public Hearings on the Proposed Minneapolis Civil Rights Anti-Pornography Ordinance.*

Post, Carole. (1982). Pornography and our self image: women speak out. *WAP Newsreport* (Spring), 1.

Prince, Stephen. (1990). Power and pain: content analysis and the ideology of pornography. *Journal of Film and Video,* 42, 31—41.

Prince, Stephen, and Paul Messaris. (1990). The question of a sexuality of abuse in pornographic films. In Sari Thomas and William A. Evans (Eds.), *Communication and Culture: Studies in Communication,* Vol. 4 (pp. 281—284). Norwood, NJ: Ablex.

Public Hearings on the Proposed Minneapolis Civil Rights Anti-Pornography Ordinance. (1983). Minneapolis: Organizing Against Pornography. The transcript of the hearings also was published as: *Pornography and Sexual Violence: Evidence of the Links.* (1988). London: Everywoman.

Queer Press Collective (Ed.). (1991). *Loving in Fear: Lesbian and Gay Survivors of Childhood Sexual Abuse.* Toronto, Ontario: Queer Press.

Radinson, Evelyn. (1986). New Playboy Club "folds" in New York City. *WAP Newsreport* VII.2 (Spring/Summer), 1.

Reilly, Kristen. (1982). WAP, NOW, Native American protest racist/sexually violent video game. *WAP Newsreport* (Fall), 1.

Reinharz, Shulamit. (1992). *Feminist Methods in Social Research.* New York: Oxford University Press.

Reisman, David. (1950). *The Lonely Crowd.* New Haven: Yale University Press

Reisman, Judith. (1985). About my study of "dirty pictures." *Washington Post, National Weekly Edition* (July), 1.

Renzetti, Claire M. (1992). *Violent Betrayal: Partner Abuse in Lesbian Relationships.* Newbury Park, CA: Sage.

Renzetti, Claire M., and Charles Harvey Miley (Eds.). (1996). *Violence in Gay and Lesbian Domestic Partnerships.* New York: Harrington Park Press.

Reti, Irene. (1993). *Unleashing Feminism: Critiquing Lesbian Sadomasochism in the Gay Nineties.* Santa Cruz, CA: HerBooks.

Richie, Beth. (1996). *Compelled to Crime: The Gender Entrapment of Battered Black Women.* New York: Routledge.

Rimmer, Robert. (1984). *The X-Rated Videotape Guide.* New York: Harmony Books.

Royalle, Candida. (1993). Porn in the USA. *Social Text,* 37 (Winter), 23–32.

Rubin, Gayle. (1993). Misguided, dangerous and wrong: an analysis of anti-pornography politics. In Alison Assiter and Avedon Carol (Eds.), *Bad Girls and Dirty Pictures: The Challenge to Reclaim Feminism* (pp. 18–40). London: Pluto Press.

Rubin, Gayle. (1984). Thinking sex. In Carole Vance (Ed.), *Pleasure and Danger* (pp. 267–319). London: Routledge and Kegan Paul.

Russell, Diana E. H. (Ed.). (1993a). *Making Violence Sexy: Feminist Views on Pornography.* New York: Teachers College Press.

Russell, Diana E. H. (1993b). *Against Pornography: Evidence of Harm.* Berkeley: Russell Publications (2018 Shattuck #118; Berkeley, CA 94704).

Russell, Diana E. H. (1988). Pornography and rape: a causal model. *Political Psychology,* 9(1), 41–73.

Russell, Diana E. H. (1986). *The Secret Trauma: Incest in the Lives of Girls and Women.* New York: Basic Books.

Russell, Diana E. H. (1984). *Sexual Exploitation: Rape, Child Sexual Abuse and Workplace Harassment.* Beverly Hills, CA: Sage.

Russell, Diana E. H. (1980). Pornography and violence: what does the new research say? In Laura Lederer (Ed.), *Take Back the Night: Women on Pornography* (pp. 218–238). New York: William Morrow.

Russell, Diana E. H., and Laura Lederer. (1980). Questions we get asked most often. In Laura Lederer (Ed.), *Take Back the Night: Women on Pornography* (pp. 23–29). New York: William Morrow.

Russo, Ann. (in press). Lesbians, prostitutes, and murder: media constructs violence constructs power. In Martha Fineman and Martha McClusky (Eds.), *Feminism, Law and the Media.* Oxford University Press.

Sanday, Peggy Reeves. (1990). *Fraternity Gang Rape: Sex Brotherhood, and Privilege on Campus.* New York: New York University Press.

Schechter, Susan. (1982). *Women and Male Violence: The Visions and Struggles of the Battered Women's Movement.* Boston: South End Press.

Scheman, Naomi. (1993). *Engenderings.* New York: Routledge.

Scholder, Amy (Ed.). (1993). *Critical Condition: Women on the Edge of Violence.* San Francisco: City Lights Books.

Scott, Joseph E., and Steven J. Cuvelier. (1987). Sexual violence in *Playboy* magazine: a longitudinal content analysis. *Journal of Sex Research*, 23(4), 534–539.

Segal, Lynne, and Mary McIntosh (Eds.). (1993). *Sex Exposed: Sexuality and the Pornography Debate*. New Brunswick, NJ: Rutgers University Press.

Silbert, Mimi H., and Ayala M. Pines. (1984). Pornography and sexual abuse of women. *Sex Roles*, 10(11/12), 857–869.

Slade, Joseph W. (1984). Violence in the hard-core pornographic film: a historical survey. *Journal of Communication*, 34(3), 148–163.

Smith, D. D. (1976). The social content of pornography. *Journal of Communication*, 26, 16–24.

Snitow, Ann. (1985). Retrenchment vs. transformation: the politics of the antipornography movement. In Varda Burstyn (Ed.), *Women Against Censorship* (pp. 107–120) . Vancouver: Douglas and McIntyre.

Sommers, Christina Hoff. (1994). *Who Stole Feminism? How Women Have Betrayed Women*. New York: Simon and Schuster.

A Southern Women's Writing Collective. (1990). Sex resistance in heterosexual arrangements. In Dorchen Leidholdt and Janice G. Raymond (Eds.), *The Sexual Liberals and the Attack on Feminism* (pp. 140–147). New York: Pergamon.

Stanko, Elizabeth. (1985). *Intimate Intrusions: Women's Experience of Male Violence*. London: Routledge, Kegan and Paul.

Statement of WHISPER Action Group Members. (1992). *WHISPER VI* 1–2 (Winter/Spring), 3.

Stivers, Camilla. (1992). Reflections on the role of personal narrative in social science. *Signs*, 18(2), 408–425.

Stock, Wendy. (1990). Toward a feminist praxis of sexuality. In Dorchen Leidholdt and Janice G. Raymond (Eds.), *The Sexual Liberals and the Attack on Feminism* (pp. 148–156). New York: Pergamon.

Stoller, Robert J. (1991). *Porn: Myths for the Twentieth Century*. New Haven: Yale University Press.

Stoller, Robert J., and I. S. Levine. (1993). *Coming Attractions: The Making of an X-Rated Video*. New Haven: Yale University Press.

Stoltenberg, John. (1989). *Refusing to Be a Man: Essays on Sex and Justice*. Portland, OR: Breitenbush Books.

Straayer, Chris. (1993). The seduction of boundaries: feminist fluidity in Annie Sprinkle's art/education/sex. In Pamela Church Gibson and Roma Gibson (Eds.), *Dirty Looks: Women, Pornography, Power* (pp. 156–175). London: BFI Publishing.

Strossen, Nadine. (1995). *Defending Pornography: Free Speech, Sex, and the Fight for Women's Rights*. New York: Scribner.

Summer, Toby. (1987). Women, lesbians and prostitution: a workingclass dyke speaks out against buying women for sex. *Lesbian Ethics,* 2(3), 33–44.

Sumrall, Amber, and Dena Taylor (Eds.). (1992). *Sexual Harassment: Women Speak Out.* Freedom, CA: Crossing Press.

Technical Report of the Commission on Obscenity and Pornography. (1971). Vol. 3. Washington, DC: U.S. Government Printing Office.

Teish, Luisah. (1980). A quiet subversion. In Laura Lederer (Ed.), *Take Back the Night: Women on Pornography* (pp. 115–118). New York: William Morrow.

Torrey, Morrison. (1993). The resurrection of the anti-pornography ordinance. *Texas Journal of Women and Law,* 2(1), 113–124.

Torrey, Morrison. (1992). We get the message—pornography in the workplace. *Southwestern University Law Review,* 22(1), 53–103.

Trees, Barbara. (1995). Like a smack in the face: pornography in the trades. In Laura Lederer and Richard Delgado (Eds.), *The Price We Pay: The Case Against Racist Speech, Hate Propaganda, and Pornography* (pp. 32–34). New York: Hill and Wang.

Velasco, Angelita, and Jeanne Barkey. (1989). OAP celebrates five years: taking pride in our past and looking forward to the future. *Organizing Against Pornography Newsletter* (Summer), 1.

Walker, Alice. (1980). Coming apart. In Laura Lederer (Ed.), *Take Back the Night: Women on Pornography* (pp. 95–104). New York: William Morrow.

Warshaw, Robin. (1988). *I Never Called It Rape: Recognizing, Fighting and Surviving Date and Acquaintance Rape.* New York: Harper and Row.

Weaver, James. (1992). The social science and psychological research evidence: perceptual and behavioural consequences of exposure to pornography. In Catherine Itzin (Ed.), *Pornography: Women, Violence and Civil Liberties* (pp. 284–309). Oxford: Oxford University Press.

Webster, Paula. (1981). Pornography and pleasure. *Heresies,* 12, 48–51.

Weyr, Thomas. (1978). *Reaching for Paradise: The* Playboy *Vision of America.* New York: Times Books.

White, Evelyn (Ed.). (1990). *The Black Women's Health Book.* Seattle: Seal Press.

White, Evelyn. (1985). *Chain, Chain, Change: For Black Women Dealing with Physical and Emotional Abuse.* Seattle: Seal Press.

Williams, Guy. (1987). Dirty business: Despite a tough new law, pornography proves the price of vice still pays huge profits. *Business-North Carolina* (April), 22.

Williams, Linda. (1993a). Second thoughts on *Hard core*: American obscenity law and the scapegoating of deviance. In Pamela Church Gibson and Roma Gibson (Eds.), *Dirty Looks: Women, Pornography, Power* (pp. 46–61). London: BFI Publishing.

Williams, Linda. (1993b). A provoking agent: the pornography and performance art of Annie Sprinkle. In Pamela Church Gibson and Roma Gibson (Eds.), *Dirty Looks: Women, Pornography, Power* (pp. 176–191). London: BFI Publishing.

Williams, Linda. (1989). *Hard Core: Power, Pleasure and the "Frenzy of the Visible."* Berkeley: University of California Press.

Williams, Patricia. (1991). *The Alchemy of Race and Rights.* Cambridge: Harvard University Press.

Wilson, Melba. (1993). *The Crossing Boundary: Black Women Survive Incest.* Seattle: Seal Press.

Winick, Charles. (1985). A content analysis of sexually explicit magazines sold in an adult bookstore. *Journal of Sex Research,* 21(2), 206–210.

Wolf, Naomi. (1993). *Fire With Fire: The New Female Power and How It Will Change the Twenty-First Century.* New York: Random House.

Wolf, Naomi. (1991). *The Beauty Myth.* New York: William Morrow.

Women's Alliance Against Pornography. (1985). *Vote "Yes" on #3 for Dignity, Justice, Respect, Honor and Equality.* Cambridge: WAAP.

Working in the body trade. (1981). *Aegis* (Autumn), 19–20.

Wriggins, Jennifer. (1983). Rape, racism, and the law. *Harvard Women's Law Journal,* 6 (1), 103–141.

Wylie, Philip. (1942). *A Generation of Vipers.* New York: Farrar and Rinehart.

Wynter, Sarah. (1989). Empowering women to escape prostitution, *WHISPER* III. 2 (Winter/Spring), 7.

Wyre, Ray. (1992). Pornography and violence: working with sex offenders. In Catherine Itzin (Ed.), *Pornography: Women, Violence and Civil Liberties* (pp. 236–247). Oxford: Oxford University Press.

Yang, Ni, and Daniel Linz. (1990). Movie rating and the content of adult videos: the sex-violence ratio. *Journal of Communication,* 40(2), 28–42.

Young, Marion Iris. (1988). Five faces of oppression. *The Philosophical Forum,* 19(4), 270–290.

Young, Olivia. (1995). A weapon to weaken: pornography in the workplace. In Laura Lederer and Richard Delgado (Eds.), *The Price We Pay: The Case Against Racist Speech, Hate Propaganda, and Pornography* (pp. 18–22). New York: Hill and Wang.

Zillmann, Dolf. (1989). Pornography research and public policy. In Dolf Zillmann and Jennings Bryant (Eds.), *Pornography: Research Advances and Policy Considerations* (pp. 387–403). Hillsdale, NJ: Lawrence Erlbaum.

Zillmann, Dolf, and James B. Weaver. (1989). Pornography and men's sexual callousness toward women. In Dolf Zillmann and Jennings Bryant (Eds.),

Pornography: Research Advances and Policy Considerations (pp. 95–125). Hillsdale, NJ: Lawrence Erlbaum.

Zillmann, Dolf, and Jennings Bryant. (1982). Pornography, sexual callousness, and the trivialization of rape. *Journal of Communication*, 32(4), 10–21.

Zita, Jan. (1988). Pornography and the male imaginary. *Enclictic*, 17/18, 28–44.

Index